Developing Interactional Competence in a Japanese Study Abroad Context

SECOND LANGUAGE ACQUISITION

Series Editor: Professor David Singleton, *University of Pannonia, Hungary and Fellow Emeritus, Trinity College, Dublin, Ireland*

This series brings together titles dealing with a variety of aspects of language acquisition and processing in situations where a language or languages other than the native language is involved. Second language is thus interpreted in its broadest possible sense. The volumes included in the series all offer in their different ways, on the one hand, exposition and discussion of empirical findings and, on the other, some degree of theoretical reflection. In this latter connection, no particular theoretical stance is privileged in the series; nor is any relevant perspective – sociolinguistic, psycholinguistic, neurolinguistic, etc. – deemed out of place. The intended readership of the series includes final-year undergraduates working on second language acquisition projects, postgraduate students involved in second language acquisition research, and researchers and teachers in general whose interests include a second language acquisition component.

Full details of all the books in this series and of all our other publications can be found on http://www.multilingual-matters.com, or by writing to Multilingual Matters, St Nicholas House, 31–34 High Street, Bristol BS1 2AW, UK

SECOND LANGUAGE ACQUISITION: 88

Developing Interactional Competence in a Japanese Study Abroad Context

Naoko Taguchi

MULTILINGUAL MATTERS
Bristol • Buffalo • Toronto

Library of Congress Cataloging in Publication Data
Taguchi, Naoko
Developing Interactional Competence in a Japanese Study Abroad Context/Naoko Taguchi.
Second Language Acquisition: 88
Includes bibliographical references and index.
1. Language and languages—Study and teaching—Japan. 2. Interlanguage (Language learning)—Japan. 3. Linguistics—Study and teaching—Japan. 4. English language—Japan. 5. Pragmatics—Japan. 6. Speech acts (Linguistics)—Japan. 7. Intercultural communication—Japan. 8. Second language acquisition—Japan. I. Title.
P57.J3T28 2015
495.680071–dc23 2015001751

British Library Cataloguing in Publication Data
A catalogue entry for this book is available from the British Library.

ISBN-13: 978-1-78309-372-4 (hbk)
ISBN-13: 978-1-78309-371-7 (pbk)

Multilingual Matters
UK: St Nicholas House, 31–34 High Street, Bristol BS1 2AW, UK.
USA: UTP, 2250 Military Road, Tonawanda, NY 14150, USA.
Canada: UTP, 5201 Dufferin Street, North York, Ontario M3H 5T8, Canada.

Website: www.multilingual-matters.com
Twitter: Multi_Ling_Mat
Facebook: https://www.facebook.com/multilingualmatters
Blog: www.channelviewpublications.wordpress.com

Copyright © 2015 Naoko Taguchi.

All rights reserved. No part of this work may be reproduced in any form or by any means without permission in writing from the publisher.

The policy of Multilingual Matters/Channel View Publications is to use papers that are natural, renewable and recyclable products, made from wood grown in sustainable forests. In the manufacturing process of our books, and to further support our policy, preference is given to printers that have FSC and PEFC Chain of Custody certification. The FSC and/or PEFC logos will appear on those books where full certification has been granted to the printer concerned.

Typeset by Techset Composition India (P) Ltd, Bangalore and Chennai, India.

Contents

	Acknowledgements	vii
1	Interactional Competence in a Japanese Study Abroad Context: An Introduction	1
	Interactional Competence: Definition and Historical Sketch	3
	Resources for Discursive Practices	7
2	Linguistic and Interactional Resources in Japanese Conversation: Speech Styles and Incomplete Sentence Endings	10
	Japanese Speech Styles	10
	Incomplete Utterance Ending in Japanese	24
3	Context of the Study: Study Abroad as a Site for Language Learning	31
4	Methods	38
	Participants	38
	Conversation Data	39
	Interview Data	43
	Supplementary Measures	47
	Data Collection Procedures	48
5	Speech Styles	50
	The Change in the Use of Speech Styles: The Polite and Plain Forms	50
	Functions of the Plain Forms	57
	Informal Speech Style: Plain Forms with Affect Keys	65
	Summary	81
6	Style-Shifting Across Discourse Boundaries	84
	Style-Shifting Between the Polite and Plain Forms Across Different Participant Structures	85
	Summary	96

7	Incomplete Sentences in Joint Turn Construction	98
	Functions of Incomplete Sentence Endings in Joint Turn Construction	99
	Summary	112
8	Case Histories of Interactional Development and Study Abroad Experience	114
	Interview Participants	114
	Findings	118
9	Conclusion	145
	Implications for the Construct of Interactional Competence and Development	145
	Implications for Study Abroad as a Site for L2 Learning	151
	Future Directions	155

Appendix A: Transcription Conventions	158
Appendix B: Conversation Task	160
Appendix C: Motivation Survey	161
Appendix D: Japanese Contact Survey	162
Appendix E: Proportion of the Utterance-Ending Forms by Individuals: Polite Forms, Plain Forms and Incomplete Endings	164
References	166
Index	174

Acknowledgements

I would like to express my gratitude to everyone who helped me write this book, provided support, helped with data collection and analysis, assisted in the editing and proofreading and offered comments and suggestions.

First and foremost, I would like to thank the Hakuho Foundation who awarded me the Japanese Language Fellowship, without which this project would have been impossible to complete. I would also like to thank the Waseda University Graduate School of Japanese Applied Linguistics for their invaluable support with participant recruitment and data collection. Special thanks to Dr Midori Ishida and Dr Chie Fukuda for their assistance with transcribing the data. I also want to thank my colleagues in the Japanese Program at Carnegie Mellon University, Dr Yasufumi Iwasaki and Dr Yoshihiro Yasuhara, for inspecting conversation excerpts for accuracy. Thanks also to Bruce Cornrich for his help with index and to everyone else, too many to mention, who supported me in this project.

The photo on the front cover was taken at Chidorigafuchi, a popular cherry blossom viewing spot in Japan. It was taken a few days after I arrived in Tokyo to begin my fellowship term. When the sight of cherry trees and boats caught my eyes, I remember quickly capturing this photo. Feverish anticipation of starting a new project in a new place still remains in my heart as brightly as the cherry blossoms in the picture. I hope to share some of the excitement throughout this book.

Sincerely,
Naoko Taguchi
February, 2015
Pittsburgh, PA
USA

1 Interactional Competence in a Japanese Study Abroad Context: An Introduction

The ability to interact appropriately and effectively in a second language is critical to both the product and process of second language acquisition. Being able to create and sustain cooperation in conversation, as well as to understand others' views and build on shared knowledge, are some of the most fundamental goals and outcomes of second language (L2) learning. This conversational interaction serves a prominent role in assisting L2 learning. When learners are engaged in meaningful, spontaneous, and active dialogues, they use whatever resources they have – linguistic, semiotic, and dialogic – in collaboration with their peers to communicate meaning, and the byproduct of this process is the development of their interactional competence.

This book reports on a study that investigates the development of interactional competence in a Japanese study abroad context. Traditional models of communicative competence consider language ability to exist within individuals as a stable trait (Bachman & Palmer, 1996, 2010; Canale & Swain, 1980). In contrast, interactional competence views language ability as a dialogic construct, locally situated and jointly constructed by participants in discourse (Hall *et al.*, 2011; Young, 2011; Young & He, 1998). Interactional competence considers participants' skillful use of a variety of linguistic and interactional resources at the task of joint meaning creation. Adapting this theoretical framework, this book illustrates the development of interactional competence as it manifests in peer-to-peer dialogues.

By adopting the framework of interactional competence, this study distances from the cognitivist approaches to SLA that view L2 learning as a individual matter. Instead, it takes a socio-cognitive approach, which suggests that L2 learning occurs through participation in social practices. Social practices here refer to recurring incidents of social interaction that structure our social realities. For example, greeting and leave-taking, ordering meals, discussing homework, and making plans for the weekend are all mundane social activities that occur in an everyday school context. Successful interaction in these contexts depends on participants' knowledge of conventions of the practices – what courses of action are expected in a specific practice, and what linguistic and non-linguistic resources are employed to construct the practice.

However, successful interaction does not result solely from individual participants' knowledge of conventions or their ability to format their linguistic and non-linguistic actions according to the conventions. It is a matter of collaborative efforts of all participants working toward the construction of shared understanding. During interaction, participants constantly monitor and regulate their contributions to the talk. When their knowledge of conventions does not align with the course of discourse, their interactional competence helps readapt their linguistic actions corresponding to the ongoing discourse. Other participants respond to this shift through acknowledgement and alignment, which is also a reflection of interactional competence. Hence, learning L2 means learning to act collaboratively with others to accomplish social actions in talk.

Following this framework, my study takes the view of language competence as a dialogical construct. I present a micro-level analysis of L2 Japanese learners' interaction with their peers. Moving away from traditional analysis of linguistic forms in isolation, my study focuses on how learners use linguistic resources in interaction to accomplish mutual understanding. A casual conversation with peers is a routine social practice, yet it presupposes intricate layers of linguistic and interactional conventions. In a Japanese conversation, learners need to know which speech style to use (plain or polite) to index social meaning of solidarity or distance. At the same time, they must understand how to mark boundaries of talk by shifting between different speech styles. They also need to know how to skilfully use incomplete sentence endings (a common feature of spoken Japanese) to involve their interlocutors to talk-in-progress and promote reciprocity. These are all critical linguistic and interactional resources that learners have to attain in order to become expert conversationalists in Japanese. By analysing these resources in peer-to-peer conversations, I will document features of interactional competence specific to Japanese language. In addition to the conversation analysis, interview data will be analyzed to reveal the nature of learners' social practices in their study abroad program. Because interactional competence develops through participation in recurring social practices, analysis of interview data will define connection among language use, language development, and context of learning.

Participants included 18 learners of Japanese enrolled in a Japanese language program at a private university in Tokyo. Learners' conversations were recorded twice during a 15-week semester. They were paired randomly and instructed to have an informal conversation for 20 minutes. The conversations were transcribed and analyzed based on Young's (2008a) interactional resources. Interviews were conducted individually with a subset of eight participants three times during the semester. The interview data were cross-examined with the conversation data to reveal different patterns of development corresponding to individuals' different social experiences.

This book has three unique features. First, the study provides a configuration of linguistic and interactional resources as they are found in Japanese. The book effectively describes what it means to be interactionally competent in Japanese by explicating what linguistic and interactional resources enable participants to construct and orient to social actions in Japanese. Second, the book not only describes changes in learners' interactional competence but also interprets these changes by complementing conversation data with interview data. A triangulated analysis of multiple data sets generates meaningful interpretations of individual variations in interactional development, and the learner-specific and contextual factors that shaped developmental trajectories. Finally, this book contributes to our understanding of contextualized SLA and study abroad learning. Study abroad programs have been claimed as a site for L2 learning, but very few studies have analysed interactional competence in relation to learners' study abroad experiences. This book offers insights about the types of learning resources available in a study abroad context and how those resources assist learners' development toward a competent speaker in the target community.

In the remaining chapter, I will first discuss the theoretical framework of interactional competence and review existing studies. Then I will introduce Japanese speech styles (the plain and polite forms) and incomplete sentence endings as primary linguistic resources through which interactional competence can be examined.

Interactional Competence: Definition and Historical Sketch

Interactional competence (Hall, 1993, 1995; Hall et al., 2011; Young & He, 1998; Young, 2002, 2008a, 2008b, 2011) has gained attention as a critical aspect of becoming a competent speaker in the target language. While the framework of interactional competence is recent, its basis goes back to the 1970s in Dell Hymes' work (Hymes, 1972). Challenging the Chomskian view of language as a system of grammar, Hymes argues that knowledge of language entails both grammatical knowledge and sociocultural knowledge. He coined the term, *communicative competence*, which refers to the ability to use language accurately and appropriately in social context.

Hymes' idea became the basis for the L2 communicative competence models emerged in the 1980s and 1990s (Bachman, 1990; Bachman & Palmer, 1996, 2010; Canale & Swain, 1980). Canale and Swain's (1980) model was a forerunner of this trend, which maintained that successful communication involves efficient integration of grammatical, sociolinguistic, discourse, and strategic competencies. Bachman (1990) and Bachman and Palmer

(1996, 2010) advanced Canale and Swain's model by providing a more elaborate classification of components of communicative competence. In Bachman and Palmer (1996, 2010), language knowledge refers to both organizational knowledge and pragmatic knowledge. Organizational knowledge deals with formal aspects of language (grammar and textual aspects), whereas pragmatic knowledge concerns language use in relation to language users and language use settings. Pragmatic knowledge is further sub-divided into functional knowledge, which enables us to interpret the relationships between utterances and the communicative goals of language users, and sociolinguistic knowledge, which enables us to interpret or create utterances that are appropriate to specific language use settings. A characteristic of these early models is that they view communicative competence as a psycholinguistic ability that exists within individuals as a stable trait, independent from context. In this view, language ability belongs to an individual who employs the ability, and it is stable across social contexts and interactional settings.

Since the 1990s, language competence has been incorporated into a broader conceptual framework that focuses on the dynamic and dialogic aspects of communication. Most notable in this trend is the emergence of the model of interactional competence (e.g. Hall, 1993, 1995; Hall *et al.*, 2011; Young & He, 1998; Young, 2002, 2008a, 2011). Drawing on Hymes' (1972) model of ethnography of speaking, Hall (1993, 1995) underscored the importance of analysing 'socioculturally-conventionalized configurations of face-to-face interaction by which and within which group members communicate' (Hall, 1993: 146). Young (2002) later elaborated on Hall's framework by proposing six components as analytical layers: (1) knowledge of rhetorical script (i.e. knowledge of how conversation is sequenced and structured); (2) knowledge of register; (3) turn-taking ability; (4) topic management skill; (5) knowledge of patterns of participation specific to a given practice; and (6) devices for signalling discourse boundaries (e.g. shifting across different speech acts).

These components are not totally in contrast with early models of communicative competence (Hall & Doehler, 2011). Knowledge of rhetorical script corresponds to the concept of discourse competence. Knowledge of register and participation patterns specific to context, and use of boundary-signalling devices reflect sociolinguistics and pragmatics considerations. However, the fundamental difference is that interactional competence rejects the view that these components are independent from each other and from social context, residing in individuals. Instead, interactional competence views these components as working in unison in a face-to-face interaction and shared among participants in interaction. Hence, an individual's ability is no longer viewed as a fixed or stable trait: it varies in correspondence with co-participants' performance. Interactional competence views language knowledge and ability as locally situated and jointly constructed by all participants in discourse. Ability and context are connected. Participants' resources are not set in advance but are dependent on the specifics of a dynamic social context. See Young's (2008a: 101) definition of interactional competence:

> Interactional competence is a relationship between the participants' employment of linguistic and interactional resources and the contexts in which they are employed; the resources that interactional competence highlights are those of identity, language, and interaction...Interactional competence, however, is not the ability of an individual to employ those resources in any and every social interaction; rather, interactional competence is how those resources are employed mutually and reciprocally by all participants in a particular discursive practice. This means that interactional competence is not the knowledge or the possession of an individual person, but it is co-constructed by all participants in a discursive practice, and interactional competence varies with the practice and with the participants.

This conceptualization finds a synergy with Hall and Doehler's (2011) definition of interactional competence. They conceptualize interaction as a goal-oriented and context-specific activity that draws on a range of participants' resources, both linguistic and non-linguistic, for the task of co-construction of meaning:

> IC [interactional competence] includes knowledge of social-context-specific communicative events or activity types, their typical goals and trajectories of actions by which the goals are realized and the conventional behaviors by which participant roles and role relationships are accomplished. Also included is the ability to deploy and to recognize context-specific patterns by which turns are taken, actions are organized, and practices are ordered. And it includes the prosodic, linguistic, sequential and nonverbal resources conventionally used for producing and interpreting turns and actions, to construct them so that they are recognizable for others, and to repair problems in maintaining shared understanding of the interactional work we and our interlocutors are accomplishing together. (Hall & Doehler, 2011: 1–2)

These definitions indicate that interactional competence conceives of language knowledge and ability shared between participants in context. It manifests in the participants' ability to design one's contribution in such a way that it responds appropriately to co-participants' previous utterances and actions. To make an appropriate contribution, one needs to understand the specifics of interaction – goals, activity types, participants' roles, and conventions of speech. At the same time, one needs to be sensitive to the sequential organization of discourse so they can align their actions to the unfolding discourse and adapt dynamically moment-by-moment. Moreover, one must continually monitor the 'direction' of ongoing talk, and revise one's understanding of preceding contribution in accordance by predicting the consequences of certain moves and actions. Hence, participants' skillful co-construction of discourse draws on their knowledge of the conventions of a given practice. And critically, these resources are shared among participants.

Participants' resources are closely related to the concept of *discursive practices*. Borrowing Tracy's (2002) term, Young (2008a: 69) defines discursive practices as 'talk activities that people do.' The structure of a practice involves 'what actions you perform, the forms of language that you use, and also gesture, eye gaze, and ways of positioning the body – how close you stand to the person you are talking to' (Young, 2008a: 58). The verbal, nonverbal, and interactional resources that participants employ to construct meaning are configured into discursive practices. Understanding discursive practices is important in SLA because L2 learning takes place within discursive practices. What is learned in the practices is interactional competence – the ability to interact effectively with others. Young (2008b) attests:

> discursive practice is an approach in which language learning is viewed not only as the changing linguistic knowledge of individual learners but also primarily as learners' changing participation in discursive practices: What is learned is not the language but the practice. (p. 138)

Under this approach, learning manifests in our changing engagement in discursive practices. We learn by participating in context-specific discursive practices. Development of interactional competence is a byproduct of this participation process.

A growing body of recent studies has applied the 'learning-as-participation' perspective to the study of interactions among L2 learners and their language development (e.g. Dings, 2014; Hellermann, 2008, 2009, 2011; M. Ishida, 2009; Markee, 2008; Masuda, 2010; Nguyen, 2011a, 2011b; Rine & Hall, 2011; Yagi, 2007; Young & Miller, 2004). Drawing on the framework of situated learning, Nguyen (2011a) documented how a learner of English used interactional resources to participate in a talk with a native speaker of English. Analysis of interactional moves between the learner and her ESL teacher revealed that at the beginning of the semester the learner's responses to the teacher's topic proffers were brief, containing simple turn construction units and non-verbal signals such as nodding and smiling. However in the later period, the learner started to produce multi-unit responses, expanding it into longer, more syntactically and lexically elaborate turn construction units. Nguyen interpreted this learner's change from a perspective of learning-as-participation. Opportunities for learning were provided by the topics nominated by the teacher, which allowed the learner to respond to the topic with expanded answers.

On the topic of situated learning, Hellermann (2011) analyzed the interactional practice of 'other-initiated repair' performed by two ESL learners in a classroom. Analysis of over 300 examples of repair sequences revealed the focal participants' change in their use of language in repair. When correcting a peer, these learners developed abilities in three areas: isolating the problem word from a longer utterance, repeating the problem word, and supporting their correction when it was not immediately taken up by their peers. In addition, there was a marked change in the learners' orientation toward different trouble sources for repair. The learners initially focused on lexical problems as repairable items, but later their orientation changed to include a broader subject, such as discourse structure and course of action for repair initiation. They also developed the ability to use a wider repertoire of methods for making other-initiated repair.

What is common in these studies is that learning is conceptualized as participation in discursive practices. L2 development is viewed as the change in ways of participating in situated practices. Participation involves the maneuvering of a collection of linguistic and interactional resources – how to manage topics, when to take turns and transfer speakership, and how to design turns in a way that they fit to the ongoing flow of conversation (Young, 2008a). These linguistic and interactional resources directly index learners' interactional competence – ability to work together with their co-participants to co-construct interactional activities.

Although these two studies are notable, longitudinal research that revealed changing patterns of talk-in-interaction is still relatively rare. A challenge of longitudinal research was pointed out by Hall and Doehler (2011) who asked: 'What are the relevant units of analysis (actions, practices, methods, linguistic items, etc.) that allow documenting change in IC [interactional competence] across time, and warrant comparability between interactional conduct at two different moments?' (p. 7)

My study responds to this question by collecting longitudinal, interactional data of L2 learners of Japanese across two comparable tasks and documenting evidence of change in their interactional practices. This study will describe Japanese-specific linguistic and interactional resources that enable participants to construct social actions in Japanese. My analyses will present both individual- and group-level change. I will illustrate what changed or did not change over time within the group, while showing individual-level data to highlight the patterns of change. At the same time, I intend to explain the changes by supplementing information about individual learners' participation in the local community gleaned from the interview data.

Resources for Discursive Practices

Interactional competence draws on a variety of resources that participants bring to the joint construction of discourse. These resources include knowledge of rhetorical scripts, lexis and syntax specific to the practice, the turn-taking system, topic management, repair, and recognition and production of boundaries between speech activities (e.g. Hall, 1993; Young, 2002, 2008a, 2008b, 2011). Young (2008a, 2008b) specifies three categories of resources: *identity, linguistic,* and *interactional. Identity resources* refer to *participant framework,* which includes participants' identities or their 'footing' (Goffman, 1979). The identity resources refer to the relative positioning of participants with respect to each other (e.g. role and status), which help us understand the social organization of the participants. Participants sometimes change their footing within a single interaction to signal a different position. This change is indexed both verbally and non-verbally.

Linguistic resources, on the other hand, refer to linguistic forms specific to activity, place, and purpose of interaction. Linguistic features such as grammatical forms, vocabulary, and pronunciation characterize a specific register for the practice. For example, certain forms and lexis co-occur frequently in a professor-student advising session and index the practice of academic advising (e.g. vocabulary such as *course nomination* and *pre-requisite,* and grammatical forms used for typical speech acts such as suggestions and refusals). While these forms are associated with specific practices, they are not pre-determined. They change in response to the specifics of context such as participants' previous experience, history of interaction, and degree of involvement in the ongoing talk. Interactional competence involves one's ability to use linguistic resources specific to practice, but it also involves one's flexibility in adjusting the use of resources corresponding to changing context.

Similar to linguistic resources, *interactional resources* also define a discursive practice. While linguistic resources focus on formal aspects of language, interactional resources attend to the ways in which participants create meaning in a collaborative manner. Interactional resources are necessary in the process of joint meaning construction, because only by successfully using these can participants display their understanding of organization of actions and their contributions to interaction. Young (2008a) presents four categories of interactional resources: *speech acts,* which involve sequential organization of a communicative act; the *turn-taking* system in which participants manage transfer of speakership; *repair* in which participants solve a communication problem; and *boundaries* in which participants distinguish the current practice from adjacent practice. Below is a summary of three types of resources (Young, 2008a: 71):

- Identity resources
  - *Participation framework*: the identities of participants in an interaction; participation framework; positioning of participants.
- Linguistic resources
  - *Register:* the features of pronunciation, vocabulary, and syntax that characterize a practice.

- *Modes of meaning*: the ways in which participants construct interpersonal, experiential, and textual meanings.
- Interactional resources
  - *Speech acts*: the selection of acts in a practice and their sequential organization.
  - *Turn-taking*: how participants select the next speaker and how they know when to end a turn and when to begin the next turn.
  - *Repair*: how participants respond to interactional problems in a given practice.
  - *Boundaries*: the opening and closing acts of a practice that distinguish a given practice from adjacent practice.

These resources serve as important guidelines for my study because they inform what units of analysis are possible when examining learners' interactional competence. My study will illustrate L2 Japanese learners' development in their use of these resources in a face to-face conversation. In translating Young's resources to the context of Japanese language, I will focus on two linguistic resources that are unique to Japanese language: speech styles (e.g. the polite and plain forms) and incomplete sentence ending. In Chapter 2, I will present descriptions of these two linguistic features and explain why they can serve as appropriate units of analysis of interactional competence in Japanese.

2 Linguistic and Interactional Resources in Japanese Conversation: Speech Styles and Incomplete Sentence Endings

Chapter 1 introduced interactional competence as a guiding theoretical framework for the present study. This chapter describes two linguistic structures, speech style and incomplete sentence structure, which formed the primary analysis of interactional competence in L2 Japanese.

Japanese Speech Styles

The polite and plain form

Japanese language has two main speech styles: the polite form (the *desu/masu* form or addressee honorifics)[1] and the plain form (informal or casual form). These two forms appear at the utterance-final position and index a range of social meanings such as politeness, formality, and affect (Cook, 1999, 2006, 2008; Ikuta, 2008; Jones & Ono, 2008; Maynard, 1991, 1993; Okamoto, 1999). Choice between these two forms is obligatory unless one opts for incomplete sentence endings. In the polite form, the copula *desu* is placed after nouns, adjectives, and adjectival verbs, and the suffix *masu* is attached as a verb ending. On the other hand, the plain form is the non-honorific counterpart of the polite form. It involves the dictionary form of verbs and adjectives, as well as *da/dearu*-ending of nouns and adverbs (can be omitted). See examples below. Both sentences have the same meaning (i.e. He is Mr Suzuki.), but the copulas attached to the noun are different: the polite form *desu* in (1) and the plain form *da* in (2).

(1) Polite form   Suzuki-san   **desu.**
                   Suzuki Mr.   COP
(2) Plain form   Suzuki-san   **da.**
                   Suzuki Mr.   COP

The polite form is usually associated with the formal register spoken among out-group members (people who are older, of higher status, and non-intimate) and the plain form is linked to the informal register shared among in-group members (people of lower status and age, or intimately related) (Harada, 1976; Ide, 1989; Niyekawa, 1991). See the excerpt and analysis below from K. Ishida (2009: 42), which illustrates the use of these two forms. The polite form (*desu/masu*) is underlined, and the plain form is in bold. See Appendix A for the transcript conventions.

(a) nihon   no   eiga   yori   <u>omoshiroi   desu</u>
    Japan   LK   movie   than   interesting   COP
    'They (American movies) are more interesting than Japanese movies.'
(b) hee   **omoshiori**
    oh   interesting
    'Oh, that's interesting.'
(c) amerikan pai   toka   <u>mimashi-ta</u>.
    American pie   and the like   see-PST
    'I saw American Pie and the like.'
(d) watashi   ne   rasshu awaa tuu   o   **mi-ta**   yo.
    I   FP   rush hour two   OBJ   see-PST   FP
    'I saw Rush Hour 2.'

In line (a), the speaker ends the sentence in the polite form as indicated by the copula *desu* attached to the adjective *omoshiroi* (interesting). In response, in line (b), the speaker ends the sentence with the plain form of the adjective *omoshiroi* (interesting). Lines (c) and (d) show the *masu* form and plain form of the verb *miru* (to see). In line (c), *mashita*, the past tense of *masu*, is attached to a conjugated form of the verb *miru*, while in line (d), the speaker ends with *mita*, the plain past tense form of *miru*. As shown here, the choice between these two speech styles is a salient characteristic of Japanese communication. Speakers' choice indicates a variety of social meanings. For instance, the use of the polite form in lines (a) and (c) conveys formality and distance, while the use of the plain form in line (d) conveys closeness. Speakers may use the plain form to express spontaneous feelings and evaluations, as in line (b).

Speech styles are important linguistic resources for a successful interaction in Japanese. The polite and plain forms signal register-appropriate language use, which help speakers construct interpersonal, ideational, and textual meaning (Young, 2008a; see Chapter 1). Because of a range of social meanings that speech styles convey, learners who are unable to use speech styles appropriately can be severely limited in their capacity to fully express themselves across different situations and discourse practices. The ability to align with different contextual specifics by using appropriate speech styles is a crucial part of interactional competence in Japanese.

In addition to the register-appropriate language use, speech styles can help signal transition between discourse boundaries. Although the traditional categorical approach associates the polite form with the formal speech and the plain form with the informal speech, the recent indexical approach argues that this dichotomy does not hold true all the time. Japanese speakers often shift between these two forms in a single context by attending not only to static contextual features but also to dynamic ones, such as sequential turns, the addressee's attitudes, and interpersonal distance (Cook, 1999, 2006, 2008; Fukushima, 2007; Geryer, 2013; Ikuta, 2008; Jones & Ono, 2008; Nazkian, 2010; Okamoto, 2011). Hence, the ability to navigate through different speech styles is a reflection of one's ability to mark boundaries across discursive practices (interactional resources in Young (2008a); see Chapter 1). Such a style-shift could signal one's sensitivity to the changing flow of interaction, as well as his/her ability to respond to contextual specifics and to transit between practices.

Acquisition of speech styles is considered challenging in L2 Japanese because it requires learners to attend to multiple levels of information, including linguistic forms, contextual cues, and sequential organization of discourse. Learners experience difficulty in using the polite and plain forms in a socially appropriate manner due to the sociolinguistic complexity of the forms. The dynamic nature of speech styles adds further demand. Speakers strategically shift between forms in order to negotiate and co-construct interpersonal relationships, affect, and distance. They also style-shift to enact different voices and social identities. Because this indexical use of speech styles is not salient or systematic, it is often difficult for learners to notice the mappings between speech forms, social meanings, and contexts. Learners' identity and subjectivity also affect their use of speech styles, because their choice of form represents the type of 'self' that one wants to project – formal or informal, distant or close.

This complexity and dynamicity involved in the use of speech styles, however, is the very reason that interactional competence is the appropriate framework when examining the acquisition of speech styles. Interactional competence assumes that learners bring in a variety of resources – both linguistic and interactional – to the act of joint meaning making. Learners orient to the specifics of context and react to change with resources. Speech styles are considered as part of their linguistic resources. By using the plain and polite forms skilfully and shifting between the two forms in occasion, learners can index register-appropriate language use and signal transitions between the boundaries.

Subcategories of the plain form: Informal style and detached style

Classification of speech styles goes beyond the dichotomy between the polite and plain form. Maynard (1993) was the first to note that the plain form has distinct properties depending on the medium of communication – speech or writing. According to Maynard, the plain form often appears with discourse markers in speech (e.g. sentence final particles), but such markers are absent when the plain form occurs in writing.

Building on Maynard's argument, Cook (2002, 2006, 2008) introduced two sub-categories of the plain form: the informal speech style and the detached speech style. The former typically co-occurs with 'affect keys', which convey the speaker's feelings, moods, and attitudes (Ochs, 1996). Those keys include sentence final particles, vowel lengthening, rising intonation, postposing of information, and coalescence (see Chapter 4 for details). In contrast, the detached style occurs in a naked form. Without affect keys, the detached form is devoid of emotion and indexes the impersonal speech style. Cook found that most instances of the plain form in conversations take the informal speech style and display the speaker's attitudes in on-going talk. In contrast, written genres such as newspapers and scientific texts display the detached style, in which writers use the plain form to foreground the referential content of a sentence.

The plain form rarely occurs without an affective key in conversation. See the excerpt below from Cook (2002: 151–152) and her analyses. This is a conversation among family members. Father (H) asks his son about his most interesting experience when he visited the US. The son (T) talks about his host family's dog as amusing experience. In the excerpt, the plain form is in bold. The affect keys are indicated by a double underline.

1 H: *Nani ga   ichiban   **omoshiro**   **katta**↑*
        What SUB   most   interesting   COP-PST
        'What was most interesting?'

2 T: *Sakki   **hanashita**   yo*
        Just now   spoke   FP
        'I just now told you, you know'
        ((several lines are omitted.))

3 T: *Deree to shite   ne,   bunnagutte   mo   okon*
        slouching-TE   FP   hit   even if   get angry

4   ***nai***   *no*
        NEG   FP
        'The dog is slouching, and does not get angry even if I hit him.'

```
5   BOTH:   ((laugh))
6   C:      Haa
            DM
            'uhuh'
7   H:      Hidee       inu   da    na.
            terrible    dog   COP   FP
            'It's a terrible dog!'
```

Most plain forms here carry affect keys. In line 1, rising intonation is used to ask a question, which indicates the speaker's uncertainty. In line 7, the coalescence *hidee* (terrible) occurs. It is derived from the dictionary form *hidoi* and indexes the speaker's affective state: in this conversation, H's rough attitude toward T's host family's dog. In lines 2, 4, and 7, the plain form accompanies the final particles *yo, no,* and *na*. According to Makino and Tsutsui (1986), these particles serve specific functions. The particle *yo* indicates the speaker's strong assertion about the topic. T's use of *yo* in line 2 demonstrates his assertion that he already talked about his most interesting experience in America. The particle *no*, on the other hand, occurs when the speaker is explaining or asking for an explanation about some information shared with the hearer. As shown in Line 4, the particle *no* appears as part of T's explanation about his host family's dog. Finally, the particle *na* amplifies emotions. H's use of this particle in line 7 is taken as an emphatic emotional marker, which indicates his opinion of the dog.

These analyses by Cook (2002) reveal that the affect keys add specific communicative effects to the utterance. The plain form co-occurring with affect keys emphasizes the speaker's affective stance toward the interlocutor or the referent, and adds the effect of informality and intimacy. The informal speech style (plain form) with affective keys is an important interactional resource for speakers of Japanese. Affective keys demonstrate the speaker's stance and alignment with the addressee, as well as his/her affective involvement in the talk-in-progress.

Style-shifting

The traditional categorical approach considers the *desu/masu* form as a polite or formal speech-level marker, and the plain form as a non-polite or informal speech-level marker. Accordingly, the *desu/masu* or polite form is associated with speech addressed to out-group members (people who are older, of higher status, and non-intimate). The plain form, on the other hand, is reserved for informal speech addressed to in-group members (people of lower status and age, and in intimate relationship) (Ide, 1989; Niyekawa, 1991; Shibatani, 1990).

However, the recent indexical approach refutes this one-to-one mapping between contextual features and speech styles, because Japanese speakers often shift between these two forms by attending to contextual dynamics such as sequential turns, the addressee's attitudes, interpersonal distance, and desired social identity (Cook, 1999, 2006, 2008; Fukushima, 2007; Geyer, 2013; Ikuta, 2008; Jones & Ono, 2008; Nazkian, 2010; Okamoto, 2011). The mixing of formal and informal speech styles is not arbitrary: speakers strategically manipulate their choice of speech style moment-by-moment to index different social meanings. For instance, shifts from the polite to the plain form can express spontaneous assertion of one's emotions and thoughts, evaluations, soliloquy-like remarks, empathy, and psychological closeness. On the other hand, shifts from the plain to the polite form can index increased psychological distance, presentation of public self, and authoritative voice. A number of studies have documented this style shifts as a common phenomenon of Japanese conversation (e.g. Chen, 2004; Cook, 1996, 1999, 2002, 2008; Fukushima, 2007; Geyer, 2013; Ikuta, 1983, 2008; Makino, 2002; Masuda, 2011; Maynard, 1991; Okamoto, 1999, 2011; Saito, 2010).

An example from Okamoto (1999: 63) below illustrates the instance of style-shifting occurring between speakers of unequal power relationship. This excerpt is a conversation between a 38-year old male professor (P) and a 23-year-old female graduate student (S). The polite form is underlined, and the plain form is in bold. If we follow the traditional view, the professor's higher status is assumed to be marked by his use of the plain form, and the student's lower status is considered to be marked by her use of the polite form. However, the data does not conform to this dichotomy. There is a considerable amount of style mixing: both the professor and the student shift between the polite and plain form turn-by-turn.

As Okamoto illustrates, in line 2, the student uses referent honorifics (the polite form), but she switches to the plain form in line 4 (*Aa, sugoi.* 'Oh, wow!') and again in line 6 (*A, honto da.* 'Oh, that's true.'). This does not mean that the student is treating the professor as a lower-status person or a close friend. Rather, it reflects her psychological state – using the plain form to show surprise. In these occasions, it is perfectly appropriate to eliminate formality by using the plain form. The professor, too, often switches back and forth between the polite and plain forms. In lines 1 and 3, he uses the plain form when explaining the photo to the student, but in his next turn in line 5, all of his utterances end in the polite form. Okamoto interpreted this switching as the professor's strategy for avoiding sounding too formal or too informal by not sticking to one form exclusively. By using the polite form occasionally, the professor acknowledges distance between himself and the student, and projects some degree of deference or formality in the office hour interaction. On the other hand, his use of the plain form is an attempt to reduce the distance with the student and to convey some level of friendliness. (The morpheme-by-morpheme gloss is omitted to reflect the original.)

1 P: *Datte moo   ni-juu-nenmo mae* **da**   **mon**. [laughter]
       'Of course, that's now 20 years ago.'

2 S: *Konna kichoona   shashin o miseteitadaite   ii   n*
       desu ka.
       'Is it all right for me to see such precious photos?'
3 P: *Uun* **betsuni**.
       'No, no problem.'
4 S: *Aa,* **sugoi**. *E, korette sensee   ga ano   tiin-ee, tiin-eejaa*
       no toki   desu   ka.
       'Oh, wow! Oh, is this when you were a teen-ager?'
5 P: *Moo   hatachi   o   sugiteimashita   kedo nee.*
       Un, koo natte kuru to   moo ima   no kao ni   nattekimasu ne
       'I was already over 20, but yeah, when it comes to this (photo), it already becomes to look like my present face.'
6 S: *A,* **honto da**.
       'Oh, that's true.'

Both parties here often shift between the plain and polite form to index their public identities, situational meaning, and social relationship. The student does not always display politeness to the professor through the use of honorifics. The professor sometimes opts for the polite form to signal certain degree of deference and present his professional identity. These Okamoto's analyses reinforce the notion that static situational elements alone cannot determine the mixing of speech styles.

Besides Okamoto's study, there is a large amount of empirical evidence supporting this observation of style-shifting (e.g. Chen, 2004; Cook, 2006; Fukushima, 2007; Geyer, 2013; Ikuta, 1983, 2008; Maynard, 1991, 1993; Nazkian, 2010). For example, Fukusima (2007) analyzed nine hours of naturalistic conversations between Japanese business people and their colleagues over different settings and personal relationships. After coding each utterance for the *desu/masu* (polite) form or the non-*desu/masu* (plain) form, she found that no conversation units consisted of exclusively one form or the other: essentially all conversations featured mixed styles. Strikingly, even people who met first time used mixed speech styles at 65% of the time, and the polite form occupied only about 35% of the conversation. These findings present counter-evidence to the common assumption that the polite form is the norm in business communication.

Mechanisms of style-shifting

Previous studies on style mixing revealed the mechanisms underlying the selection of one speech style over the other. These studies focused on why speakers style shift within a single sequential discourse in which the situational conditions (e.g. subject matter, setting, and conversation participants) remain constant. An early study by Ikuta (1983) revealed interpersonal distance as primary cause of style-shifting. Based on the analyses of a TV interview program, she showed that the polite form indicates larger interlocutor distance [+distance] and that the plain form indicates smaller distance [−distance]. However, speakers optionally switch from one form to the other in order to project different levels of interpersonal distance and empathy. For example, the use of the [−distance] level (plain form) helps the speaker express closeness to his interlocutor, whereas the use of the [+distance] level (polite form) represents the speaker's attitudinal remoteness. When empathy is expected (i.e. when the speaker shows strong agreement or positive evaluation of his interlocutor's statement), he often employs the [−distance] level (i.e. plain form) to add a genuine effect of the empathy. In contrast, when the speaker asks personal or sensitive questions about the interlocutor, he/she avoids using the [−distance] level because the empathy conveyed by this speech level could violate the other person's privacy. In these occasions, the speaker purposefully uses the [+distance] level (i.e. *desum/masu* form or polite form) to demonstrate attitudinal independence or objectivity.

While Ikuta found that empathy and attitudinal distance determine the shifting of speech levels, other studies have identified factors that contribute to style-shifting. By analyzing spoken conversation and written prose, Maynard (1991, 1993) found that the speaker's choice of the speech style is closely associated with the degree of the speaker's sensitivity toward 'others.' When the speaker and the listener are in a close relationship and share a sense of bonding, the speaker finds less need to address his/her interlocutor as a separate entity. As a result, the speaker is more likely to use the plain form. In contrast, when the speaker is aware of the addressee as a separate entity, he/she is more likely to use the polite form. Based on this analysis, Maynard proposes six circumstances in which the level of awareness of 'others' is low, and as a result, the plain form is more likely to be used: (1) when the speaker recalls something abruptly; (2) when the speaker expresses sudden emotions; (3) when the speaker expresses inner thoughts; (4) when the speaker jointly creates utterances with the listener; (5) when the speaker presents information that is semantically congruent to background information; and (6) when the interlocutors are in an intimate relationship.

However, Cook (1996, 1999) argues that Maynard's argument is inadequate because it cannot explain why the plain form sometimes appears when the interlocutors do not share a sense of psychological closeness. In authentic data, people who are involved in a quarrel often use the plain form to each other because they are angry and are not concerned with their public self-presentation (Cook, 1999). On the other hand, in an intimate mother-child relationship, a mother sometimes uses the polite form with a child when teaching social norms or disciplining the child because the polite form indexes the speaker's 'on-stage' identity acting a 'role' (Cook, 1996). Cook's analyses advanced Maynard's interpretation of speech style mixing by showing that it is not the interlocutors' psychological closeness per se that affects the choice of the speech form. Other contextual conditions such as the speaker's enacting of a role and the speaker's display of a public persona affect the choice.

As described above, Ikuta (1983), Maynard (1991, 1993), and Cook (1996, 1999) all explain the mechanisms of speech style-shifting and reveal the contextual conditions for style-shifting. Contextual parameters such as interpersonal distance and empathy, sensitivity and awareness of 'the other,' and role taking and self-presentation have been found to be the key factors that guide one's choice of speech style. These findings emphasize that context is a dynamic, complex entity and that speech style does not assume a direct, one-to-one correspondence between the form and contextual features. Contextual parameters change moment-by-moment during any single interaction, and style-shifting is one linguistic phenomenon that reflects this change.

While these studies revealed the extent of speech style mixing, more recent research has revealed how speakers use particular speech styles to co-construct discourse with their interlocutor (e.g. Cook, 2006, 2008). Cook (2006) analyzed academic consultation sessions between three male Japanese professors and their students at universities in Tokyo. She focused on the students' choice of the speech style at a transition relevance place (TRP) (Sacks *et al.*, 1974). When the professor comes to a TRP with a turn marked in the plain form, the student can choose either the polite form or the plain form in the next turn to construct a particular type of relationship with the professor. Of note in Cook's findings was the student's use of the plain form in the co-construction of knowledge with the professor. See the excerpt from Cook (p. 281) and her analysis for illustration. (The morpheme-by-morpheme gloss is omitted to reflect the original.)

12   P: ...*Kurisuchan   no   kazu   to   hon:toni kurabemononi*
         naranai kurai   [kirisutokyoo   ga
         '... compared with Japan, (in Korea), the number of Christians is'
13 → S: [*ooi*
                         many
                         'large'
14   P: *shinja   ga   **ooi***
         '(the number of) believers is much larger'.

In this conversation, the professor is assisting the student with his thesis topic. When the professor comes to a TRP in line 12 (talking about the number of Christians in Korea), the student anticipates the predicate and takes over the turn with the plain form in line 13 (*ooi* 'many'). Here, the student's turn is embedded in the professor's utterance. The student uses the plain form as a resource for the joint creation of knowledge. At the same time, this strategy keeps the student from playing the subordinate role and passively observing the institutional hierarchy expected in the academic setting.

More recently, Okamoto (2011) illustrated the speaker's agency affecting the choice of speech style. Analysis of blog postings and conversations among

Japanese speakers provided convincing evidence that there are no socially agreed-upon rules of honorifics that all speakers follow blindly corresponding to contextual specifics (e.g. hierarchy, social distance). Rather, speakers have different beliefs as how honorifics should be used, and 'it is ultimately the speaker and not the context that determines the choice of honorific and plain forms' (Okamoto, 2011: 3686). The speaker's choice of a particular speech style reflects the affective stance that the speaker strategically projects toward the listener in situation. Data revealed that the speaker's choice of the polite form often reflected his/her deferential stance toward the listener and contextual parameters (e.g. setting and type of speech act performed). Absence of such a stance often resulted in the choice of the plain form. Okamoto claimed that the meanings of speech forms are diverse and ambiguous, reflecting one's language ideology and contextual contingencies.

Geyer (2013) also supports the argument regarding the diversity and dynamicity of speech styles. However, she maintains the position that there is the default usage of speech styles that are generally agreed upon among speakers. By analyzing conversations in different social settings and participant memberships, she documented the baseline use of the polite and plain forms, as well as instances in which the speakers deviated from the normative usage. Her analysis suggests that contextual features do affect the use of speech styles at the baseline level, but they also serve as a reference point with which the speaker's deviations from the norm is assessed. Norms affect the speaker's choice of speech styles, but at the same time the speaker constructs norms regarding the use of speech styles during interaction.

In summary, a series of key studies in the past three decades have produced evidence against the traditional standpoint, which simply associates the use of the polite and plain form with fixed situational categories (i.e. formal vs. informal). Instead, these studies have revealed speech forms as resources available for speakers to adapt to dynamically changing interaction and to construct social identities. Under this indexical approach, the speaker is not a passive observer of social conventions but rather an active participant who makes choices to express social meaning and stance (Cook, 2006; Okamoto, 2011). A shift from one speech form to another occurs in a range of functions, reflecting conversation participants' relationship, distance, affect, stance, identity, and the 'self' that they wish to project.

Below is a list of conditions in which the speaker is likely to shift from the polite to plain form as found in the literature (Chen, 2004; Cook, 1996, 1999, 2002; Fukushima, 2007; Geyer, 2013; Ikuta, 2008; Jones & Ono, 2008; Makino, 2002; Masuda, 2011; Maynard, 1993; Nazkian, 2010; Okamoto, 1999, 2011; Saito, 2010; Usami, 1995). The speaker typically uses the plain form when:

(1) Expressing feelings and thoughts
(2) Showing empathy/sympathy

(3) Indicating closeness to the interlocutor
(4) Exploring common interests and topics
(5) Talking to themselves
(6) Emphasizing
(7) Hedging
(8) Adding to the interlocutor's information
(9) Adding to own information
(10) Correcting self
(11) Repeating the interlocutor's utterance
(12) Recalling something
(13) Summarizing or paraphrasing the interlocutor's speech
(14) Listing facts
(15) Teasing
(16) Complaining indirectly
(17) Advocating the interlocutor's feelings and ideas
(18) Negotiating for meaning
(19) Completing the interlocutor's turn-in-progress

Acquisition of speech styles in L2 Japanese

Because of the dynamicity and complexity involved in speech styles, mastery of the plain and polite forms presents a considerable challenge for learners of Japanese. Learners have to acquire not only the complex grammatical patterns of the speech forms according to clause types, but also have to know how these two forms can co-exist in a single interaction. They also have to understand when and for what functions people shift from one form to the other by attending to the utterance and situational meanings that arise in communication. Because appropriate choice of speech style is obligatory in Japanese conversation, the knowledge of different speech forms and ability to distinguish them in a spontaneous interaction are essential in the process of becoming a competent speaker in Japanese. In short, speech style is a tool for self-expression and interactional management. The ability to respond to contextual specifics (i.e. setting, relationship, psychological distance, attitudes, shared knowledge, and sequential turns) by using the appropriate speech style is a critical aspect of interactional competence in Japanese.

A number of previous studies have examined Japanese learners' use of the polite and plain forms (Atsuzawa-Windley & Noguchi, 1995; Chen, 2004; Cook, 2001, 2008; Iwasaki, 2010, 2011; Masuda, 2011; Marriot, 1995; Masuda, 2011; McMeekin, 2007, 2011; Uenaka, 1997). Because Japanese textbooks typically introduce the polite form first and do not introduce the plain form until much later, learners tend to stick to the polite form as their default style and do not attempt to use the plain form. Previous studies revealed learners' skewed use of one speech style over the other (Chen, 2004; Masuda, 2011; Maynard, 1993; McMeekin, 2011). These studies also demonstrated the cases of learner-specific style shifts. Chen (2004) analyzed conversations between graduate students of L2 Japanese and native Japanese speakers. He found that, while native speakers used the plain form for self-correction and exclamation at the rate of 70–100%, L2 speakers' rates in these two functions remained only 20 to 50%. Instead, they showed a tendency of using the plain form to solve communication problems.

This L2-specific shifting was also found in McMeekin's (2011) data. Conversations between learners and their host family members revealed learners' predominant use of the polite form. However, learners often shifted from the polite to plain form when they were negotiating meaning. See the excerpt below for illustration. This is a conversation between Brad (B), a learner and his host mother (HM). The polite form is underlined and the plain form is in bold. (The morpheme-by-morpheme gloss is omitted to reflect the original version.)

1 B: *ah itsumokazokutoissho ni <u>atsumemasu</u>*
        'Ah (we) always get together with the family.'
2 HM: *fu::n*
        'Hmmm.'
3 B: *sore karawatashi no ah watashi no nan to **iu**?*
        'Then my ah my ah what do you call it?'
4 HM: ***itoko**?*
        'Cousin?'
5 B: *no ah kazoku ah **jinrui**?*
        'No ah family ah jinrui?'
6 HM: ***shinrui**?*
        'Relatives?'
7 B: *hai shinrui no ie ni <u>ikimasu</u>*
        'Yes, we go to the relative's house.'

Although the host mother's utterances consistently carry the plain form, Brad's utterances contain a mixture of the plain and polite forms. Brad starts out with the polite form (*desu/masu* form) in line 1, but shifts to the plain form in lines 3 and 5 when seeking vocabulary help (searching for the Japanese term for 'relatives'). After the lexical problem gets solved, he shifts back into the *desu/masu* form in line 7 to complete his utterance. This negotiation sequence is characterized by Brad's use of the plain form (lines 3 through 6) while solving his lexical problem. Brad's return to the polite form in line 7 indicates that the negotiation sequence is over and that the main thread of the conversation has resumed. McMeekin refers to the use of the plain forms in communication problems as an 'embedded subspace' – a sequence subordinate to the main thread of the conversation. In a circumstance like this, interlocutors suspend concerns for politeness and instead concentrate on the problem being solved. Learners' shifts to the plain form in these negotiation exchanges suggest their implicit understanding that the plain form can be used in this situation without causing a threat to politeness.

As shown above, existing findings suggest that L2 learners' style shifts do not always produce the communicative effects that Japanese speakers produce, like showing psychological closeness or expressing sympathy. Similarly, they do not always contribute to collaborative co-construction of an utterance with the interlocutor. Instead, learners' style shifts are often characterized as their communication strategies – the plain forms being employed to compensate for a communication breakdown. Observation of these L2-specific uses of the plain forms makes us wonder whether learners are aware of the social meanings and indexical functions of the speech styles. It could be that learners resort to the plain forms simply as a tool to cope with communicative pressure, because these forms are linguistically simple and do not carry elaborate morphological markings. A question remains on learners' shifts to the plain forms beyond compensatory strategies – whether or not learners understand the indexical functions of the plain forms and are able to use them proactively to project their desired social personae.

Learning speech styles in a study abroad setting

Learning speech styles is a demanding task, but what types of experience could facilitate the acquisition? Previous findings point to opportunities to observe and practice speech styles in diverse social settings as a condition for acquisition. Because these opportunities are likely to exist in the target language community, previous research has examined study abroad settings as a context for the development of speech styles. Masuda (2011) found higher production rates of the plain form among learners who had studied in Japan than among those with no study abroad experience. The findings suggest that exposure to different speech styles and communicative situations could help learners move away from the default polite style and incorporate the plain form in their linguistic inventory.

Learners' greater tendency to use the plain form was indeed found in several other studies in a study abroad setting (Caltabiano, 2008; Hashimoto, 1993; Iwasaki, 2010; Marriott, 1993; Marriot & Enomoto, 1995). When exposed to the plain forms through informal interaction with peers and host family members, learners probably abandoned the default use of the polite forms that they learned in the classroom and adapted the plain form in their linguistic repertoire. However, these studies also revealed that learners often overuse the plain form after studying abroad, which suggests that socialization into the pragmatically appropriate use of speech styles did not fully take place.

Iwasaki (2011) conducted interviews with five male learners of Japanese to gain insights about their experiences with speech styles during study abroad. Interview data revealed a variety of social contexts that facilitated learners' understanding of the formal and informal speech: club activities involving the junior-senior hierarchy and corresponding status-appropriate language use; host family members' use of honorific forms when talking to out-group members; and home stay interactions that encouraged the expression of mood and emotion with informal language use. Interactions in these contexts played a prominent role in learners' socialization into the appropriate use of speech styles. Notable in the data was learners' emerging awareness and appreciation of style mixing. When observing senior-junior interaction, one learner commented that juniors do not always use the polite form (*desu/masu* form) to seniors. He realized that the use of the *desu/masu* form does not always mark hierarchy or politeness. Although this learner was yet unable to articulate rules behind style-mixing, he was at least aware that speech forms are not bound to any fixed contextual features.

While participants' awareness of the speech styles was evident in Iwasaki's study, their learning process also revealed a complex picture resulting from constraints imposed by the local community. Perceptions toward foreigners, especially toward male Americans, constrained the learners' practice of different speech forms. Local Japanese people did not expect learners to use formal language because of the essentialist view of Americans being casual and friendly. At the same time, some learners reported that they were not allowed to use 'vulgar' male speech because they were L2 speakers. As a result, they were restricted to only use gender-neutral language and had to stay away from using 'male language' that could index playfulness. In another occasion, learners' subjectivity and identity mediated their cultivation of speech styles. Learners knew the appropriate speech style to use, but struggled with conforming to the norms due to their desire of maintaining their identity. Some learners wanted to project the image of a formal self and resorted to using the polite forms, while others wanted to sound casual and chose to use the plain forms to index friendliness.

These findings point to a number of factors that affect the learning of speech styles in a study abroad program: input, feedback, modeling, perceptions and expectations of the local community, and learner identity and subjectivity. Quality of exposure and social contacts in a wide range of settings could assist acquisition of speech forms and their social meanings, but equally influential are learners' subjectivity and investment in those experiences. How they construct themselves as L2 speakers and what identities they wish to project could facilitate or bind their access to opportunities for practice.

Other study abroad studies provided micro-genetic analyses of learners' interactions with community members to reveal how speech styles are learned in social activities (e.g. Cook, 2008; McMeekin, 2011). Cook (2008) analyzed dinnertime conversations between nine learners of Japanese and their host family members during a year-long study abroad program.

Although family members predominantly used the plain form at home, they occasionally shifted to the polite form as a way to project different identities. For instance, a host mother switched to the *desu/masu* form when she was serving the food that she had just prepared, signaling her identity as the 'person in charge.' In another occasion, a host mother shifted to the polite form when she was explaining to a learner about Japanese social customs, which highlighted her identity as a knowledgeable person. Another instance of style-shifting was found when family members directly took on the voices of others, for example mimicking the voice of a mailman or a customer. Through observation of these instances, learners were implicitly socialized into the target-like use of the speech styles.

McMeekin (2011) also revealed linguistic socialization in a home stay setting. Learners opted to use the polite form at home, although the host family members predominantly used the plain form. However, a small increase in use of the plain form occurred through their participation in daily activities. For example, through a routine talk about food with a host mother, a student learned that spontaneous, emphatic utterances like *oishii* ('It's delicious.') take the plain form because they index self-directed thoughts. The student gradually adopted the plain form with these emphatic expressions by repeating after her host mother. Language socialization occurred following the host mother's modeling of the appropriate speech style in context, her prompting for participation in the exchange, and repetition of the exchange.

This chapter has described two primary forms of Japanese speech style, the polite form (*desu/masu* form) and the plain form, as linguistic resources contributing to interactional competence. I have presented their structures and functions, as well as conditions in which these two forms mix and shift between one another. Learners of Japanese experience difficulty in using these forms in a register-appropriate manner because of the linguistic and sociocultural complexity involved in the forms. Japanese speakers strategically shift between speech styles in order to negotiate and co-construct interpersonal relationships, affect, and interpersonal distance, as well as to index different social identities or to mark discourse boundaries. Because this indexical use of speech styles is not salient in naturalistic, face-to-face interactions, learners often face challenge in understanding the mappings among speech forms, meanings, and contexts. Modelling and feedback from local members may facilitate socialization into the appropriate use of speech styles. A study abroad context that offers opportunities to interact in a variety of social settings can be an optimal environment for the acquisition of speech styles.

Incomplete Utterance Ending in Japanese

While the polite and plain forms are the major clause-ending forms in Japanese conversation, there is another category of sentence forms that cannot be neglected – incomplete sentences. In Japanese conversation, speakers choose between the polite and the plain form at sentence-final position, but they can also opt for an incomplete ending. The pervasiveness of ellipsis and incomplete endings is a characteristic of Japanese communication. Maynard (1989) contests that the Japanese language is known for its frequent ellipsis of particles, and verbal and nominal phrases. See the example:

1 A: *Seattle   wa   kirei   da.*
       Seattle   TOP   beautiful   COP
       'Seattle is a beautiful city.'
2 B: *Honto. Watashi   mo   ki-ta   no   hajimete   da*   **kedo.**
       Really I   too   come-PST   NOM   first time COP   but
       'Really. This was my first time to come here **but**'

In line 2, Speaker A's utterance is marked by the conjunction *kedo* (but), but the reminder of the sentence is missing. By leaving out a clause that follows *kedo*, Speaker A avoids saying what is already understood and leaves some space for the listener to fill in his/her own interpretations of the missing clause. Maynard claims that the function of *kedo* here is not grammatical but interactional. By using incomplete sentences, the speaker can involve the listener in the talk and develop a shared understanding.

Incomplete sentences also appear in the co-construction of turn or turn-sharing. See another example from Maynard (1989):

1 A: *Ichikawa   tte   yatsu   ga   iru   janai?*
       Ichikawa   QT   guy   SUB   exist   isn't he
       'Ah, you know the guy Ichikawa?'
2 B: *Un,   un.*
       yes   yes
       'yes, yes'
3 A: *Aitsu   ga   ne*
       that guy   SUB   FP
       'that guy'
4 B: *shushoku*   ←
       employment
       'employment'
5 A: *shi-nai   mitai* ←
       do-NEG   seems like
       'seems not to do so.'

Here, after Speaker A introduces the topic (Mr Ichikawa), Speaker B adds the object noun phrase (*shushoku*) in line 4, because the topic is about getting a job after graduation. Following B's contribution, in line 5, Speaker A completes the sentence by supplementing the verb predicate (*shinaimitai*).

Incomplete sentences are pervasive in Japanese conversation. Tadokoro (2012) discovered that, at 25–50% of the time, Japanese speakers left their utterances incomplete, while the range was 30–45% in Nazkian's (2010) data in formal interview situations. Masuda (2011), on the other hand, revealed Japanese college students using incomplete endings about 35% of the time during their conversations with a Japanese professor.

Usami (1995) defines the incomplete ending form as an utterance that is grammatically unfinished but completes transmission of information. It includes a case of predicate omission, or in the case of a compound sentence, an omission of the main clause introduced by a subordinating particle. Chen (2000) provides more detailed categories of incomplete utterances and their functions. By analyzing four conversations among Japanese speakers, he identified six types of particles and conjunctions that often occur at utterance-final position and mark incomplete endings. See Table 2.1 for the list adapted from Chen (2004: 130–137). Incomplete endings are marked in bold.

Incomplete sentences serve a variety of interpersonal functions (Chen, 2010; Maynard, 1986; Usami, 1995). The speaker uses incomplete endings to avoid being definite, to allocate a turn to the next speaker, or to avoid an explicit marking of the polite or plain speech style. They also function as a strategy of economy: the speaker leaves a sentence incomplete when missing information is understood based on the shared knowledge and context of conversation. Incomplete sentences also assist with turn projection and turn allocation, especially when they occur at the transference of speakership. At the practice of turn-taking, participants monitor a turn-at-talk to identify a possible point of completion. They project and anticipate the possible speaker transition point, or what Sacks *et al.* (1974) called transition relevance place (TRP), before it actually occurs. Participants coordinate their contributions with one another to determine who should speak next and for how long (Sindnell, 2010). Hence, turn construction is a product of interaction between the speaker and the hearer.

Incomplete sentences characterize the practice of co-construction of an event. When the speaker produces an incomplete sentence, the listener orients to it and then responds to it. The listener's response can take a variety of formats, including: providing backchannel cues to encourage the speaker to continue with his or her talk; completing the utterance initiated by the speaker in a form of joint turn construction; or treating the incomplete sentence as a turn completion signal and starting a new turn (Hayashi, 2003, 2014; Hayashi & Mori, 1998; Lerner, 2004). In all of these occasions, incomplete sentences function as interactional resources. They reflect the speaker's choice as to how to design a turn in such a way that it becomes understandable and acceptable to the listener. At the same time, the listener's response or follow-up on these sentences signals his/her active involvement in the talk. In short, incomplete sentences are conversational phenomena that

Table 2.1 Common morpho-syntactic markers of incomplete endings (adapted from Chen, 2004)

(1)	Conjunction particle *te* and *de* (and)
	JF1: *Kotsuhitoka de okane kasegema-sen deshi-ta?*
	transportation fee by money can earn-NEG COP-PST
	'Couldn't you earn some money by (saving) transportation fee?'
	JF2: *De, tomodachi nankani tomare-ba, momarumouke tteiu kanji-**de** ...*
	And friend something stay-if save a lot QT like-TE
	'And if you stay at friend's house or something, you can save a lot ...'
(2)	Conjunction particle *shi* and *node* (so/because)
	JF2: *Chigaimasu yo ne.*
	different FP FP
	'It's different, right?'
	JF1: *Tokuni daigakuintte senmontekina tokoro na **node** ...*
	especially graduate school specialist place COP because
	'Especially because a graduate school is a specialist place ...'
(3)	Conjunction particle *to* and *ba* (functioning as if-clause)
	JF1: *Mattaku chigau node yoku shirabe-te*
	completely different because thoroughly check-TE
	*haira-nai **to** ...*
	enter-NEG if
	'It's completely different, so if you don't enter without a thorough check ...'
(4)	Quotation particle *to* (....say that....)
	JM2: *Mae ni susumou **to** ....*
	forward to go QT
	'You are saying that you are going forward ...'
	JM1: *U...n sonotsumori desu **kedo** ...*
	u...n intend COP but
	'Yes, I intend but ...'
(5)	Topicalization with particle *wa* and *tte*
	JM1: *Onamae **wa** ...*
	name TOP
	'Your name is ...'
	JF2: *Sato desu*
	sato COP
	'Sato.'
(6)	Listing examples with the conjunction particle *toka* (and/or/like)
	JF2: *Nantoka hodaraa **toka** ... (laugh)*
	something hodaraa like
	'Something like *hodaraa*, and ...'
	JM1: (laugh)

reflect elaborate processes in which the participants constantly monitor each other's turns and collaboratively develop ongoing talk.

The connection between interactional competence and collaborative turn completion was made recently in Dings's (2014) study. She examined the development of interactional resources related to alignment activity in L2 Spanish conversations during study abroad. According to Atkinson *et al.* (2007: 169), alignment is 'the complex means by which human beings effect coordinated interaction and maintain that interaction in dynamically adaptive ways'. Collaborative turn completion (i.e. a participant completing another participant's utterance) reflects a high degree of alignment because the hearer projects how the speaker is going to end an utterance and adopts the speaker's point of view by completing his/her utterance (Nofsinger, 1991). The participant, Sophie, developed ability to produce collaborative completions during study abroad. When her interlocutor displayed difficulty in finding the right word, Sophie provided a turn completion in a precisely timed, perfectly grammatical manner. Sophie's evolving contributions of collaborative turn completions provided evidence that she became able to play a more active role in the co-construction of discourse as her time abroad progressed.

Through alignment activity, participants exhibit their 'intersubjectivity, by showing each other that they are understanding each other and are being understood' (Dings, 2014: 744). Alignment moves demonstrate shared understanding among participants, as well as their ability to adopt the other's point of view and speak in the other's voice. In Japanese, alignment activity through collaborative completions is found in the use of the conjunctive particle *te*. *Te*-ending connects multiple clauses and serves a range of conversational functions, including: developing an interactive chain of clauses and joint turn completion (Hashimoto, 2007); signaling the continuity of a topic or subject matter (S. Iwasaki, 1993); and narrating a story (Iwasaki & Ono, 2007). *Te*-form functions as a turn projection device by signaling the syntactic shape of the unfolding turn and the possible place of its completion. Because *te* indicates that the current turn is not yet over and that the predicate is to follow, the current speaker can continue speaking or invite the listener to take over the turn.

Hashimoto (2007) demonstrates how *te*-form ending sentences contribute to the projection of unfolding turns and the accomplishment of co-construction of turns. The excerpt below (Hashimoto, 2007: 253) illustrates how speakers use *te*-form repeatedly and systematically in talk-in-progress. (The glosses are from the original.)

```
6    Tomi:    ohiru ka-
              lunch or
7    (0.2)
8             nanka wo tabete::
              something ACC eat:TE
              '((we)) eat lunch or something TE,'
9    Aya:                    ohiru tabete:::
                             lunch    eat:TE
                             'eat lunch TE,'
```

10		*chotto: omise* *nozoi**te**:::,*
		SOF shop peek:TE
		'take a quick peak at shops TE,'
11	Tomi:	*nozoi**te**::,*
		look into:TE
		'peek ((at shops)) TE,'
12	Aya:	*saigo purikura* *tot**te**::,*
		lastly purikura take:TE
		'lastly ((we)) take purikura TE,'
13	Tomi:	***te**::,*
		TE
		'TE,'

This excerpt displays six instances of the particle *te* conjoining a series of clauses. After the first appearance of the *te*-form in line 8 by Tomi (*nanka wo tabete*), in line 9, Aya takes over the turn with the same *te*-ending construction (*ohiru tabete*). Simultaneously, in line 10, she continues the turn by adding on to the topic-in-progress with another *te*-form unit (*omise nozoite*), which is followed by Tomi's repetition of the utterance in line 11. Finally in line 12, Aya indicates the end point of the activity listing by producing an entire clause with *te*-form (*saigo purikura tot**te*** 'lastly we take purikura'). Following this, in line 13, the first speaker contributes to the co-construction of talk by adding the particle *te* only. Although producing this bound morpheme *te* alone is ungrammatical, in this context of joint turn construction, the speaker's contribution of *te* is perfectly suitable, adding to the interactive nature of the conversation. Participants build a conversation collaboratively by producing utterances in concert with one another by using *te*-form in incomplete endings.

Although the use of incomplete sentences is a major characteristic of Japanese conversation, L2 learners have difficulty in using incomplete sentences skillfully. Even advanced-level learners (e.g. graduate students in a Japanese university or the Japanese Language Proficiency Level 1 holders) cannot produce incomplete sentences as frequently or skillfully as native speakers of Japanese. For instance, Chen (2004) analyzed conversations between L1 Chinese graduate students in a Japanese university and native Japanese speakers, and found that incomplete sentences occupied only about 12% of the utterance-ending forms. The rest were complete sentences in the polite or plain form. The use of the incomplete endings becomes much smaller in the case of elementary to intermediate-level learners. Masuda (2011) analyzed L2 Japanese learners' conversation data and found only about 4% of incomplete sentences produced by the learners.

To recap, incomplete sentences serve a prime interactional function by presenting an opportunity for alignment activity and co-construction of talk. By leaving a sentence unfinished, the speaker signals a point of transfer of speakership. Responding to this signal, the listener may complete the sentence initiated by the speaker (joint turn construction), or may acknowledge the end of the talk and initiate a new topic. Given this interactive nature, collaborative use of incomplete sentences serve as an indicator of interactional competence in L2 Japanese. Knowledge of incomplete sentences and the ability to use them to co-construct a turn-in-progress is a critical part of linguistic and interactional resources that learners bring in to the process of joint meaning making.

The present study examines L2 learners' changes in the use of incomplete sentence endings in face-to-face conversations, as well as their changes in their use of the polite and plain forms over a semester study abroad. The next two chapters present background and methods used in this investigation. Chapter 3 presents an overview of study abroad programs as a site for language learning. Chapter 4 describes the methods used in this study.

Note

(1) The term 'polite form' and *'desu/masu* form' are used synonymously in Japanese to refer to the same speech style. In this book, I will use the term 'polite form' throughout.

3 Context of the Study: Study Abroad as a Site for Language Learning

Study abroad settings have been studied extensively in SLA research as a promising venue for examining language use and development (for a review, see Collentine & Freed, 2004; DuFon & Churchill, 2006; Freed, 1995a, 1998; Kinginger, 2009, 2011; Llanes, 2011). This context's popularity stems from the belief that L2 learners benefit both culturally and linguistically by studying in the target speech community. Beginning with Freed's (1995a) seminal volume, *Second Language Acquisition in a Study Abroad Context*, researchers have investigated the ways in which studying abroad contributes to L2 learning. The study abroad context presents a rich environment for language learning because learners are exposed to a community full of linguistic and cultural practices that are not easily available in a domestic, formal classroom setting. Exposure to target language input and practice is considered a prime feature of the study abroad context that can facilitate second language acquisition.

Existing study abroad research mainly falls into two categories: (1) studies that investigated benefits of this context by analyzing linguistic outcomes, and (2) studies that documented learners' social participation and experiences during study abroad. Previous studies confirmed notable progress made by students in a study abroad program, particularly in the areas of oral skills, vocabulary, and sociolinguistic/pragmatic competence (e.g. Barron, 2003; Collentine, 2004; Dewey, 2008; Freed, 1995b; Llanes, 2010; Llanes & Munoz, 2010; Matsumura, 2001; Regan *et al.*, 2009; Schauer, 2006; Segalowitz & Freed, 2004; Taguchi, 2011; Taguchi *et al.*, 2013). Freed (1995b) analyzed L2 French learners' oral fluency and found that those who have studied abroad spoke at a faster speech rate. Llanes (2010) compared oral and written productions of children and adults who learned English in a domestic, formal instructional setting and in a study abroad program. She revealed that the study abroad context was superior to the domestic context for both groups of learners in the area of oral abilities. Regan *et al.* (2009) investigated the use of sociolinguistic features among L2 French learners in a study abroad program. They found that the negative morpheme *ne* deletion was observed more frequently in learners' speech after a year abroad. They also found that learners started to follow native speaker patterns of variation according to linguistic-internal factors (e.g. clause type). Matsumura (2001), on the other hand, examined L2 English learners' ability to recognize appropriate advice-giving expressions. After a four-month stay in Canada, more students in the study abroad group chose appropriate expressions than the group in a domestic setting. Schauer (2006) also revealed positive effects of study abroad. German learners of English increased their ability to detect pragmatic errors in speech acts during their stay in England, almost reaching the native speaker level.

Although existing findings largely favor study abroad learning, some studies revealed no conclusive evidence of study abroad effects in L2 development (e.g. Dewey, 2004; Freed, 1990; Mendelson, 2004). Freed (1990) found no general connection between language use and proficiency development in L2 French during study abroad, although she did find that lower-proficiency learners in France benefited more from interaction with native speakers than advanced learners. Similarly, Mendelson (2004) found no significant relationships between language use and proficiency gains. Dewey (2004), on the other hand, compared development of reading abilities between L2 Japanese learners in a study abroad and immersion setting, measured by a self-assessment, reading test, and vocabulary test. Study abroad participants outperformed the other two groups on the self-assessment measure, but not on other measures.

These inconclusive findings in the existing literature have led to a general consensus that studying abroad is not a uniform experience for all learners. Rather, it is subject to a complex set of variables, both personal and social, which in turn leads to great individual variation in the size and rate of linguistic gains. In fact, as early as two decades ago, Huebner (1995) argued that the study abroad context intensifies individual variation in learning process and outcomes. Following this claim, more recent studies have conducted a simultaneous analysis of linguistic gains and study abroad experiences, and revealed learners' changes in relation to individual and contextual characteristics. The central question addressed in these studies is what makes the study abroad context unique for second language development. The study abroad program, typically defined as a pre-scheduled, temporary stay in a foreign country for educational purposes, is different from a sojourn or a domestic classroom environment in that learners have access to both formal instruction in class and authentic communication outside the class. However, this simplified description does not say much about the specifics of the study abroad context that actually facilitate learning. In pursuing a more focused analysis of the context-learning connection, a number of studies have investigated what contextual features in the study abroad – nature, type, and intensity of social contact and experience – lead to linguistic achievement.

Social contact and experience have been examined in a variety of settings, including home stay, extracurricular activities, and social networking in a local community. Among these, homestay settings and other informal social networks have been thoroughly documented in the literature (e.g. Cook, 2008; Diao & Freed, 2012; Hernandez, 2010; Isabelli-Garcia, 2006; M. Ishida, 2009, 2011; Iwasaki, 2011; Kinginger, 2008, 2013; Kinginger & Farrell, 2004; Knight & Schmidt-Rinehardt, 2002; McMeekin, 2011; Schmidt-Rinehardt & Knight, 2004; Shively, 2011, 2013; Tanaka, 2004; Wilkinson, 1998, 2002). For example, Isabelli-Garcia (2006) examined how learners' social networks promoted their oral communication skills and accuracy. She found that involvement in local social networks led to learners' strong motivation in language learning, because social networks provided a platform for learners to align themselves with the new culture and accept cultural differences, which in turn produced learning.

Several other studies have adapted the language socialization approach (Duff, 2007; Schieffelin & Ochs, 1986) and the concept of community of practice (Lave & Wenger, 1991; Wenger, 1998) to reveal the interaction among learners' social contact, community involvement, and linguistic development. Lave and Wenger (1991) define community of practice as a group of people who share a concern or interest and gather to learn things as they interact regularly. They argue that only through the process of sharing information and experiences with the group, the members develop themselves personally and professionally. Language socialization theory, on the other hand, attests that linguistic and sociocultural knowledge develop simultaneously through social interaction in a local community (Duff, 2007; Schieffelin & Ochs, 1986).

Following these frameworks, several studies have provided micro-generic analyses of learners' interaction with community members and revealed how linguistic features are taught in situated social activities (e.g. Cook, 2008; Diao, 2014; DuFon, 2010; Iwasaki, 2011; McMeeken, 2011; Nguyen, 2011a; Shively, 2011, 2013). For example, Cook (2008) and McMeekin's (2011) studies, cited in Chapter 2, documented learners' socialization into the use of speech style through their daily interactions with host families. Numerous instances were found in which host family members explicitly and implicitly socialized learners into target-like uses of the plain and polite forms. In another study, Shively (2011) examined service encounter transactions among learners of Spanish while studying abroad in Spain. The learners carried a digital voice recorder and recorded their interaction in shops, restaurants, and other local settings. A total of 113 naturalistic recordings of service encounter exchanges were analyzed. Some learners acquired the knowledge of appropriate request-making forms in service exchanges by observing other customers' request-making forms and adapted them to their practice, while others learned the request forms through feedback from their host families. Diao (in press), on the other hand, focused on a college dorm as a place for socialization. She analyzed conversations between American learners of L2 Chinese and their Chinese roommates in a dorm in Shanghai and described instances of peer socialization of gendered Mandarin practices. Her analysis revealed the participants' use of affective sentence-final particles and their discussion about the social meaning of sexuality and gender that the particles project.

These studies illustrated how learners, as new members in the target community, became socialized into the practices of community. The social contacts and experiences built around the homestay and other local networks present a community into which learners integrate themselves. The socialization process occurred when learners entered the new community, took up a new role as a host family member, a customer or a friend, and participated in the role in recurrent practices of social interaction. Linguistic gains were the byproduct of this socialization process. These studies analyzed some of the key elements of a study abroad context – opportunities for input and interaction, feedback on and modeling of linguistic behaviors, and exposure to varied linguistic norms and practices – in conjunction with learners' linguistic growth. Findings generated a meaningful interpretation of what resources were available in the context of study abroad and how they supported L2 development.

The connection between context and learning revealed in these studies, however, is not always straightforward, because there is no guarantee that learners can successfully establish a membership in a local community while abroad and gain access to opportunities for practice. Learners' success depends on a range of factors, including their personalities, beliefs, and attitudes. In other words, contextual features alone do not tell us much about their impact on learning. What is important is the interaction between context and individuals, and changes within the interaction. As Larsen-Freeman and Cameron (2008) claim, context is not a stable background variable outside of individuals that affects their linguistic choices. Instead, the individual and context are interconnected at multiple levels, and every change to the individual is influenced by context. Hence, explanations of language development should come from two separate but complementary resources: (1) internal, or within the learner resources (e.g. proficiency, personal perspective and attitudes, motivation), and (2) external, or outside the learner resources (e.g. environment, input, interacting agents, time, materials, reinforcement). Interaction and adaptations of these resources form a basis to explain change in linguistic abilities.

Several studies have revealed this complex interplay among context, individuals, and language development in a study abroad setting. Tanaka (2004), for instance, showed that proficiency gains during study abroad were affected by both learners' beliefs about language learning and opportunities that helped transform their beliefs to actual learning behaviors. Although Japanese students in New Zealand in his study made notable gains on a proficiency test and oral narrative tasks, there was considerable individual variation within the group. Interview and diary data showed that some students did not talk to their host family because of their shyness and weak English skills. As a result, these students had little opportunity to interact with their hosts, which consequently affected their learning outcomes. These findings suggest that study abroad does not bring about uniform linguistic gains across learners. Learners' agency and other individual characteristics (e.g. personality and proficiency) mediate their access to social contact and experience, and shape their language development as a result.

Similar findings were reported in Kinginger's (2008) study that examined L2 French learners' awareness of sociolinguistic forms during a semester abroad in France. Pre- and post-test comparisons revealed considerable individual variation in 17 learners' development. Qualitative data revealed how learners negotiated their membership in the community. For example, one learner, Louis, had a host family who preferred a quiet environment. To compensate for the lack of conversation at home, he actively developed a social network in French by talking to his peers in French and participating in volunteer activities. Liza's case was the opposite. She developed a close relationship with her host mother, but ended up spending a substantial amount of time speaking in English because her family and friends visited her in France. She also maintained strong links to home online. These findings reveal the types of learning resources available in host communities and learners' various reactions toward them. Although learners might initially treat the study abroad as an opportunity for L2 learning, they might get discouraged from unexpected home stay arrangements or close connections they maintain with their home country peers. In those circumstances, it is the learners' agency that re-shapes the context and learning opportunities available during study abroad.

So far I have described learner-side factors that may constrain learners' participation in linguistic and social practice. Adding to this body of literature, previous research has also revealed host community-side factors that may limit learners' access to practice while abroad. Several studies found that race and gender-discrimination constrained learners' access to the host community (Polanyi, 1995; Talburt & Stewart, 1999) and living arrangements (Churchill, 2003; Knight & Schmidt-Rinehart, 2002). Other studies showed that cultural stereotypes function as a barrier to providing and receiving target language input. Members in the host culture may treat international visitors differently than in-group members, and interact with them using different pragmatic norms (Brown, 2013; Hassall, 2013; Iino, 1996; Siegel, 1994).

In Siegal's (1994) study, a participant, Mary, was a visiting scholar at a Japanese university. She used the polite modal verb *deshoo* frequently in her interaction with a Japanese professor. *Deshoo* is an epistemic marker indicating that the information is known to the addressee. However, it sounds condescending when used with someone who is not in a close relationship with the speaker, because – depending on intonation – it sounds as if the speaker is challenging the addressee's knowledge. Mary used *deshoo* purposefully to express a polite stance, but her strategy failed in the eyes of native Japanese speakers. However, Mary's inappropriate speech was not perceived as a pragmatic failure because she was categorized as a *gaijin* (foreigner) who had no obligation to conform to the norm – which was not her chosen identity, but the identity assigned by the members in the local community.

Brown's (2013) study on L2 Korean honorifics revealed a gap between the learners' prescriptive knowledge of how honorifics should be used and the way they actually used honorifics during their one-year stay in Korea. This gap emerged because native-like patterns of interaction were not available to the learners: their position as exchange students and foreigners resulted in the belief on Korean interlocutors that the norms of honorifics did not apply in interactions with them. For example, one of the participant's instructors used *panmal* (honorific forms) when addressing Korean students, whereas she always used *contaymal* (non-honorific forms) when addressing the learner. The 'foreigner' identity assigned to the participants positioned them in the 'peripheries of Korean society' (p. 290), which resulted in patterns of honorific use that flouted native speaker norms.

Similarly, Hasall's (2013) study showed how the 'foreigner' identity constrained study-abroad participants from adopting local norms of address forms during a seven-week sojourn in Indonesia. He showed that the participants were positioned in the target language as *bule*, an Indonesian term used to refer to western foreigners which bears a disparaging tone. This identity of 'outsiders' assigned to them led to learners' belief that they do not have to practice appropriate use of the address term system.

From this collection of studies, it is clear that there are more than just contextual features to examine in the study abroad setting. Potential impact of the study abroad experience on learning is quite apparent, but the variation in learning outcomes and learners' experiences found in previous studies reminds us that success is not always guaranteed for everyone: learners' 'takeaway' in a study abroad setting depends on their degree of investment in the context. The context may offer a variety of venues for social contact and interaction, but it is the product of contextual affordances and learners' positioning that determine whether learners can take advantage of the context to grow linguistically while abroad. This intricate relationship among linguistic gains, individual differences, and context can be revealed through a longitudinal study that combines systematic data collection on change in learners' abilities combined with qualitative analyses of context and individuals.

I present my study as an example of such research. I take the position that language development is an interactive process, ratified by real-life experiences. Following this stance, I adopt a mixed methods approach in a longitudinal design and present a combined analysis of descriptions of linguistic change and factors affecting the change in a study abroad setting. I will describe development of interactional competence among 18 participants during a three-month study abroad program in Japan as indexed by their use of linguistic and interactional resources in face-to-face conversations. Analyses from the conversation data are complemented with interview data collected from a subset of individuals about their social experiences during study abroad. A triangulated analysis of multiple data sets help us interpret individual variations in the development of interactional competence and understand the learner-specific and contextual factors that helped shape developmental trajectories.

This methodology is particularly fitting in the analysis of interactional competence. Interactional competence capitalizes on the belief that language learning is fundamentally social and people learn by participating in context-specific discursive practices. Language knowledge is locally situated and jointly constructed by participants in a discursive practice (Young, 2002, 2008a, 2011). If interaction is conceptualized as a situated, goal-oriented activity that draws on a range of participants' resources, it makes most sense to look into participants' actual social practices to understand their development of interactional competence. Because ability to interact depends on learners' understanding of how actions are organized within specific communicative events or activity types, the range of social practices that learners are engaged in, together with the nature, type, and intensity of those practices, could provide lenses through which interactional competence is examined. Practice-specific communication patterns, such as how turns are taken and actions are ordered, and how linguistic and semiotic resources are conventionally used to produce meaning, are learned and acquired through participation in those communicative situations. Because the verbal, nonverbal, and interactional resources that learners employ are configured into discursive practices, analyzing learners' social practice and experience in the host community should help discern the facets of the discursive practices that learners are routinely engaged in. In turn, we can see how these facets contribute to the development of interactional competence.

Following this approach, the present study describes the nature of interactional development and social affordances in a study abroad context that may assist learners' access to practice. The next chapter (Chapter 4) presents methods used in this investigation.

4 Methods

Specifics of the methodology in this study are described in the following section that encompasses three parts: participants, data and data analysis methods, and data collection procedures.

Participants

Participants included 18 international students enrolled in an intensive Japanese language program at a large private university in Tokyo. The program was one of the biggest in Japan, with 1600 students enrolled. The program had eight levels and offered over 800 classes per week. Four male and 14 female students participated, with an average age of 22 ranging from 19 to 29. The group included six Chinese, three Taiwanese, three Americans, two Singaporeans, one New Zealander, one Brunei, one Korean, and one French. They came from a variety of majors: psychology, computer science, English literature, Japanese, East Asian studies, journalism, environmental science, economics, political science, business administration, comparative studies, and international studies. Based on the standardized placement exam results, they were judged to be intermediate-level and were placed in the Level 3 or 4 of the eight levels in the Japanese program. None of the students had studied in Japan previously. All students had received formal Japanese instruction in their home countries before coming to Japan (three years on average). At the time of data collection, 10 students were living in an international dormitory, five had a home stay arrangement, two were living alone in an apartment, and one was in a shared house. They received 4000 yen (about $48) for participation.

Participant recruitment took place according to the following procedures. First, participants were recruited from a group of intermediate-level students who had already learned the polite and plain form in class. I distributed a flyer to all students enrolled in Level 3 or 4 to solicit their participation (a total of 233 students). Of about 100 students who volunteered, I excluded the students who had studied in Japan before or who were continuing coursework from the previous semester. In addition, because the test instructions were given in English, I excluded the students who did not indicate much confidence in their English skills. After this screening process, 18 students remained in the study.

From the group of 18 participants, eight students were recruited as informants for the interview. In determining the informants, I took the following steps. First, I asked the 18 participants about their interest in participating in the interviews. Eleven participants indicated interest. Of the 11, I selected eight participants who demonstrated diversity in nationality, gender, length of previous Japanese study, living arrangements, and purpose of study abroad. The participants were interviewed three times during the period of the study (one semester). In this book, I will report findings from four participants. See Chapter 8 for their background.

Conversation Data

Participants' conversations were recorded at the beginning and end of the semester on a Macintosh computer in a quiet office on campus. Participants were paired randomly and were instructed to have a free, informal conversation with their peer on everyday topics for 20 minutes. Appendix B includes a copy of the task directions given to the participants. The pairs of interlocutors were intentionally selected from students who were enrolled in different classes. This was done to reduce the effect of participant familiarity and to attribute learners' performance changes to development in interactional competence, rather than to increased familiarity among the interlocutors. Because none of the students presumably had known each other prior to the study, I incorporated a ten-minute warm-up session before the recording.

I participated in the conversation occasionally to introduce variation as the conversation was progressing. Because previous literature revealed that people switch speech styles by attending to dynamic contextual features (e.g. psychological distance with the addressee, the addressee's behavior and attitudes; see Chapter 2), my goal was to see whether or not students' speech styles change to correspond with changing participant structure: between the moment when they conversed only with their peer and the moment when they conversed with their peer and the researcher.[1] The students' style-shifts across these different participant structures were considered to provide a window through which I could analyze their ability to mark discourse boundaries – part of the interactional resources in Young's (2008a, 2008b) framework (see Chapter 1). While the majority of the conversation was two-way (between students), about 40% of the conversation was three-way (see Chapter 5). The conversations were transcribed following the conventions adapted and modified from Sacks *et al.* (1974) (see Appendix A for the transcription conventions).

Interactional competence (Young, 2008, 2011) was the theoretical model that guided the analysis of conversation data in this study. Interactional competence requires participants to make a skillful use of a variety of linguistic and interactional resources for the task of joint meaning making. Under this framework, I analyzed learners' production of two primary speech styles (polite and plain forms), focusing on the functions that each performs and participants' shift between these forms. In addition, I analyzed participants' use of incomplete sentence endings in the practice of turn projection and turn allocation. I analyzed how participants used incomplete sentences collaboratively for the purpose of turn co-construction and joint meaning making. Below, I will explain the coding criteria used for the analysis.

Speech styles: The polite and plain form

Prior to the analysis, an utterance was defined as a 'single semantic and structural unit bounded by pauses, intonation counters, or turns' (Fukushima, 2007: 30). Participants' utterances were analyzed for complete and incomplete sentence ending forms. First, all the incomplete sentences were identified. Remaining sentences (excluding fragments) were categorized as complete sentences. Complete sentences included two types: the polite form (*desu/masu* form) and the plain form. Percentages of these forms were compared between the first and second recordings to track change. Table 4.1 displays the criteria used to classify the plain and polite forms, which were adapted from the previous literature (e.g. Cook, 2006; Iwasaki, 2010; Tadokoro, 2012).

Although utterance endings are the primary indicators of speech styles (polite or plain), clause endings also index a certain level of formality or informality. Thus, in addition to the utterance endings, I analyzed the

Table 4.1 Categorization criteria for the complete sentences: Polite and plain forms

Category	Forms
Polite form	***desu/masu* form ending** (*desu/deshita/deshou/masu/mashita/mashou/masen/masendeshita*) e.g. *Kirei desu.* (It's beautiful.); *Wakarimasen.* (I don't understand.); *Dekimasu.* (I can do it.); *Dokodesu ka?* (Where is it?) ***desu/masu* form followed by sentence final particles (*ne, na, yo, yone, ka*)**[2] e.g. *Suki desu ne.* (I like it.); *Tanoshii desu yo.* (It's fun.); *Iijyana-idesu ka* (It's fine, isn't it?); *Mimasu ne* (I watch it.)
Plain form	**dictionary form, including one-word utterance and word stems** e.g. *Tanoshii.* (It's fun.); *Ryugaku?* (Study abroad?); *Erai.* (Great.); *Honto* (It's real.); *Kuyashikatta.* (It was regrettable.) **dictionary form followed by sentence final particles (*ne, na, yo yone, kana, ya*)** e.g. *Samu katta yo.* (It was cold.); *Yaritai na.* (I want to do it.); *Naiyo ne.* (There isn't any, is it?); *Sugoi na.* (It's great.); *Watashi gurai kana.* (Maybe it's just me.)

endings of clauses including those with *kara* (so/because), *kedo* (but), and *node/nde* (therefore). I excluded the followings from the analysis: backchannels, laughter, exclamations, parroting and simple repetition, and formulaic expressions (e.g. *gomen* 'sorry'; *sodesu ka* 'Is that right?'; *doshiyo kana* 'I don't know what to do.'). Ungrammatical forms were omitted from the analysis (6.4% of the data). I coded the data for the polite or plain form and calculated percentage of each category. I completed three rounds of coding over different days to ensure accuracy.

Functions of the plain form

In addition to coding the data for the polite and plain forms, I conducted more detailed analysis of the participants' use of the plain form – how often they used the plain form and for what purposes they used it. Previous studies identified a number of functions served by the plain form in conversation (Chen, 2004; Cook, 1996, 1999, 2002, 2008; Fukushima, 2007; Ikuta, 2008; Jones & Ono, 2008; Maynard, 1991, 1993; Makino, 2002; Masuda, 2011; Nazkian, 2010; Okamoto, 1999; Saito, 2010; Usami, 1995). Although previous findings found instances of the plain form specific to L2 interaction, such as the negotiation of meaning and accommodation toward the interlocutor's speech (Chen, 2004; Masuda, 2011; McMeekin, 2011; see Chapter 2), this study examined whether learners' choice of the plain form extends beyond these ordinary functions to expressing different social meanings and discourse functions.

I developed the original taxonomy for this analysis. The first step in the process was to survey existing literature and compile a list of the plain form functions identified in the previous studies. The original list of 19 functions appears in Chapter 2. While not exhaustive, the list displays common conditions under which the plain form occurs in conversation. Based on this list, I developed macro-categories by grouping similar functions together and elevating them to an independent category. Then, after coding all the plain forms in the present data, I assigned a function to each plain form. This manual coding process required multiple readings of the plain forms occurring in the data to check initial judgments and confirm coding decisions. Once the coding was complete, the frequency of different functions of the plain form was determined, along with their representative examples. Table 4.2 displays the list of the five sub-categories that emerged from this process. The plain forms are in bold in the examples.

The plain forms with affect keys

In addition to the functions of the plain form, I analyzed the plain forms for the presence or absence of affect keys (i.e. linguistic resources that signal the speaker's feelings, moods, and attitudes). Affect keys are a reflection of the speaker's affective stance toward the addressee or the

Table 4.2 Taxonomy of the plain form functions

1.	**Request for information or confirmation from the interlocutor** The plain form is used to ask questions or to solicit information and reaction from the interlocutor. (e.g. *Sono eiga do **omotta?*** 'What did you think about the movie?')
2.	**Joint meaning making** The plain form is used to add to the interlocutor's speech, to complete the interlocutor's turn-in-progress, to advocate the interlocutor's feeling or wish, to expand on the interlocutor's speech, and co-construct information and knowledge. A: *Takusan asondara mata. . .* (if you play a lot, you can again. . .) B: *Benkyo **dekiru.*** (can study.)
3.	**Presentation of information** The plain form is used to present information, add to own information, explain something, or self-correct information. e.g. *Kurasu ga hitotsu atta. Sokode nihon no odori o **shita.*** (I had one class. We did Japanese dance there.)
4.	**Expression of inner self** The plain form is used to express feeling, surprise, sympathy/empathy, and evaluation. The plain form is used for self-talk and conviction. e.g. ***Sugoi!*** (Great!); *Iito **omou.*** (I think it's good.); *A, **wakatta**!* (Oh, I got it!)
5.	**Response to questions** The plain form is used to respond to the question. A: *Shukudai no ryo wa do?* (How is the amount of homework?) B: *Takusan **aru.*** (There is a lot.)

referent, and emphasize the tone of informality and intimacy (Cook, 2002, 2006, 2008). Because affect keys are considered important interactional resources in Japanese conversation, I analyzed the learners' use of them as an indicator of their interactional competence. Based on Cook's (2002) taxonomy, the following affect keys and their interpersonal functions were coded along with the plain form. In the examples, plain forms are in bold, and affect keys are double-underlined. Sentence final particle is shown as FP.

(1) Sentence final particle that functions to facilitate the addressee's involvement in the conversation (e.g. *ne, yo*) (marker for interpersonal relation)
    e.g. Mou   **hanashi-ta**   yo.   (I told you already.)
         already   talk-PST   FP

(2) Postposing information or placement of information at post-predicate (device for floor management)
    e.g. **Kichat-ta**   Suzuki-san   ga.   (Mr Suzuki has come.)
         came-PST   Mr Suzuki   SUB

(3) Rising intonation (marker of uncertainty)
    e.g. Eiga   do   **dat-ta**↗   (How was the movie↗)
         movie   how   COP-PST

(4) Coalescence (merging of two or more phonological segments into one) (signal of affective states)

e.g. <u>Hidee</u>   **inu**   **da**   <u>na</u>   (*hidee* derived from *hidoi*)
terrible   dog   COP   FP

Cook's taxonomy includes the fifth category, vowel lengthening, in which case the vowel is lengthened to show emotional intensity (e.g. in *soide nee*, the vowel [e] in the final particle *ne* is lengthened as in *nee*). I excluded this category from the analysis because in L2 speech it is ambiguous as to whether the vowel lengthening is implemented intentionally to signal emotional intensity, or whether it is produced unintentionally due to L2-specific constraints (e.g. hesitation and mispronunciation).

Incomplete sentence ending

In addition to the two primary speech styles (i.e. the plain and polite form), this study analyzed incomplete sentences as resources of interactional competence. Usami (1995) defines an incomplete sentence as a sentence that is grammatically unfinished but semantically finished. It includes a case of predicate omission, or in case of a compound sentence, an omission of a clause. I also used Chen's (2000) categorization of incomplete utterances as guidelines in the coding of incomplete sentences. See Chen's categorization of morpho-syntactic markers of incomplete endings below. Table 2.1 (Chapter 2) presents the complete list with example sentences.

(1) Conjunction particle *te* and *de* (and)
(2) Conjunction particle *shi*, *node*, and *kara* (so/because)
(3) Conjunction particle *to* and *ba* (functioning as if-clause)
(4) Quotation particle *to* (…say that…)
(5) Topicalization with particle *wa* and *tte*
(6) Listing examples with the conjunction particle *toka* (and/or)

Using this classification as my reference, I coded all incomplete endings in conversation transcripts and analyzed changes over time both quantitatively and qualitatively. I conducted three rounds of coding over different days in order to ensure accuracy.

Interview Data

In addition to the conversation data, this study collected interview data from a subset of eight participants with the purpose of gaining insight into the relationship among interactional competence, types of sociocultural experiences, and individual differences in these experiences. I conducted three interviews with each informant. The interviews were conducted in English in a quiet on-campus office for 40–60 minutes and were recorded on the Macintosh computer. The interviews were semi-structured to include certain pre-selected themes but allowed flexibility in incorporating themes nominated by the informants. In all three interviews, my questions revolved around three themes: (1) Japanese study, (2) study abroad experience, and (3) cultural contact and communication.

The first interview (conducted at the end of the first month in the semester) focused on the informants' educational background and experiences. I asked questions about their formal Japanese study in their home country (e.g. the number of class hours, medium of instruction, and similarities and differences from their classes in Japan), amount of contact with native Japanese speakers before they came to Japan, goals of their Japanese study, and their perceived improvement in their Japanese skills after they came to Japan. In the area of study abroad experiences, I asked questions related to the degree of their adjustment to the new environment (both academically and socially), as well as the extent of their satisfaction with their study abroad program. I asked the informants what kind of expectations they had before coming to Japan and how those expectations had changed through their immersion in Japan. I also asked what they considered to be their most valuable experience in Japan. Finally, on the theme of cultural contact and communication, I asked questions about the participants' degree of social networking (e.g. types of community activities they were involved in and the number of Japanese-speaking friends they had). I asked how much time they spent speaking Japanese every week, with whom, for what purposes, and on what occasions.

Many of these questions were recycled in the second interview conducted half way in the study period, but the topic was extended to more detailed accounts of the participants' communication opportunities with local community members. I asked questions about the participants' perceived importance of Japanese speaking skills in establishing relationships and networks with local people. I also asked about the influence of those social relationships and contact on their Japanese skills – whether, and in what ways, their Japanese abilities improved because of their social involvement. I added a new category in the second interview: participants' reflection on their intercultural competence. I asked about the skills and personal qualities that they thought were important in order to integrate into the Japanese community, and whether they had made any improvement in those areas.

The last interview was conducted at the end of the semester, a few days after the last data collection session. I revisited the questions from the first and second interviews to gain information about the participants' changes over the semester. Because the use of speech styles was the primary focus of this study, my questions directly focused on this area. I asked what they knew about the polite and plain forms, what observations they had about Japanese speakers' use of them, what experiences they had in their own use, and whether they experienced any difficulties in the use. See below for the list of the interview questions in each time period.

(1) Interview questions, Time 1

Japanese study

- How long have you been studying Japanese?
- How many hours do you spend studying Japanese? What do you study?
- Is studying Japanese important to you? Has it changed after you came to Japan?
- What aspects of Japanese skills do you think you have improved most since you came to Japan?
- How would you compare learning Japanese in US and in Japan?

Study abroad experience

- What expectations did you have about your study abroad before you came to Japan?
- Has your experience overall met your expectations? In what ways?
- What has been the highlight of your study in Japan?
- Have you experienced any difficulties living in Japan?

Communication and cultural contact

- On a typical day, how much time a week do you speak Japanese outside class?
- With whom do you speak Japanese with? For what purposes?
- With whom do you speak Japanese most frequently? What do you usually talk about?

(2) Interview questions, Time 2

Japanese study

- Do you think your Japanese skills have improved since you came to Japan? What aspects of Japanese skills do you think you have improved and why?

Communication and cultural contact

- With whom do you usually speak Japanese?
- Do you think Japanese ability is important in establishing relationships with local people? If so, in what ways?
- Do you think your Japanese ability has improved because of your relationships with local people? If so, what aspects do you think you have improved most?

Study abroad experience

- How would you evaluate your study abroad experience so far? Tell me about your highlights and difficulties. Do you have any episodes to share?

Intercultural competence

- What abilities, skills, or personal qualities do you think are important to function effectively and appropriately when interacting with Japanese people? Why do you think so? Do you have any episodes to share?
- Do you think you have developed those abilities and skills?

(3) Interview questions, Time 3

Japanese study

- Do you think your Japanese skills have improved since you came to Japan? What aspects of Japanese skills do you think you have improved and why?

Communication and cultural contact

- With whom do you usually speak Japanese?
- Do you think Japanese ability is important in establishing relationships with local people? If so, in what way?
- Do you think your Japanese ability has improved because of your relationships with local people? If so, what aspects have improved most?

Study abroad experience

- How would you evaluate your study abroad experience this semester? Do you feel good about it, or do you have any regret? Tell me about your highlights and difficulties.

Intercultural competence

- What abilities do you think are important to function effectively and appropriately when interacting with Japanese people? Why do you think so?
- To what extent have you developed those abilities?

Speech style

- Japanese language has two main speech styles: plain and polite forms. What do you know about these forms?
- What is your observation of Japanese people using these two speech styles?
- What are your experiences with using these speech styles in Japan?
- Have you found it difficult to use these two different speech styles? Why?

Interviews were recorded on a Macintosh computer and transcribed. The data were analyzed using the strategy of content analysis and analytic induction. I examined the interview data for impressions and trends by noting salient, recurring comments and grouping the comments by similarity. Because the same questions were used for all participants, I coded their responses and compared them across participants for similarities and differences.

The purpose of the interview was to seek a possible link between the participants' degree of social involvement – especially, the nature and domains of the opportunities to speak Japanese – and the change in their interactional competence in Japanese. To achieve this goal, I selected four participants who demonstrated different degrees of change in the target linguistic and interactional resources and cross-examined their experience during study abroad. These four cases demonstrated idiosyncratic developmental trajectories, and variations were explained based on different types of learning opportunities and resources available to individuals.

Supplementary Measures

In addition to the conversation task and interviews, I collected data using two additional instruments: a motivation survey and a Japanese contact survey. Data from these measures were used to supplement interview data by providing a more detailed profile of interview informants.

Motivation survey

This study used a survey adapted from Fantini (2005) that measures participants' overseas experiences and intercultural competence. The survey aims to assess various outcomes of intercultural service experiences: the level of intercultural competence developed by participants, the effects on their lifestyle choices, and participants' impact on communities and other individuals after returning home. I adapted questions from one section – motivation and options – in order to assess participants' motivation and interest toward the host culture. See the sample question below. Appendix C displays all the questions. The survey was given at the beginning and end of the semester.

Item 1: How would you characterize your motivation toward the host culture while in Japan? Indicate the level of your agreement/disagreement with each statement below.

		strongly disagree	strongly agree
(a)	I sometimes wanted to return home.	1------2------3------4------5	
(b)	I felt I was not learning very much.	1------2------3------4------5	

Japanese contact survey

A modified version of the Language Contact Profile (Freed et al., 2004) was administered in English at the beginning and end of the semester in order to document the amount of out-of-class contact with Japanese. The survey asked participants to indicate how many days per week and how many hours per day they spent using four language skills in Japanese (i.e. speaking, reading, writing, and listening). The product of these two numbers (i.e. the number of days per week and hours per day) provided an estimate of total hours per week in Japanese. The survey also included open questions asking participants about their classes, the number of Japanese friends they had, and type and nature of their communication in Japanese. See below for sample questions. Appendix D provides a copy of the survey.

Item 1: How much time do you spend communicating in Japanese with your teachers outside of class?

Typically, how many days per week?   0   1   2   3   4   5   6   7
How many hours per day?   0   0-1   1-2   2-3   4-5   more than 5

Item 2: How much time do you spend communicating in Japanese with your classmates, friends, or host family outside of class?

Typically, how many days per week?   0   1   2   3   4   5   6   7
How many hours per day?   0   0-1   1-2   2-3   4-5   more than 5

Data Collection Procedures

Below is an overview of the data collection process, which took place in the academic year of 2012. The Japanese academic year begins in April. The first semester ends in July.

April   Conversation task ($n = 18$)
         Motivation survey ($n = 18$)
         Japanese contact survey ($n = 18$)
May   Interview 1 ($n = 8$)
June Interview 2 ($n = 8$)
July   Conversation task ($n = 18$)
         Interview 3 ($n = 8$)
         Motivation survey ($n = 18$)
         Japanese contact survey ($n = 18$)

The next chapter (Chapter 5) reports on the first part of findings. I will present changes in the distribution of the complete (i.e. polite and plain forms) and incomplete ending forms over a semester as found in the 18 participants' peer-to-peer conversations. I will describe how the proportion of each utterance ending type changed over time according to the participants' understanding of the type of task that they were engaged in (i.e. informal, peer-to-peer talk) and how this change characterized their interactional development in the ability to use linguistic resources that are appropriate to register.

Notes

(1) Style-shifting within conversation between peers was beyond the scope of this study and thus was not analyzed in this study.
(2) See Tanaka (1999) for the functions of sentence final particles and sentence final expressions.

5 Speech Styles

This chapter describes how participants' proportion of the polite and plain forms changed over the semester and how this change characterized the participants' interactional development in the ability to use language that is appropriate to a specific register.

The Change in the Use of Speech Styles: The Polite and Plain Forms

Table 5.1 summarizes the percentage of the complete sentences (ending in the polite or plain form) and incomplete sentences that appeared in 18 participants' conversations at pre- and post-test (see Chapter 4 for the definitions of these sentence forms and coding frameworks). Figure 5.1 graphically displays the change. There were 1536 sentences at pre-test and 1919 sentences at post-test. Because the length of the conversation was the same in both sessions (20 minutes), the results show a large increase in the participants' oral production and fluency over a 12-week period. At pre-test, the polite and plain forms comprised the majority of the utterance ending forms (about 48% and 46%, respectively). Incomplete sentences appeared only at 5.7%. However, at post-test, the use of the polite form dropped to about 15%, while use of the plain form increased to almost 70%. The most striking change was the increase in incomplete sentences. The percentage almost tripled from pre- to post-test (from 5.7% to 16.7%).

Interestingly, the distribution of these utterance-ending types was almost exactly the same between the two-way conversation (when the students talked with a peer) and the three-way conversation (when the researcher joined the conversation), indicating that no drastic style-shifts occurred over the change of the participant structure. In sum, change over a semester is summarized as follows: a decrease in the polite form, an increase in the plain form, and an increase in the incomplete utterances. The sharp increase in the use of the plain form at post-test indicates that the students became able to adapt to the situational requirement and used the informal register (casual speech style) when speaking with their peer about an everyday topic.

Table 5.1 Proportion of the polite, plain, and incomplete forms at pre- and post-test

	Complete ending		Incomplete ending	
	Polite form	Plain form		Total
Pre-test				
Total	48.2% (740)	46.2% (709)	5.7% (87)	100% (1536)
2-way	47.1%	47.2%	5.6%	
3-way	49.6%	44.3%	6.1%	
Post-test				
Total	14.6% (281)	68.4% (1312)	16.7% (326)	100% (1919)
2-way	14.4%	70.0%	15.6%	
3-way	15.2%	66.1%	18.7%	

Note: The numbers in the parenthesis are raw counts. 2-way: conversation between students. 3-way: conversation between students and the researcher.

Learners' development was evident in their increasing ability to control speech styles across discourse segments. At the beginning of the semester, there was a considerable mixing of the polite and plain forms, and the shifts were random and haphazard, demonstrating no discernible trend in their switching from one form to another. The excerpt below between W (female New Zealander) and A (female Singaporean) illustrates this point.

In all transcripts to follow, the polite forms are underlined, the plain forms are bold-faced, and the incomplete sentences have a wavy underline. Appendix A contains the transcription notations. See Chapter 4, Table 4.1 for the coding guidelines. Laughter, backchannels, exclamations, simple repetition, and formulaic expressions were not coded.

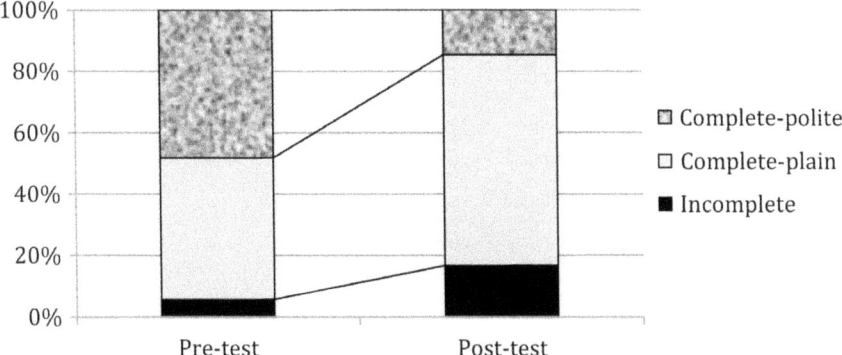

Figure 5.1 Proportion of the polite, plain, and incomplete forms

Excerpt 5.1 (pre-test) W and A are talking about their club activities

1 **A:** *soo   desu   ne   >ishuukan<   wa   nankai   <u>ikimasu ka</u>*
           so   COP   FP   one week   TOP how often go   Q
           'I see. How often do you go in a week?'

2 **W:** *hhh   renshuu   wa   shuu nikai, ga   <u>arimasu</u>.*
                   practice   TOP   week twice   SUB exist
           'We practice twice a week.'

3 **A:** *oo:*
           DM
           'oh'

4 **W:** *ikkai   wa: **nijikanhan**.*
           one time   COP   two and a half hours
           'Two-and-a-half-hours at a time.'

5 **A:** *nijikanhan.*
           two and a half hours
           'Two-and-a-half-hours.'

6 **W:** *un. hai.*
           yes yes
           'Yes, yes.'

7 **A:** *konaka-tta   **suru***
           come-NEG   do
           'Sometimes you don't come.'

8 **W:** *soshite   Tai-chan   wa   shuumatsu nani wo **suru**? (1.0)*
           And then   Tai-chan   TOP   weekend   what   O   do
           'And, what do you do on weekend, Tai-chan?'

9 **A:** *a,   >shuumatsu desu ka?<   hai.*
           ah   weekend   COP Q   yes
           etto:: saikin   wa: ano,   tenisu sa:kuru ni   <u>hait-te:</u>
           DM   recently   TOP   DM   tennis club   in   join-TE
           'Oh, weekend? Yes. Well, recently, I joined the tennis club.'

10 **W:** *hai hai.*
           Yes yes
           'yes, yes.'

11 **A:** *doyoobi: wa   tenisu dei   <u>desu</u>.*
           Saturday   TOP   tennis day   COP
           'Saturday is tennis day.'

12 **W:** *hai.   hai.   jaa,*
           yes.   yes.   DM
           'Yes, yes, then'

13 **A:** *u:n,   tenisu,   n::   hoka ni   nanika?*
           Yes   tennis   other   anything
           'You mean, anything other than tennis?'

14 **W:** hhh tenisu wa   [mita koto ga: <u>arimasu</u> kedo:
           tennis TOP   saw NOM SUB have (seen) but
      'I have seen tennis but'
15 **A:**   [(hokani nani ka⌢)
                       other   anything
                     'Other than tennis⌢'
16 **W:** nanka heta-de   anmari   hhh **shi-nai**.
      DM   poor-TE   not very   do-NEG
      'I'm not good, so I don't play much.'

In this excerpt, while A uses the polite form throughout (except for her self-talk in line 7), W's speech style lacks consistency, and her style-shifts do not reflect any patterns. In line 2, W responds to A's question using the polite form (*arimasu*), but when she asks a question in line 8, W switches to the plain form (*suru⌢*). In line 14, she switches back to the polite form, but in line 16, once again, she goes back to the plain form (*shinai*). W's ambivalence with her speech style could be due to her peer's speech style. Because A consistently uses the polite form, it is possible that W is uncertain about which form to use. At pre-test, A used the polite form about 70% of the time, plain form about 25%, and incomplete sentences 5%. W used the polite and plain form at a similar frequency (about 44% of the time). Incomplete sentences appeared about 12%.

These cases of ambiguous style mixing largely disappeared at post-test because the plain form became the participants' base-form (used almost 70% of the time). In the case of A and W, the distribution of A's sentence forms at post-test changed to 12% for the polite form, 70% for the plain form, and 18% for the incomplete ending, whereas the distribution of W's sentence forms changed to 7% for the polite form, 70% for the plain form, and 25% for the incomplete sentences.

Excerpt 5.2 illustrates this marked development in these learners' control of sentence ending forms. Although A primarily used the polite form at pre-test, she consistently used the plain form and incomplete endings at post-test. In response to W's polite-form question about A's favorite food in line 3 (*nan deshoo⌢*), A responds in the plain form (*niku ryoyi*) and gives examples of the food using the conjunction particle *toka* (and/or). She also asks a question in the plain form in line 18 (*nanifuu⌢*) – which is in stark contrast to the pre-test data, in which A used the polite form *desuka* in most of her questions.

Similarly, in W's speech, arbitrary switching between the plain and polite form disappeared at post-test. She uses the plain form consistently (lines 11, 13, and 15). Particularly noteworthy is the plain form used for the self-question in line 19, *nandaroo* (What would that be⌢). In the preceding turn (line 18), A asked W what style of *okonomiyaki* she likes. Not sure about *okonomiyaki* varieties, W responds to this question with the auxiliary *daroo*, the informal conjecture form of the copula *da* (to be), which expresses feeling of uncertainty. The use of informal/plain form *daroo* is appropriate here because the expression of uncertainty is directed to herself, not to her interlocutor. This usage contrasts with W's conjecture in line 3, where she employs *deshoo*, the formal/polite version of the copula *da*, when guessing or speculating about A's favorite Japanese food. The polite form *deshoo* is appropriate here, because this conjecture is directed to A and is used to make inference about A's state of mind by implying, 'I wonder what kind of food you might like.' This excerpt shows that W has two forms of the conjecture, *daroo* and *deshoo*, – the plain and polite version – in her repertoire, and she has developed the ability to distinguish these forms depending on their functions and the context of use.

Excerpt 5.2 (post-test) A and W are talking about their favorite Japanese food.

1 W: *jaa   sukina*
       well then   favorite
       'well then, favorite'
2 A: *un.*
       yes
       'yes'
3 W: *ryoori wa   nan   deshoo↑*
       cuisine TOP   what   COP
       'What is your favorite food?'
4 A: *sukina   ryoori↑   u:n   yappari: niku   **ryoori.***
       favorite   cuisine   uhmm   after all   meat   cuisine
       yakiniku: toka.
       barbeque   like
       'Favorite food? Uhmm, after all, meat cuisine, like barbeque.'
5 W: *aa   yakiniku.*
       ah   barbeque
       'Oh, barbeque'
6 A: *shabushabu: toka.*
       shabu-shabu   like
       'like *shabu-shabu*'
7 W: *un.*
       yes
       'yes'
8 A: *tonkatsu   mo.   u:::n (1.0)   tokidoki   **sushi:↑***
       tonkatsu   too   uhmm   sometime   sushi
       un   soo   da   ne. (1.0)   un,   Wu-san   wa↑
       yes   so   COP   FP   yes   Ms.Wu   TOP
       '*Tonkatsu* too. Uhmm… sometimes *sushi*? Yes, that's right. How about you, Ms Wu?'

9 **W:** wa(.)ta(.)shi(.)   wa:
       I   TOP
       'I'
10 **A:** un.
       yes
       'yes'
11 **W:** sushi   ga   **daisuki**   tokuni: **kaitenzushi**=
       sushi   SUB like a lot   especially   kaitenzushi
       'I like sushi, especially *kaitenzushi* (conveyer belt *sushi*).'
12 **A:** =*kaitenzushi*¿
       kaitenzushi
       '*kaitenzushi*¿'
13 **W:** un,   jibun no   sukina   sushi o   erabu   no   wa: **suki**.
       yes   own   LK   favorite   sushi O   choose NOM   TOP like
       'Yes, I like choosing my own favorite *sushi*.'
14 **A:** un.
       yes
       'yes'
15 **W:** soshite: okonomiyaki mo: hh   **suki**=
       and   okonomiyaki too   like
       'And, I like *okonomiyaki* too.'
16 **A:** =okonomiyaki [:
       okonomiyaki
       '*okonomiyaki*'
17 **W:**   [u:n.
                   yes
                   'yes'
18 **A:** onkonomiyaki.   e¿   **nani fuu**¿
       okonomiyaki   what?   what style
       '*Okonomiyaki*. What¿ What style¿'
19 **W:** **nan   daroo**¿   hhh   yoku   **wakara-nai:**   hh   kedo
       what   AUX   well   understand-NEG   but
20   oko:nomiyaki   no   resutoran   ni   it-te:
       okonomiyaki   LK   restaurant   LOC   go-TE
21   soshite tomodachi   to   isshoni   okonomiyaki   o
       and   friends   with together okonomiyaki   O
22   tsukuru   no   wa   omoshiroi na: to=
       make   NOM   TOP   fun   FP   QT
       'What would that be¿ I don't understand well, but going to the *okonomiyaki* restaurant and making *okonomiyaki* together with friends is fun.'
23 **A:** =u:n.
       yes
       'yes'

24 **W:** <u>omot-te</u>.
    think-TE
    'I think.'
25 **A:** soo   da   ne,   soo   da   ne.   jibunde   <u>tsukut-te:</u>,
    so   COP   FP   so   COP   FP   by yourself   make-TE
    'That's right, that's right. You make it by yourself.'
26 **W:** un.
    yes
    'yes.'
27 **A:** omoshiroi   to: motto   oishii   koto   to: **kanjir-areru**=
    fun   QT   more   delicious   thing   QT   feel-can
    'It can feel fun and more delicious.'

Although the majority of the learners dramatically increased their use of the plain form after a semester in Japan, there was individual variation in their usage. Figures 5.2 and 5.3 display the distribution of the three utterance-ending forms across 18 learners at pre- and post-test. The letters (A–R) represent participant IDs. Appendix E contains actual percentages. As shown in Figure 5.3, two participants (B & G) did not follow the majority norm at post-test: as opposed to other students, who used the plain form as base form, these two learners used the plain and polite forms at almost equal proportion (about 40–50%). In the case of G, her use of the plain form decreased by about 15% from pre to post-test, while the use of the plain form increased by about 15% from pre to post-test for the majority of learners. After the post-test, I asked G why she used the polite form when her peer (H) was speaking to her mostly in the plain form. She responded that the polite form is her default form, and switching to the plain form spontaneously was difficult. These individual-level analyses indicate that not all learners made a shift to the plain form as a normative style of peer-to-peer

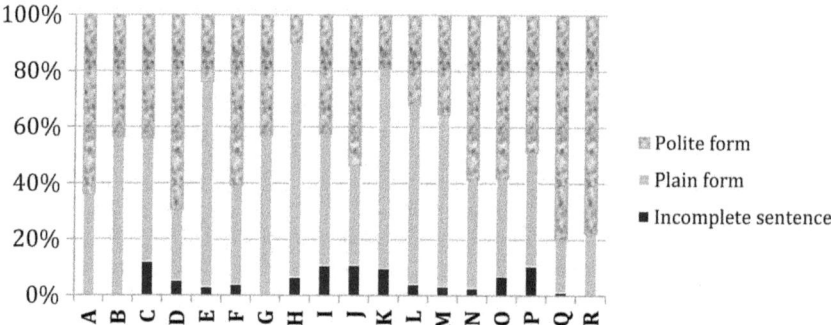

Figure 5.2 Proportion of the polite, plain, and incomplete sentences by individual, Pre-test

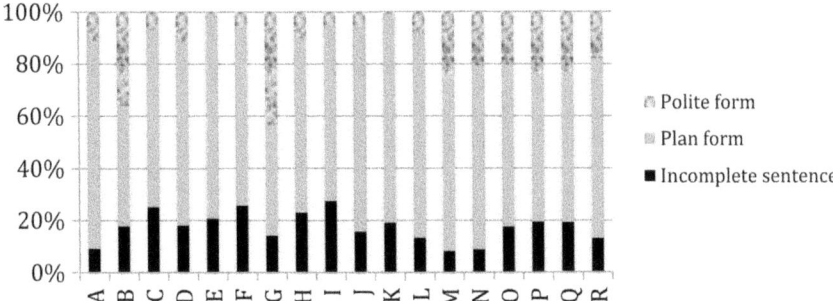

Figure 5.3 Proportion of the polite, plain, and incomplete sentences by individual, Post-test

interaction after a semester of study-abroad. Some learners – albeit, the minority – remained ambivalent about the use of casual speech style and continued with the default polite form that they were most familiar with from their formal instruction. I will discuss this individual variation in the process and outcome of learning speech styles in Chapter 8.

Functions of the Plain Forms

As shown in the previous section, the major change in learners' use of the speech styles was found in their increased use of the plain form. This section illustrates learners' development in their functional abilities with the plain form – whether or not they became able to use the plain form in a wider range of communicative functions. Below is the coding framework used in this analysis. (See Chapter 3 for the descriptions of these functional categories of the plain form.)

(1) Request for information, response or confirmation from the interlocutor.
(2) Joint meaning making.
(3) Presentation of information.
(4) Expression of inner self.
(5) Response to questions.

Using this taxonomy, I coded the 18 students' plain forms as they appeared in the conversations. The coding criteria were made as conservative as possible: only the plain forms that clearly belong to each function type were categorized. As a result, there were about 2% of the plain forms that were removed from the analysis. Table 5.2 displays the distribution of the five functions. Figure 5.4 is a graphic illustration of the distribution.

Table 5.2 Proportion of the functions of the plain forms at pre- and post-test

	Pre-test	Post-test
1. Request for information, response, and confirmation	13.8% (96)	15.5% (201)
2. Joint meaning making	6.2% (43)	9.7% (125)
3. Presentation of information	35.6% (248)	30.4% (394)
4. Expression of inner self	31.3% (217)	28.6% (371)
5. Response to questions	13.3% (93)	14.9% (193)
6. Others	0	0.7% (9)
TOTAL	100% (697)	100% (1293)

Note: The numbers in the parentheses are raw counts. There were a total of 709 plain forms at pre-test and 1312 plain forms at post-test. The numbers in this table are smaller than the observed counts because some plain forms with ambiguous functions were excluded from the analysis.

At both pre- and post-test, the learners mostly used the plain form to present information and express their inner self. Each function occupied about 30–35% of their plain form usage. The function of information presentation occurs purely for the purpose of information transmission: the speaker uses the plain form to present information, explain, or self-correct information. Expression of inner self, on the other hand, involves the plain form being used to express feeling, surprise, sympathy/empathy, and evaluation (including self-talk and conviction).

The excerpt below from G (female American) and H's (male Korean) conversation illustrates these two functions. In his first turn (line 1–4), K uses two plain forms: *aru* (verb expressing one's experience, meaning 'have done something') and *dekiru* (verb meaning 'can do'). These two forms serve to present information: K reports his experience of having been to Hiroshima

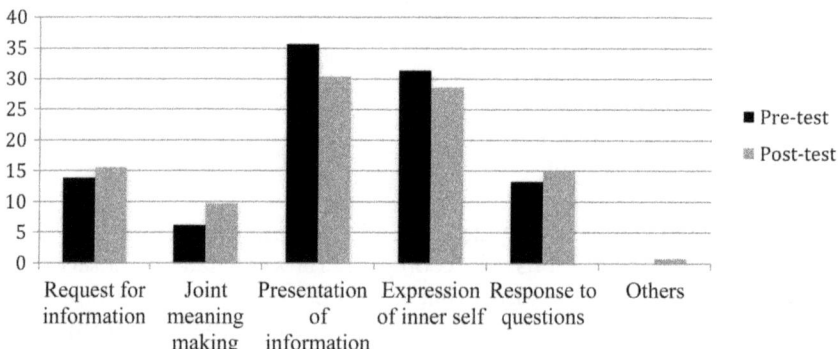

Figure 5.4 Functions of the plain forms

and his observation about people in Hiroshima. H continues with this topic in line 6–7 by comparing people in Hiroshima and Tokyo. Here, the function of the plain form *tsumetai* (cold) is seen as an expression of inner thought because it conveys H's evaluation of Tokyo people.

Similar to H, G also uses plain forms for multiple functions. In line 10, after agreeing with H's assessment of people in Tokyo, G presents her own assessment of Tokyo (There are many people in Tokyo.). Here, the plain form *omou* (I think) explicitly marks her opinion. In the subsequent turn, she expresses her surprise with the plain form, *bikkurishita* (I was surprised.), and again in line 19. In line 17, G uses another plain form *chiisai* (It is small.) and offers the size of her hometown as a reason why she was surprised with the high density in Tokyo. This plain form is coded as a simple presentation of information.

Excerpt 5.3 (pre-test) I and J are talking about Hiroshima and Tokyo.

```
1  H:  un.   demo   hiroshima         no:
       yes   but    Hiroshima         LK
2      datte maeni: Hiroshima itta         koto    ga   aru   kedo:.
       DM    before Hiroshima go-PST       thing   SUB  have  but
3      demo  hiroshima   wa:  sono:  minna       kekkoo      (1.0)
       but   Hiroshima   TOP  DM     everyone    reasonably
4      nn:   nakayoku    dekiru.
             get along   can
       'Yes but Hiroshima…Well, I have been to Hiroshima before, but
       Hiroshima, well, everyone can reasonably becomes friends.'
5  G:  [hai. un.
       yes, yes.
       'Yes'
6  H:  [suguni.
       immediately
       'Immediately.'
7      (aa)  tookyoo     wa:   cho(h)tto      tsumeta(h)i(h)
       ah    Tokyo       TOP   a little       cold
       'Ah, Tokyo (people) is a bit cold'
8  G:  [ha:i. =
       yes
       'Yes'
9  H:  [un.
       yes
       'yes'
10 G:  demo (4.3)  tookyoo    wa    hito     ga    °ip°pai.  to   omou
       but         Tokyo      TOP   people   SUB   many     QT   think
       'But I think there are many people in Tokyo.'
```

11 **H:** *u:n=.*
    yes
    'yes'
12 **G:** *=to: (1.0)   °tote°mo: **bikkuri-shi-ta(h)**   hh=*
    QT   very   surprise-do-PST
    'I was very surprised.'
13 **H:** *= (watashi   mo)*
    me   too
    'Me too.'
14 **G:** *hai. hai.*
    yes   yes
    'Yes, yes.'
15 **H:** *[un.*
    'Uh.'
16 **G:** *[watashi   wa:. watashi   no   machi wa   totemo*
    I   TOP   I   LK   town TOP   very
17   ***chiisai.**   dakara:.*
    small   so
    'I...My town is very small, so...'
18 **H:** *un. (2.3)*
    yes
    'Yes.'
19 **G:** *(h)ee:: (hai)   **bikkuri-shi-ta***
    yes   yes   surprise-do-PST
    'Yes, yes, I was surprised.'
20 **H:** *soo.*
    I see
    'I see.'

These two functions – information presentation and expression of inner self – occupied the majority of the learners' plain form usage at both pre- and post-test. Other functions – request for information, response to question, and co-construction of talk – occupied a small proportion, ranging from 6% to 15%. In fact, although the frequency of the plain forms almost doubled at post-test, the overall distribution of the function was almost the same between the two test sessions. These findings indicate that frequency increase was the major indicator of learners' development in plain form usage. The range of the functional categories of the plain forms and distributions of the forms across categories remained largely the same within the same time frame. The learners were able to use the plain form for a range of functions, which were all critical for developing conversation: sharing information and experiences, asking and responding to questions, expressing feeling, and collaborating in meaning-making.

However, a small change was observed in the learners' slight gain in their use of the plain form for joint meaning-making. Under this function, the plain form is used to add to the interlocutor's speech, to complete the interlocutor's turn-in-progress, to advocate for the interlocutor's feeling, or to expand on the interlocutor's speech and co-construct knowledge. This is a highly interactive function, because – in order to collaboratively construct meaning – both the speaker and listener need to monitor each other's contribution closely and infer what is expected in the next turn. The increase from 6.2% to 9.2% in this particular function suggests the learners' developing interactional competence: learning how to act collaboratively to accomplish social actions in talk.

See Excerpt 5.4 for illustration. This is a conversation between I and J – two female Chinese students. In line 1–9, on the topic of going to Mt. Fuji during the break, the learner I is trying to explain that hotels around Mt. Fuji are a little expensive. After I stops at the word *chotto* (a little) in line 7, J anticipates the word *takai* (expensive) coming after *chotto* and supplies the first syllable of the word (*ta*) in line 8. Following the syllable, I completes her turn and produces the word *takai* in line 9. Here, the learners are orienting to the same word *takai* and co-constructing the knowledge (Hotels around Mt. Fuji are a little expensive.). The plain form functions effectively in building shared understanding.

Excerpt 5.4 (post-test) I and J are talking about their travel plans during the break.

```
1  I:   watashi:: (1.0) daitai:  a     sono   mae     wa:.
        I               about   ah    that   before  TOP
2       Fujisan    ni    iku   tsumori      [desu  kedo:.
        Mt. Fuji   LOC   go    intention    COP    but
        'Before that I have an intention to go to Mt. Fuji, but...'
3  J:                                       [aa
                                            uh huh
                                            'uh-huh'
4  I:   demo    chotto     sono mawari     no:   ryokan toka
        but     a little   DM   around     LK    inns   like
5       hoteru   ga    yachin    ga
        hotel    SUB   fee       SUB
        'But fees of inns or hotels around there are a little'
6  J:   aa.=
        ah
        'ah'
7  I:   =chotto
        a little
        'a little'
```

8 J: °a°   °ta°
       ah   ex
       'ah, ex...'
9 I: **takai.**
       expensive
       'expensive'
10 J: *u::n.*
       uh-huh
       'uh-huh'

Of the 18 learners, N most frequently used the plain form for the function of joint meaning-making. There were 15 instances of this function in her speech at post-test, although the frequency was only 5 at pre-test. N used this function skillfully to add to her interlocutor's information and expand on the topic in progress. See Excerpt 5.5 for illustration. In the preceding dialogue, M told N that her father is visiting her in Japan for an entire month because he is a university professor and can take a long vacation during summer. In line 1–2, M says that it would have been impossible to take a long vacation if her father were a businessman. Starting line 4, after a brief laugh, N presents a comparison between a businessman and teacher. In line 6–7, she says *natsuyasumi ga aru kara* (they have summer vacation, so...) using the plain form. This comparison extends the on-going topic and develops into shared knowledge between M and N (the nature of a teacher's job compared to a businessman's job). This shared understanding is evident in M's contribution in line 8. M overlaps with N's turn and co-constructs the turn by supplying the main clause in the plain form (*daijyoobu* 'it's all right'). Here, M infers what is in N's mind in line 4 and anticipates what comes next. The plain forms appear throughout this process of collaborative meaning-making. Although the overall increase of this function was small at group-level (6% at pre and 10% at post-test), we recognize a tendency toward more interactive use of the plain form, as shown in this excerpt.

Excerpt 5.5 (post-test) M and N are talking about M's father's visit to Japan.

1 **M:** *sarariiman*   *to-*   *nara:.*
           businessman   with   if
2   *muri de(h)s [(h)*
           impossible
           'if a businessman, it's impossible'
3 **N:**   hh hh hh.
                     (laughter)
4   *aa.   demo   sensee   toka*
           ah   but   teacher   like
           'ah, but like teacher'

```
5  M:  sen[see
       teacher
       'teacher'
6  N:     [ga-  gakusee     to     isshoni,   natsuyasumi      ga
           stu  student     with   together   summer vacation  SUB
7      aru           ka[ra
       exist         so
       'there is summer vacation together with students, so'
8  M:                [ha:i.  **daijoobu**
                     yes    all right
                     'yes, it's all right.'
```

The five functions in the original taxonomy accounted for most cases of the plain form. However, a few new categories emerged at post-test, which further indicates the learners' functional development of plain form usage. These new categories were grouped together as 'others' in Table 5.2 (0.7% or nine instances in total). These nine instances involved five new functions: making a request, giving a suggestion, changing topics, and evaluating others.

See Excerpt 5.6 for the example of giving a suggestion. I is telling J about her travel plans during the summer break. I explains that she plans to go to Karuizawa with members in the Japan-China association and to come back to Tokyo alone (*jibun de kaeru* 'coming home by myself'). Surprised with this information, in line 3, J asks a clarifying question by repeating a portion of I's utterance (*jibun de kaeru↑* 'Coming back by yourself↑'). J asks the question again in line 6 with a tone of disbelief, which is marked with a sharp rise in pitch (↑). Following this, in line 8, J raises a concern about I's coming home alone. Here, the utterance, *yabakunai↑* (Isn't it problematic↑), is a youth slang that conveys strong tones of informality and closeness. Furthermore, this utterance functions as a pre-expansion: an expansion of an adjacency pair. In Conversation Analysis, an adjacency pair involves two mutually-dependent turns (e.g. suggestion–acceptance) (Sacks et al., 1974; Schegloff, 2007). A pre-expansion is an expansion of a sequence before the first pair part and anticipates the projected work to be done in the adjacency pair (Schegloff, 2007). In this excerpt, the utterance (*Yabakunai↑*) is a pre-suggestion. It purposefully raises a concern about the action that I plans to take: coming back to Tokyo alone. By using this pre-suggestion, J checks a condition for the likelihood of success in her upcoming suggestion. In line 10 – following I's mild acknowledgement of the problem in line 9 – J proceeds with her suggestion, *tomodachito kaereba ii* (It'd be good if you come home with your friends.). The plain form *ii* (good) is appropriate here because the polite equivalent (*iidesu* or *iideshoo*) sounds too imposing and almost forceful. By using the plain form, the illocutionary force of the suggestion is softened. In her succeeding turn (line 11–14), however, I does not heed this suggestion and provides her reason as refusal (She doesn't know the people at the event.). In line 15, J responds by maintaining her suggestion and points out that, after spending three days, everyone will get to know each other. Here, J leaves her utterance incomplete with the conjunction *kedo* (but), with no clause to follow. By omitting a clause, J leaves some space for I to fill with her own assessment of the suggestion. This is shown in line 16, when I takes over the incomplete turn and responds with agreement, *so dane* (You're right.), which completes the adjacency pair, suggestion–acceptance sequence.

Excerpt 5.6 (post-test) I and J are talking about their travel plans during the break.

```
1  I:  ma   karuizawa  kara   ano   tookyoo  made  jibunde
       DM   Karuizawa  from   well  Tokyo    to    by myself
2      kaeru.    to yuu      koto-de
       return    QT say      thing-TE
       'I will come back to Tokyo from Karuizawa by myself.'
3  J:  e      jibunde       [kaeru↿
       what   by yourself   return
       'what↿ Return by yourself↿'
4  I:                       [jibunde
                            by myself
5      cho-  chotto  sore  wa   watashi  wa   ima   komat-te(h) iru
       a     a bit   that  TOP  I        TOP  now   get in trouble-RES
       'By myself. I'm a bit worried about that now.'
6  J:  ↑jibunde      [kaeru↿
       by yourself   return
       'return by yourself↿'
7  I:                [jibunde
                     by myself
                     'by myself.'
8  J:  yabaku-[nai↿
       problematic-NEG
       'Isn't it problematic↿'
9  I:         [maa
              'well'
10 J:  demo  tomodachi  to     isshoni    kaer-eba      ii
       but   friends    with   together   come home-if  good
       'It'd be good if you come come with friends.'
11 I:  ma    shikashi  ano   sono  ibento  sanka-shi-ta
       well  but       well  that  event   participate-do-PST
12     kata    wa    ano   minna
       people  TOP   well  everyone
       'well, but people who participated in the event are all'
```

13 J: *nn*
   uh
   'uh'
14 I: *shiranai* °*hito*°
   unfamiliar people
   (1.2)
   'unfamiliar people.'
15 J: *demo mikkakan atode minna* [*shit-teru kedo,*
   but three days after everyone get to know-RES but
   'But after three days everybody knows each other, but'
16 I: [*aa: soo da ne,*
   ah so COP FP
   'Ah, you're right.'

To summarize, the overall frequency of the plain forms increased from pre- to post-test conversation, which indicates the learners' developing understanding of register-appropriate language use (i.e. peer-to-peer conversation) and their ability to mark informal, casual speech with the plain forms. The learners used plain forms over a variety of functions, but a majority of their use was allocated to the functions of presenting information and expressing inner thoughts (e.g. feeling, empathy and evaluation). Although the distribution patterns of the functions remained the same at pre- and post-test, there was an emerging upward trend of the plain forms being used for interactional, collaborative functions.

Another noteworthy change was found in the expansion of the plain forms' functions. Although small in frequency, learners became able to perform a wider range of speech acts like suggestion illustrated in the excerpt above. In those speech acts, the plain form played a critical role by demonstrating solidarity and mitigating the force of imposition. These findings indicate that increased use of the plain forms is an indicator of learners' developing ability to use language appropriately according to the talk type. At the same time, the increase is a sign of learners' emergent ability to deal with a range of speech functions spontaneously in talk-in-interaction.

Informal Speech Style: Plain Forms with Affect Keys

The previous sections reported findings on the frequency and functions of the plain forms. In this section, I will discuss additional analysis conducted on the plain forms – informal speech style. According to Cook (2002, 2006, 2008), the plain form involves two subcategories: the informal and detached speech style. The informal style co-occurs with affect keys – linguistic resources that signal the speaker's feelings and moods. The

66 Developing Interactional Competence in a Japanese Study Abroad Context

detached style, on the other hand, occurs without affect keys and indexes the impersonal manner of speaking. My analysis here focuses on the former type: the informal style with affect keys. Using Cook's (2002) taxonomy, I coded learners' plain forms for the following affect keys. See Chapter 4 for details and examples.

(1) Sentence-final particle (e.g. *ne, yo*) that facilitates the addressee's involvement in the conversation (marker for interpersonal relation).
(2) Postposing information or placement of information at post-predicate (device for floor management).
(3) Rising intonation (marker of uncertainty).
(4) Coalescence (merging of two or more phonological segments into one) (signal of affective states).

Table 5.3 displays the frequency of the plain forms with affect keys (i.e. informal speech style) at pre- and post-test. Figure 5.5 illustrates the frequency data by individual learners.

As shown here, the overall proportion of the informal speech style was relatively small (about 20–23%), which means that the majority of the plain

Table 5.3 Frequency of the informal speech (plain forms with affect keys) at pre- and post-test

	Total frequency of informal speech	Total plain forms	%
Pre-test	137	709	19.3%
Post-test	310	1312	23.6%

Note: The percentage refers to the proportion of the informal speech style within the total number of plain forms.

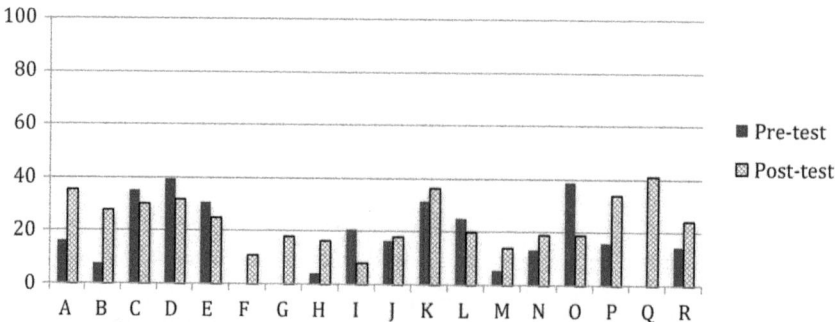

Figure 5.5 Proportion of the plain form with affect key (informal speech style) by individual

Table 5.4 Frequency of the plain form with affect key (informal speech style) by category

	Pre-test	Post-test
Sentence-final particle	4.7% (33)	4.6% (61)
Postposing	0.4% (3)	2.2% (29)
Rising intonation	13.4% (95)	16.2% (213)
Coalescence	0.8% (6)	0.5% (7)
Proportion of informal speech style	19.3% (137)	23.6% (310)
Total plain forms	709	1312

Note: The numbers in the parentheses show raw counts.

forms occurred without affect keys. Although there was an upward trend from pre- to post-test, the increase was minimal (4.3%). There was considerable individual variation, however. As shown in Figure 5.5, several learners produced affect keys more than 30% of the time at pre-test (C, D, E, K, and O), while others did not employ affect keys at all (F, G, and Q). Although all learners became able to use affect keys at post-test, the degree of their use varied from 7.8% (I) to over 40% (Q). In the case of six learners (C, D, E, I, L and O), the frequency dropped at post-test.

Table 5.4 displays the distribution of informal speech style across categories. Figure 5.6 is a graphic display of the distribution and change from pre- to post-test.

Similar to the plain form functions, the pre-post comparison did not yield a dramatic change in any of the subcategories of the informal speech style. Plain forms with sentence-final particles and coalescence appeared at the same rate at pre- and post-conversation, while a slight change in

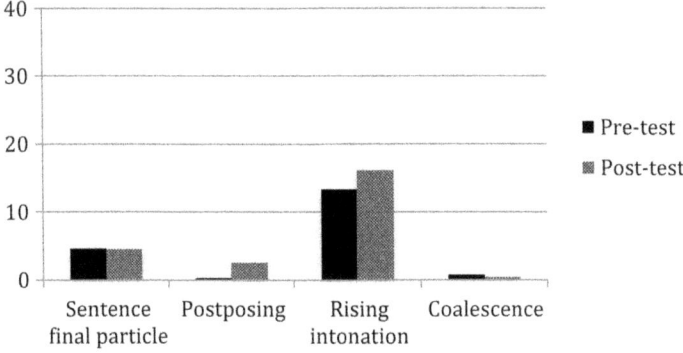

Figure 5.6 Proportion of the plain form with affect key (informal speech style) by category

frequency was found in the categories of postposing and rising intonation. The next section presents a discussion on these two affect keys.

Rising intonation

The most common affect key found in the data was rising intonation. This occupied 69% of the affect keys both at pre- and post-test (about 13–16% of the total plain forms). Although the overall frequency of rising intonation was similar between the two conversation sessions, a notable difference was found in its function. Rising intonation typically occurs when asking a question or marking inquiry. However, this typical role was not as common at pre-test, because 45% of the rising intonation was non-question. In other words, rising intonation marked a question in plain forms only 55% of the time. In fact, the learners used rising intonation mostly as a comprehension check at pre-test. When they were not confident in their use of vocabulary or meaning they intend to convey, or when they were not clear about their understanding, they used rising question to appeal to their peer for confirmation.

As an illustration, consult Excerpt 5.7 from pre-test. Rising intonation is noted with the question marker (¿) in bold face. E (an American male) is explaining his relationship with his host family to F (a Chinese male) and the researcher (R). In line 1–2, E brings up his plan of leaving his host family and moving into an apartment. In line 5, the researcher asks why. In lines 6–7, E responds by explaining that his relationship with his host family is not very good – and, after two seconds of pause, he provides another reason (i.e. the house is far from school). E uses rising intonation with the plain form adjective *tooi* (far) and waits for his interlocutors' reaction. E is not asking a question here. E is either checking his interlocutors' understanding or requesting their acknowledgement with the meaning he is trying to convey. F parrots E's word (*tooi*) twice in lines 8 and 10, which signals his comprehension problem. Similarly, the researcher returns only mild acknowledgement in line 11. Responding to these reactions, E elaborates on his word *tooi*. In line 13, E asks whether the interlocutors know of apartments in Adachi district (suburb of Tokyo). Here again, E uses rising intonation (*kono Adachi-ku no apaato¿* 'This apartment in Adachi district¿'). This rising intonation with the word *apaato* (apartment) occurs in the middle of the sentence, and thus does not serve the function of a question. Rather, it occurs as topic introduction by drawing the interlocutors' attention to the topic (apartment in Adachi district). A true question immediately follows this intonation marker with the question particle *ka* (*shitteimasu-ka¿* 'Do you know¿'), but this time in the polite form. As illustrated here, at pre-test, rising intonation attached to the plain form occurs largely for comprehension check and clarification request. This function of rising intonation could be considered a sign of learners' limited linguistic competence and greater reliance on communication strategies. By using rising intonation, the learners were checking their interlocutors' understanding in order to ensure that meaning is being communicated and that the conversation is moving to the intended direction.

Excerpt 5.7 (pre-test) E is talking about his host family to F and the researcher (T).

```
 1 E:  ee    boku  wa    ima    hosuto famirii  ni     isshoni    sun-deiru
       yes   I     TOP   now    host family     LOC    together   live-PROG
 2     kedo:. nanka: (1.0) tabun     apaato   ni     hikkos:u::=
       but    DM           maybe     apartment LOC   move
       'I'm living with my host family now, but well, maybe I will move to
       an apartment.'
 3 F:  °hikkosu:,°=
       move
       'Move...'
 4 E:  =aa    mada    kimetei-nai      kedo:
       ah     still   decide-NEG       but
       'well, still not decided, but...'
 5 T:  sore   wa    dooshite:↗
       that   TOP   why
       'Why is that↗'
 6 E:  ee::   sukoshi:.   nanka:   boku  no    hosuto famirii to:    no: (1.0)
       HES    a little    DM       I     LK    host family    with   LK
 7     kankee       wa:    maamaa       yoku-nakute: (2.1)   sukoshi  tooi↗
       relationship TOP    so so        good-NEG             a little distant
       'a little, well, my relationship with host family is not so good, a little
       distant↗'
 8 F:  [tooi
       distant
       'distant.'
 9 E:  [(toshi)     da      kara       to[oi
       city         COP     because    distant
       'it's distant because it's a city.'
10 F:     [tooi=
           distant
           'distant'
11 T:  =aa::=
       ah
       'ah'
12 E:  =etto: adachi-ku:          no:   etto:  kono    apaato↗
       DM     adachi-district     LK    DM     this    apartment
       (1.3)
```

13   shitte- <u>shitteimasu   ka:⸴</u>
        kno   know   Q
        'well, this apartment in the Adachi district. Do you know⸴'
14 **T:**   °**shiranai**°   <u>shira-nai-des.</u> [(un.)
        know-NEG know-NEG-COP
        'I don't know. I don't know.'

This function of rising intonation changed at post-test: over 80% of the rising intonation with plain forms occurred in its original function – asking a question. In the case of E from the previous excerpt, there were 19 instances of rising intonation, of which 18 instances occurred in question form. Excerpt 5.8 below illustrates this. In line 1, E produces two questions in the plain form: *doo⸴* (How's going⸴) and *nani shiteta⸴* (What have you been doing⸴). Both forms carry rising intonation. A 1.3 second pause following these questions indicates F's lack of understanding, which is further signaled by his negative response (request for repetition) in line 2. In an attempt to repair the trouble source, E repeats his question in line 3. But this time, intonation is flat, perhaps because this is a repeated question, and a query was already made in his first attempt. F understands E's question this time and responds that he hasn't done anything lately. In line 6, F asks another question in the plain form with rising intonation. This is a question that confirms F's response – but at the same time elaborates on it, because E adds two words: *tanoshiikoto* (fun thing) and *zenzen* (not at all) to F's statement. F says that he doesn't remember doing anything fun. E presents his assessment in the following turn (It's a pity.).

Excerpt 5.8 (post-test) E and F are talking about what they did during the break.

1 **E:**   ***doo⸴*** *nani* **shi-te-ta⸴**
        how   what   do-PROG-PST
        'how's going⸴ What have you been doing⸴'
        (1.3)
2 **F:**   *n⸴*
        huh
        'huh⸴'
3 **E:**   *saikin   maa   nani*   **shi°-te-ta,**°
        these days   well   what   do-PROG-PST
        'these days, well, what have you been doing.'
        (1.0)
4 **F:**   *saikin   wa::* (2.5) *tabun   nanimo   s:::hi-nai   to(h)*
        these days   TOP   maybe anything do-NEG   QT
5   ***shi-naka(h)t-ta***   *hh hh=*
        do-NEG-PST
        'these days maybe don't do anything, didn't do anything.'

6	**E:**	*tanoshii*	*koto*	*zenzen*	***shi-nakat-ta:↑=***		
		fun	thing	at all	do-NEG-PST		
		'didn't do fun thing at all?'					
7	**F:**	=*tanoshii*	*koto*	*wa:*	(1.6) °*chotto:*°	*rokugatsu*	*wa::* (4.4)
		fun	thing	TOP	a little	June	TOP
		oboe-nai.	*obo[e-nai*				
		remember-NEG	remember-NEG				
		'Fun thing is, well, I don't remember, I don't remember in June.'					
8	**E:**		[*o(h)*	***zannen***			
			DM	pity			
			'Oh, it's a pity.'				

Postposing

The previous section described change in rising intonation from pre- to post-test data. The affect key that changed the most, however, was postposing. In postposing, pre-predicate elements are dislocated to their post-predicate position. This structure was almost absent at pre-test (only three instances in 18 students' conversations), but it appeared 29 times at post-test. Essentially all 18 learners except two used postposing. Although the overall proportion is small (2.2% of all the plain forms; 9.1% of the plain forms with affect keys), the emergence of this structure in later conversation is notable, considering that it was almost completely missing at the beginning of the semester. Combined with previous cross-sectional findings which revealed that higher proficiency learners produced postposing more often than lower-level learners (e.g. Tomiyama, 2009), greater use of postposing found in this longitudinal investigation indicates that the use of postposing can be a distinct sign of developing interactional competence.

We should also note that this structure is restricted to casual, spoken Japanese. Because written Japanese rarely exhibits this feature, Japanese textbooks – particularly at the intermediate-level – do not typically provide grammatical explanation or explicit instruction on postposing. This is supported by the near absence of this form at pre-test, when the learners first came to Japan. After being immersed in authentic communication and non-prescriptive discourse structures during study abroad, the learners probably incorporated this construction into their linguistics repertoire and started using it in interaction.

Before I discuss the learners' development, a brief background about the structure and functions of postposing is in order. Japanese is canonically a head-final language and is strictly predicate-final (Kuno, 1973; Shibatani, 1990). However, colloquial speech exhibits a construction that violates this predicate-final requirement. Non-predicate elements (e.g. subject noun phrases, pronouns, adverbial clauses, and prepositional phrases) sometimes come after the main clause verbs and occupy the sentence-final position

(Kuno, 1973; Matsumoto, 1995; Shibatani, 1990; Shimojo, 1995; Simon, 1989). Example (1) illustrates the normative, predicate-final (verb final) structure, while (2) shows the postposing pattern in which the subject noun phrase (*Yoko-ga*) is dislocated to the sentence-final position. (In all examples, postposed part – the tail – appears in bold face.)

(1) *Yoko-ga   sensyuu   computer   o   kat-ta   yo*
    Yoko-Nom last week computer   O   buy-PST   FP
(2) *Computer   o   sensyuu   kat-ta   yo   **Yoko-ga***.
    Computer   O   last week buy-PST   FP   **Yoko-SUB**
    'Yoko bought a computer last week.'

This postposing phenomenon is not rare in spoken Japanese. Takahara and Peng (1981) report that 9.7% of utterances contained this form, while Matsumoto (1995) found that, in a 45-minute conversation, 84 instances of postposing were observed, which occupied 5.5% of intonation units. Other scholars (Clancy, 1985; Nomura, 2007) showed that postposing occurs in children's speech as early as two-years old, suggesting early pragmatic/discourse competence and increasing sensitivity with information structure.

Why do Japanese speakers use postposing? Scholars have presented a range of motivations underlying the use of postposing. For example, Shibatani (1990) introduced memory constraints coming from on-line speech processing as motivation. Speaking is a process of translating concepts into linguistic units and articulating them on-line. Because this process occurs quickly, lapses in planning sometimes happen, which could lead to the omission of a linguistic element from a sentence. When the speaker considers that the omitted element is crucial for the listener's understanding, he/she appends it to the post-predicate position as 'afterthoughts,' which results in the postposing structure.

Based on Ono and Suzuki (1992), Nomura (2007) proposed discourse/pragmatic accounts of postposing and presented four major categories of postposing: pragmatic repair, grammatical repair, deliberate defocusing, and sophisticated pragmatics. The first type, *pragmatic repair*, corresponds to the 'afterthought' type postposing originally proposed by Shibatani. The tail part (post-posted element) provides information that is missing from the body (main predicate), but that is crucial for understanding the meaning. This function is typically identified when the noun phrase (NP) or prepositional phrase (PP) – which either appears in the sentence for the first time, or is ambiguous in meaning – is postposed. In the Example (3) below, the PP, *gakko-ni* (to school) is appended to the end after the predicate. This is because the location phrase is new information, and without the post-predicate element, the listener may or may not understand the reference point. In order to avoid potential ambiguity from the information and to clarify the meaning, the speaker postposes the element.

(3) Itsu   ki-ta?   **Gakko ni.**
     When   come-PST school to
     'When did you come to school?'

The second category of postposing is called *grammatical repair*. This occurs when the speaker makes a grammatical mistake in the body and tries to correct it in the tail. As shown in (4), the speaker mistakenly attaches the nominative marker in the main body *–ga* to the noun *hyooka* (evaluation). Then, he corrects his mistake in the tail by replacing *–ga* with *–o* (accusative marker).

(4) Hyooka   ga   shite-nai. **Hyooka   o.**
     evaluation SUB   do-NEG   evaluation O
     '(Someone) hasn't done the evaluation.'

The third type of postposing is called *deliberate defocusing*, which originated with Clancy's (1985) idea that the speaker sometimes deliberately defocuses an element that is already shared and presupposed by the listener by postposing the element. This category of postposing typically occurs with demonstratives in a single intonation counter, without a break between the body and tail. Different from pragmatic repair, the postposed element in this type is clearly known and jointly attended to by the speaker and listener. See (5) for example. The postposed noun *ocha* (tea) follows a demonstrative *kono* (this). Because demonstratives' referents typically exist within immediate discourse context, the noun *ocha* is shared information.

(5) Nigai **kono ocha**.
     Strong. This tea.
     'This tea is strong.'

The last category of postposing, which Nomura calls as *sophisticated pragmatics*, involves the use of postposing for five purposes: providing extra information, elaborating on the predicate, expressing emphasis, linking information, or contrasting the body and tail part. This type of postposing can be identified by the following criteria (adapted from Nomura, 2007): (a) repetition of an NP/PP that forms old, shared information; (b) paraphrase of a body element; (c) postposing of adverbials, adjectivals, or conjunctions; and (d) unrepeated postposing of a personal pronoun. See Example (6). Here, the postponed element is a paraphrase of the main body (*hikooki* 'airplane', which forms old information. The speaker repeats it in the tail position to emphasize the element and to elaborate on the expression in the body.

(6) hikooki   ga   tonde-ru. **Ookii hikooki   ga.**
     airplane SUB   fly-PROG   big airplane   SUB
     'A big airplane is flying in the sky.'

Table 5.5 Frequency of postposing by category, post-test

Type	Raw frequency
Pragmatic repair	3
Grammatical repair	0
Deliberate defocusing	5
Sophisticated pragmatics	21
Total postposed utterances	29

Using the criteria above, I classified the 29 postposed sentences that appeared in the post-test data into the four functional categories. Table 5.5 displays the frequency of each type.

By far, the last category – sophisticated pragmatics – was the most frequent, occupying 70% of the postposing cases. Close analysis of individual cases in the data revealed that a variety of linguistic elements (e.g. arguments of the preceding clause, adverbs, adverbials, demonstratives, temporal and locative phrases, noun phrases) were placed in the post-predicate position, motivated by cognitive, interactional, and emotive factors.

Excerpt 5.9, a case of pragmatic repair, is an example (in the excerpts in this section, symbols for speech styles and incomplete endings are omitted. Postposed parts appear in bold face). In line 1, J brings up a new topic, *natsumatsuri* (summer festival). J asks I if she has been to a summer festival somewhere (line 3–4). J uses postposing in this question. She first says *itta?*, the plain form of the verb 'went' with question intonation in line 3, and then adds *dokokano natsumatsuri* (summer festival somewhere) after the verb in line 4. This postposed element, the locative adverbial phrase, specifies the content of the question. This element is critical for I's comprehension, because without understanding the object of the question, she cannot say 'yes' or 'no.' Although the term *natsumatsuri* was already introduced in line 1, after observing I's neutral response in line 2 – and a slight confusion in her negative response (request for repetition) in line 5 – J realizes I's problem and adds the explicit post-predicate of location (*natsumatsuri*) to eliminate ambiguity (line 6). J's use of postposing here is an indication of her orientation to ongoing conversation and her sensitivity to a potential communication breakdown. After introducing *natsumatsuri* in line 1, J assumes that the topic is jointly attended to, and the object in her question (which *natsumatsuri*) is mutually understood. However, I's reaction signals that this assumption may not hold. Responding to this, J provides a pragmatic repair by making the object explicit in the post-predicate position. This analysis indicates that post-predicate elements are interactionally constructed. They emerge from a sequential context where both parties orient to the direction of conversation and the relevance of each other's response in order to achieve mutual understanding.

Excerpt 5.9 (post-test) J and I are talking about summer festivals.

```
1  J:  natsumatsuri      ni       it-ta.
       summer festival   LOC      go-PST
       'I went to a summer festival.'
2  I:  aa.
       ah
       'ah.'
3  J:  it-ta¿
       go-PST
4      do[koka           no              ←
       somewhere         LK
       'did you go¿ somewhere'
5  I:  [e¿       ii::
       huh¿      go...
       'huh¿ go...'
6  J:  natsumatsuri                      ←
       summer festival
       'summer festival.'
7  I:  °natsumatsuri¿°
       summer festival
       'summer festival.'
8  J:  °un.°
       yes
       'yes'
9  I:  °natsumatsuri.°
       summer festival
       'summer festival'
```

Sophisticated pragmatics was another common function of postposing in the data. Under this category, postposing occurs in a variety of interactional and discoursal functions: emphasizing information, elaborating, linking information, and strengthening the speaker's stance toward the proposition. See Excerpt 5.10. Q expresses his difficulty with finding a job in Japan, but he is determined to find one. In line 8, he says that it is hard to find a job in Japan. In this utterance, the adverb *ima* (now) is postposed and occurs after the predicate, *nihonde mitsukenikuinda* (It's hard to find in Japan.). The postposed adverb *ima* functions to add emphasis to this statement.

Excerpt 5.10 (post-test) Q is telling R that he is looking for a job in Japan.

```
1  Q:  demo: mada   shuushoku      no    tokoro    wa:  tashikani:
       but   yet    employment     LK    place     TOP  certainly
```

```
2        wakara-nai.           sore    wa:    do-    dokodemo       sagashite-iru.
         understand-NEG        that    TOP    HES    everywhere     look for-PROG
         'but I don't know yet where I can find employment. I'm looking
         everywhere.'
3  R:    aa,            aa.
         uh-huh         uh-huh
         'uh-huh, uh-huh.'
4  Q:    un.
         yes
         'yes.'
5  R:    (inaudible)=
6  Q:    =nihon  wa     totemo:         a:     nihon   ni     totemo   i-tai.      demo:
         Japan   TOP    very            ah     Japan   LOC    very     stay-want   but
7        nihon   de     mitsukeru       no     ga:     chotto: nihon    de
         Japan   LOC    find            NOM    SUB     a little Japan   LOC
8        mitsuke-nikui  n       da      ima.             ←
         find-hard      NOM     COP     now
         'Japan is very, ah, I want to stay in Japan very much. But finding (a
         job) in Japan is a little... It's hard to find in Japan now.'
```

See Excerpt 5.11 for another example. Prior to this excerpt, C expressed that she is stressed out from the large amount of homework and asked D for tips on stress reduction. In line 3, D starts sharing advice by listing a series of activities with the conjunction *toka* (and). Postposing occurs in the last piece of advice in line 13, *shitaikotowo suru* (Do whatever you want to do.), which is followed by the adverbial clause *nanimo kangaenaide* (without thinking anything) in line 15. This is postposing because in Japanese the adverbial clause typically comes before the verb. This post-posed element elaborates on the suggestion made in the preceding predicate. After D presents her advice in the first clause, she decides to add more information to it in the form of a post-predicate. Note that after C's request for suggestion in line 1–2, D holds the floor throughout the conversation. This is because the first pair part of the adjacency pair (request for suggestions) nominates D as the speaker of the next turn. This sets the stage for D to produce a multi-turn unit and become the primary speaker (by providing suggestions requested by C), while C becomes the recipient of this discourse unit. Conforming to this structure, C provides a series of backchannel cues without interrupting D, showing her orientation and attention to D's talk. This sequential organization seems to contribute to the occurrence of postposing. Because D is folding the floor, she is in the position where she can expand her speech by adding elements and providing more details *post hoc*. She tacks the adverbial phrase on as a post-predicate unit to elaborate on her suggestion. This is additional evidence that postposing is interactionally constructed. Learners orient to the unfolding discourse and to their participant roles, and they use postposing skillfully to expand on the topic-in-progress and construct shared knowledge.

Excerpt 5.11 (post-test) C and D are talking about stress management.

```
1  C:  sono   ichinichi         wa    nani   o     suru¿
       well   one day           TOP   what   O     do
2      ano    sanpo:            toka¿
       well   taking a walk     like
       'What should I do one day? Like taking a walk?'
3  D:  un.    chotto   dake   de    wa    naku:   tabun    dokoka
       yes    a little only   COP   TOP   NEG     maybe    somewhere
4      iki-tai         tokoro         e      iku:    toka.
       go-want         place          LOC    go      like
       'yes, not only a little, maybe like you go somewhere you want to go.'
5  C:  un.
       yes
       'yes.'
6  D:  eto:    oishii         tabemono     tabe-tai      toki
       well   delicious       food         eat-want      when
       'well, when you want to eat delicious food'
7  C:  aa
       uh-huh
       'uh -huh'
8  D:  jaa            oishii        tabemono       toka:
       well then      delicious     food           like
       'then like delicious food'
9  C:  aa.
       uh-huh
       'uh-huh'
10 D:  sono   ato     tomodachi     to      dokoka:        isshoni:     iku:
       that   after   friends       with    somewhere      together     go
11     ano (1.0)      kaimono       toka:¿
       well           shopping      like
       'After that you go somewhere together with your friends, like shopping?'
12 C:  un     un.
       yes    yes
       'yes, yes'
13 D:  shitai         koto     o     suru.
       do-want        thing    O     do
       'You do what you want to do.'
```

14 **C:** a::.
        ah
        'ah...'
15 **D:** *nanimo*   ***kangae-nai-de***.   ←
        anything   think-NEG-TE
        'not thinking anything.'
16 **C:** *hahaha*.
        (laugh)

The final example below involves two cases of postposing produced by two different speakers. It comes from a conversation between K and L about *Odaiba*, a popular entertainment district in Tokyo Bay. In line 1, L introduces the topic, saying that there is a festival going on in *Odaiba*. K shows interest in her experience by giving a series of backchannel cues of both mild and strong surprise, starting in line 2. After explaining what she saw in *Odaiba*, in line 12, L makes a direct suggestion: *zehi itte* (You should definitely go.). K does not immediately accept this suggestion. Continuing with her suggestion, L adds a conditional clause *jikan attara* (if you have time) in line 21, which mitigates the imposition of the suggestion. More specifically, this conditional clause is postposed from the suggestion statement in line 12.

This postposing arises from a negotiation sequence between L and K that spreads over a number of turns. L's direct suggestion in line 12 – the first pair part of the suggestion-response sequence – does not meet the preferred response (acceptance of suggestion) in the following turn. Following this, L adds more information about *Odaiba* to extend her suggestion further, but K only provides backchannels with no explicit acceptance. L elaborates on her suggestion, but K does not provide a preferred response (acceptance), so L elaborates more. Hence, the appearance of the postposed clause in line 21 (if you have time) is almost conditioned in this sequence, in which L pursues a preferred response (acceptance): it arises from L's necessity to mitigate the force of suggestion because K does not take L up on her suggestion.

Excerpt 5.12 (post-test) K and L are talking about *Odaiba* (a popular district in Tokyo Bay).

1 **L:** *saikin   ano: odaiba   ga   matsuri   ga   aru   yo.*
        Recently well Odaiba   SUB festival   SUB exist FP
        'well, recently there is a festival in Odaiba.'
2 **K:** (.)*uso:!*
        lie
        'No kidding!'
3 **L:** *un,*
        uh-huh
        'uh-huh'

4 **K:** *he::::.*
   DM
   'Oh'
5 **L:** *sokode   wanpi:su   no: >nanka<   sugoi   mono*
      there   one piece   LK   DM   amazing   thing
6   *ga   at-ta.*
      SUB   exist-PST
      'there was an amazing One Piece thing there.'
7 **K:** *hhh a:::::. nanka   kyarakuta: no:*
         ah   DM   character   LM
      'ah, characters. . .'
8 **L:** *un,   ano: tatoeba: ningyohime:¿ totemo(.)   ookii   nor-eru*
      yes   well for example   mermaid   very   big   ride-can
      'yes, well, for example, mermaid¿ very big. You can ride on it.'
9 **K:** *he::[::*
   DM
   'oh'
10 **L:**   [*ahaha*
      'ha ha'
11 **K:** *a,   soo.*
      ah   really
      'really.'
12 **L:** *zehi   it-te.*
      by all means   go-TE
      'go, by all means.'
13 **K:** *he::::.*
   DM
   'oh'
14 **L:** *un,   kashu   mo   iru.*
      yes   singers   too   exist
      'yes, there are singers too.'
15 **K:** *kashu¿*
   singers
   'singers¿'
16 **L:** *un.*
   'yes.'
17 **K:** *fu::n.*
   I see
   'I see.'
18 **L:** *nanka: senshuu   no   doyoobi   kara: tabu:n*
      DM   last week   LK   Saturday   from   maybe
19   *natsu   ga   owaru   made:*
      summer   SUB   ends   until
      'well, from last Saturday until maybe the summer ends.'

20 K: *fu:::n.*
    I see
    'I see.'
21 L: *ja-   dakara   **jikan   at-tara:***   ←
    well then so   time   have-if
    'well then, so, if you have time'
22 K: *aa. soo na   no.*
    ah   so   COP FP
    'ah, really.'
23 L: *un.*
    'yes.'
24 K: *soo   ne,   saikin   wa:*
    right FP   recently   TOP
    'right, recently'
25 L: *hehehe.*
    (laugh)
26 K: *totemo   isogashii   kedo:*
    very   busy   but
    'very busy, but'
27 L: *un.*
    yes
    'Yes'
28 K: *maa   jikan   ga   ar-eba:*
    well time   SUB   exist-if
    'well, if I have time'
29 L: *un.*
    yes
    'yes'
30 K: *itta   hoo   ga   ii   ne:,   **odaiba.***   ←
    go-PST   way   SUB   good   FP   odaiba
    'better to go to Odaiba.'

K finally accepts L's suggestion in line 30 – but, interestingly, K produces postposing in her turn here. She first produces the predicate *itta hoo ga iine* (I should go.) and then adds the location (where to) in the post-predicate position. The location, *Odaiba*, is clearly understood here after a long sequence (29 turns) of talk surrounding this topic. L's post-expansion on her initial suggestion in line 21 (if you have time) also produces the expectation that K will respond to her suggestion about *Odaiba* in the next turn. Despite this presupposition, K still adds *Odaiba* after the predicate. The motivation of this postposing is clearly not to clarify the topic. Rather, it is to add emphasis. By specifying the location, K's intention of accepting L's suggestion becomes clear. The postposed *Odaiba* demonstrates K's orientation to the on-going topic and her alignment to L's suggestion. Combined with the analysis of the first postposing in this excerpt, the data here reveals the important nature of postposing: Postposing is interactionally constructed and arises from the sequential organization of talk-in-progress.

Summary

This chapter has presented data on 18 participants' change in their use of speech styles (the polite and plain forms) in a spontaneous peer-to-peer conversation over 12 weeks of study abroad. A major change was found in their dramatic increase in their usage of the plain form and their decrease in the polite form. This change conforms to the register-appropriate language use. Because the conversation task was set up as a casual talk between peers, a certain degree of informality was expected. The general shift to the plain form use conforms to this expectation. The learners studied here demonstrated a major change in their dominant speech style between the beginning and end of the semester, which is an indication of their development of interactional competence. Speech styles served as their linguistic resources to signal 'talk type' and to construct interpersonal meaning in this particular discourse.

Although group-level shift to the plain form is notable, there was considerable individual variation in their choice of the speech style. Several learners used the plain form as their base from the beginning of their study, while others maintained their primary polite style even at the end of the study abroad period (see Figures 4.2 and 4.3). These individual variations, in part, come from the learners' unfamiliarity with the plain form (using polite form as default style) – but, more importantly, the variations could also reflect the individuals' stances toward speech styles. The polite form is typically associated with the formal register, and the plain forms are linked to the informal register, but these prescriptive views do not always hold true in real-life communication. A recent indexical approach claims that speech style is not a fixed, idealized form; rather, it indexes the speaker's stance, attitudes, and affect, which change during the course of interaction. This current view could explain the individual variation observed in the frequency of plain forms. As expressed by one participant, some learners may not have perceived their peer-to-peer conversation as informal and casual. They might not have developed enough familiarity with their peer in order to 'act out' a casual, informal interaction. They might have felt more comfortable sticking to their familiar polite forms because they wanted to present themselves as a formal and distant conversant. Unfortunately, this study did not collect data on individual learners' perceptions toward the speech style or to the task, so the role of subjectivity in the choice of speech style remains only suggestive.

In addition to the frequency data, this chapter has described functional-level analyses on the learners' use of the speech style. As opposed to frequency, only a small change was found in the distribution of the five plain form functions (i.e. request for information, joint meaning making, presentation of information, expression of inner self, and response to questions). The data revealed two tendencies: (1) Learners performed a variety of conversational functions with plain forms from the very early stage of their study abroad; and (2) Several functions (i.e. presentation of information and expression of inner thought) occupied primary use of the plain forms, and other functions did not appear as much in conversation. Although the overall distribution was relatively stable, the learners' development was observed for evidence of two changes: (1) increased use of the plain forms for joint meaning-making and (2) emergence of a wider range of speech acts performed through the plain forms. Joint meaning-making involves using the plain form to add to the partner's speech (or complete his/her turn), to develop topic-in-progress, or to advocate for the partner's feeling. A slight increase observed in this function is an indication of learners' developing ability to work collaboratively to construct meaning and move conversation along. The emergence of a wider range of communicative functions (e.g. speech acts of suggestions and corrections) at post-test is also a sign of their interactional development. The learners expanded their functional abilities with the plain forms: They conveyed different types of illocution and co-constructed speech events collaboratively with their peers.

Interactional development was further observed in learners' use of affect keys in plain forms (informal speech style). The overall proportion of the four affect keys (i.e. sentence-final particles, rising intonation, postposing, and coalescence) was very small both at pre- and post-test, and the increase over a semester was rather trivial (4.3%). However, a noteworthy change was observed in the emergence of postposing in most learners' data at post-test. This structure was almost absent at pre-test, but it appeared 29 times in the post-test data. More importantly, qualitative analyses of individual cases demonstrated that the postposed elements served a range of discourse-pragmatics functions (i.e. repair, clarifying ambiguity, adding extra information, elaborating on the topic, and expressing emphasis), indicating the learners' functional development. Another important finding is that postposing emerged out of interaction. The postposed element was a product of the sequential organization of talk in which the learners, as both the speaker and listener, monitor each other's contribution to talk and respond to each other. When responding to their peers' reaction, some learners added an element after the predicate in order to intensify or reduce the force of their intention encoded in the predicate (e.g. suggestion). Other learners used postposing as a repair. In reaction to their peers' negative response (e.g. expression of confusion and non-understanding), the learners provided the referent explicitly in the post-predicate position and clarified ambiguity of the referent coming from a wrong assumption. These instances of postposing illustrate learners' interactional competence. Using postposing as their linguistic resources, the learners responded to the changing flow of conversation skillfully and maximized their contribution to the collaborative meaning-making process.

The next chapter (Chapter 6) provides further evidence for the learners' interactional development from the point of style-shifting between the polite and plain forms.

6 Style-Shifting Across Discourse Boundaries

Interactional competence draws on a variety of resources that participants bring to the joint meaning-making process. These resources include: understanding of participant organization, knowledge of register-appropriate language use, knowledge of conversation management (e.g. topic control, repair, and turn-taking system) and recognition and production of boundaries between speech activities (Young, 2002, 2008a, 2008b, 2011). This chapter focuses on the last resource – the ability to mark discourse boundaries.

Young (2007) defines boundaries as 'opening and closing acts of a particular practice that serve to distinguish a given practice from adjacent talk' (71). In authentic communicative situations, different sets of resources are called for according to contextual and interactional specifics of a particular discourse practice. For instance, the ways in which openings and closings are handled in a service encounter situation differ from the ways in which they occur in an academic advising session between a professor and a student. The task of L2 learning involves developing linguistic and interactional abilities to signal boundaries between different discourse practices and move across boundaries efficiently.

The concept of boundaries reinforces that L2 learners' linguistic and interactional resources are not pre-determined but are dependent on the specifics of the context that change within a single interaction. For example, certain linguistic forms usually co-occur in academic advising sessions and characterize the discourse of academic advising (e.g. vocabulary such as 'credits,' 'course selection,' and 'pre-requisite,' and grammatical forms for common speech acts of suggestions and refusals). However, these forms are not fixed or pre-determined before interaction. They might change according to the specifics of a context. Professor–student relationships, history of interaction, similar previous experiences on advising, degrees of involvement in the ongoing talk are all contextual specifics that may change during the course of interaction and directly affect participants' linguistic choice. Participants' interactional competence enables them to respond to these changing contextual figurations skilfully and transit between interactional practices.

This chapter presents analyses of learners' act of signalling boundaries between transitions corresponding to different participant structures within a single interactional setting. Specifically, this chapter examines learners' style-shifting between the plain and polite forms across different participant structures. Although the conversation task was arranged as a 20-minute peer-to-peer interaction, I (the researcher) participated in the conversation sporadically and introduced variation as the conversation was progressing. While a large proportion of the conversation was two-way (between learners), about 40% of the conversation was three-way (between learners and the researcher).

When the third person of a different background joins in the middle of the conversation, it changes the flow of interaction, requiring participants to respond to this change skilfully. In this study, participant structure changes between the moment when the conversation takes place among just students and the moment when the researcher participates in the conversation. In the peer-to-peer conversation, a certain level of informality and closeness might be expected because of the shared background between students, but this structure might change in a conversation when the third person with a different background (the researcher is an older Japanese professor) is present.

Speech styles (plain and polite forms) could function as linguistic resources that signal changes in the participant structure. Japanese speakers often switch speech styles by attending to dynamic contextual features such as interpersonal distance and the addressee's attitudes, which may change during interaction. For instance, people shift from the polite to the plain form to express emotions and thoughts, evaluations, soliloquy-like remarks, and closeness. Shifts from the plain to the polite form, on the other hand, can index psychological distance, presentation of public self, and authoritative voice (Chen, 2004; Cook, 2002, 2008; Fukushima, 2007; Ikuta, 2008; Makino, 2002; Okamoto, 1999; Saito, 2010; see Chapter 2 for details). This study investigated whether or not learners changed their speech styles between the time when they conversed only with their peers and the time when they conversed with their peers and the researcher. Learners' style-shifting between these two types of participant membership reflects their sensitivity and reciprocity toward the changing state of ongoing discourse. Skillful switching between different speech styles is a reflection of learners' ability to mark discourse boundaries, a vital resource in interactional competence.

Style-Shifting Between the Polite and Plain Forms Across Different Participant Structures

Chapter 5 reported on the distributions of the 18 learners' polite and plain forms at pre- and post-conversation session (see Table 5.1 and Figure 5.1). At pre-test, the polite and plain forms appeared at the same rate, 48%

and 46% respectively, but at post-test, the plain forms increased to almost 70%, whereas the polite forms dropped to 15%. Despite this marked change, the distribution of the plain and polite forms remained the same between the two-way conversation when the learners talked with a peer and the three-way conversation when the researcher joined the conversation. Hence, there were no instances of marked group-level style-shifts over the change of the participant structure (See Table 5.1, Chapter 5).

However, at the individual level, several students demonstrated signs of sensitivity to the changing participant structure and ability to differentiate speech styles according to the addressee. The following excerpt among K (female American), L (female American), and the researcher (T) illustrates this observation. In all transcriptions to follow, the polite forms are underlined, the plain forms are bold-faced, and the incomplete sentences have a wavy underline.

Excerpt 6.1 (post-test): K and L are talking about their favorite experiences in Japan.

```
1    L:   demo   ichiban:        ureshi:kat-ta   koto        wa
          but    most            happy-PST       thing       TOP
          'But the happiest thing was'
2    T:   un.
          uh huh
          'uh huh'
3    L:   a:     watashi         wa
          ah    I                TOP
          'ah, I'
4    T:   un.
          hu huh
          'uh huh'
5    L:   fu:pu, tookyoo   no    fu:pu   dansu   no   sa:kuru   o
          foop   Tokyo     LK    foop    dance   LK   club      O
6 →       mitsukemashi-   [ta.
          find-PST
          'Foop, I found the foop dance club in Tokyo.'
7    K:                   [aa::
                          ah
                          'ah'
8    T:                   [aa::
                          ah
                          'ah'
9         nanka  it-te-ta         yo    ne:
          DM     say-PROG-PST     FP    FP
          'You were saying something about that, weren't you?'
```

10	K:	*un.*						
		yes						
		'yes'						
11	T:	*harajuku*	*de*	*ya(.)t-te-ta*		*desho¿*		
		Harajuku	LOC	do-PROG-PST		COP		
		'You were doing it in Harajuku, right¿'						
12	L:	*soo*	*soo*	*soo*	*soo.*			
		so	so	so	so			
		'yes, yes, yes, yes.'						
13	T:	*soo*	*ne.*					
		so	FP					
		'yes.'						
14	L:	*soo*	*soo.*					
		so	so					
		'yes, yes'						
15	T:	*a,*	*honto.*	*aa, ja*	*moo*	*zutto*	**yatt-en**	**n**	**no**
		ah	really	ah DM	already	long time	do-PROG	NOM	FP
16		*sore¿*							
		that							
		'Really. Well, so you are doing it for long time¿'							
17	L:	*soo*	*soo*	*soo.*					
		so	so	so					
		'yes, yes, yes.'							
18	K:	*e:::,*	**omoidashi-ta.**	**sugoi**	**yo**	**ne:.**			
		HES	remember-PST	great	FP	FP			
		'I remembered. It's great, isn't it¿'							
19	T:	**sugoi yo**	**ne.**						
		great FP	FP						
		'It's great, isn't it¿'							
20 →	L:	*soo*	*desu.*	*ano:*					
		so	COP	DM					
		'Yes, well'							
21	T:	**tanoshii¿**							
		fun							
		'Is it fun¿'							
22 →	L:	*honttoni*	*tanoshii*	*desu.*					
		really	fun	COP					
		'It's really fun.'							
23	T:	*a:::.*							
		ah							
		'Ah'							
24	L:	*ano:*							
		DM							
		'Well'							

25	K:	oo:: takusan tomodachi **deki-ta:**¿
		oh many friends make-PST
		'Oh. Did you make many friends¿'
26 →	L:	un minna fu:pu dansu **suru:** kara:
		yes everyone foop dance do because
		'Yes, because everyone does foop dance'
27	K:	un.
		yes
		'yes'
28 →	L:	san, sengetsu watashi mo happyoo *shimashi-ta*.
		last month I too presentation do-PST
		'Last month I did presentation too.'
29	K:	aa:: **soo** **na** **n** **da:**
		ah so COP NOM COP
		'Oh, I see.'
30	T:	hee::
		DM
		'Oh.'

At post-test, when talking to K alone, L used the plain form about 96% of the time and the polite form only about 4%. However, when the researcher participated in the conversation, L changed her speech style and used the polite form almost six times more. Excerpt 6.1 above is a good example. Although L maintained the plain form in backchannels and short responses, in line 6, L responds to my questions with the polite form. L also uses the polite form in line 20 when she acknowledges the joint assessment from K and the researcher in the plain form (*sugoiyone* 'It's great.'). Although her stance in sticking to the polite form is evident, in line 26, she suddenly switches to the plain form when she answers K's question. This demonstrates perfect alignment with her peer's question asked in the plain form. However, in her subsequent turn in line 28, another style-shift occurs: L imparts new information about her last month's dance presentation using the polite form. This shift again emphasizes L's stance in her choice of speech style in the three-party interaction: the polite form is the base-form when she presents information to the researcher.

Like L, several other students showed style-shifting across different participant structures. Table 6.1 summarizes the proportion of the plain and polite forms produced by individual learners. Three students showed a marked style-shifting between the time when conversing with their peers (two-way conversation) and the time when conversing with their peers and the researcher (three-way conversation) at post-test: Student I, L, and R. In the case of Student I, the polite form appeared in only about 2% of her speech during a two-way conversation, but the frequency jumped to over 20% when the researcher joined the conversation. Student R was also able to style-shift

Table 6.1 Individual comparisons of the polite and plain form distributions across participant structures

	Two-way				Three-way			
	Pre-test		Post-test		Pre-test		Post-test	
	Polite	Plain	Polite	Plain	Polite	Plain	Polite	Plain
A	50.8% (32)	49.2% (31)	11.1% (7)	86.8% (46)	69.7% (23)	30.3% (10)	11.1% (4)	89.2% (33)
B	54.8 (17)	45.2 (14)	47.6 (20)	52.4 (22)	23.5 (4)	76.5 (13)	36.4 (8)	63.6 (14)
C	44.1 (26)	55.9 (33)	7.1 (3)	93.0 (40)	73.3 (11)	26.7 (4)	13.0 (3)	87.0 (20)
D	73.6 (53)	13.9 (19)	13.3 (6)	86.7 (39)	97.4 (38)	2.6 (1)	15.2 (5)	84.8 (28)
E	6.5 (2)	93.5 (29)	3.3 (2)	96.7 (59)	42.4 (14)	57.6 (19)	4.0 (24)	96.0 (1)
F	67.9 (19)	32.1 (9)	2.9 (1)	97.1 (33)	56.5 (13)	43.5 (10)	14.8 (4)	85.2 (23)
G	41.2 (21)	58.8 (30)	50.0 (31)	50.0 (31)	45.5 (10)	54.5 (12)	52.9 (9)	47.1 (8)
H	16.7 (5)	83.3 (25)	14.9 (13)	85.1 (74)	7.3 (4)	92.7 (51)	8.8 (3)	91.2 (31)
I	52.3 (23)	47.7 (21)	2.0 (1)	98.0 (49)	42.5 (17)	57.5 (23)	21.1 (4)	78.9 (15)
J	54.7 (35)	45.3 (29)	5.2 (4)	94.8 (73)	68.2 (30)	31.8 (14)	11.5 (3)	88.5 (23)
K	13.5 (7)	86.5 (45)	1.1 (1)	98.9 (90)	31.4 (11)	68.6 (24)	2.4 (1)	97.6 (40)
L	25.5 (12)	74.5 (35)	3.8 (3)	96.2 (75)	46.2 (12)	53.8 (14)	23.5 (8)	76.5 (26)
M	31.8 (21)	68.2 (45)	35.9 (28)	64.1 (50)	54.5 (12)	45.5 (10)	14.3 (5)	85.7 (30)
N	60.0 (42)	40.0 (28)	26. v3 (20)	73.7 (56)	57.8 (26)	42.2 (19)	16.7 (8)	83.3 (40)
O	61.2 (41)	38.8 (26)	27.5 (14)	72.5 (37)	62.5 (10)	37.5 (6)	20.6 (7)	79.4 (27)
P	61.9 (26)	38.1 (16)	25.9 (14)	74.1 (40)	45.5 (20)	54.5 (24)	38.1 (8)	61.9 (13)
Q	87.5 (42)	12.5 (6)	35.1 (13)	64.9 (24)	72.2 (26)	27.8 (10)	19.2 (5)	80.8 (21)
R	94.4 (17)	5.6 (1)	2.2 (1)	97.8 (44)	82.6 (19)	17.4 (4)	50.0 (14)	50.0 (14)

Notes: The numbers in the parentheses are raw counts. Two-way refers to a portion of a conversation between learners only, while three-way refers to a portion when the researcher joined the conversation.

effectively to signal transitions and distinguish a given discourse from an adjacent discourse. The style-shifting was more dramatic in this student's case: she used the polite form less than 2% of the time during a two-way conversation when talking only with her peer, while the frequency was almost 50% during a three-way talk with the peer and the researcher. Hence, we can conclude that in these three students' cases, speech style mixing was not arbitrary. They took into account both static and dynamic features of the interaction (e.g. status, interpersonal distance) and strategically manipulated their speech styles moment-by-moment in order to project different social meanings across contexts.

Excerpt 6.2 illustrates Student R's style-shifting from a dyad to triad. In this excerpt, R is explaining her experience working part-time in a Japanese restaurant to the researcher (T) and to her peer, Student Q. The polite forms are underlined, and the plain forms are bold-faced. When conversing with her peer alone (line 1–9), R marks every ending of her utterance with the plain form, although her peer is asking questions with the polite form (see lines 1 and 3). Here R is making a conscious choice to use the plain form: she opts for the plain form although her speech style does not align with her peer's speech style in questions directed to her. By using the plain form in response to her peer's polite form, R is deliberately signaling her understanding of the interactional situation (peer-to-peer talk) and the speech style that typifies such interaction (i.e. the plain form).

Excerpt 6.2 (post-test): R is talking about her work experience at a Japanese restaurant.

```
1 Q:  a,      dono    resutoran       deshi-ta      ka?
      ah      which   restaurant      COP-PST       Q
      'Ah, which restaurant was it?'
2 R:  otoya   to yuu                  resutoran.
      otoya   called                  restaurant
      'Restaurant called Otoya.'
3 Q:  uh huh. waseda          no      chikaku   desu   ka?
      uh-huh  Waseda          LK      near      COP    Q
      'Uh-huh. Is it near Waseda?'
4 R:  uun,    ie      no      chikaku.    un.    ie     kara:  ano,
      no      house   LK      near        yes    home   from   DM
5     resutoran       made    arui-te     tabun  juppun        kakaru.
      restaurant      to      walk-TE     maybe  ten minutes   take
      'No, near my house. Yes, from home to restaurant, maybe it takes
      10 minutes walking.'
6 Q:  uh huh.
      uh-huh
      'Uh-huh.'
```

7 **R:** a,   demo: senpai   koohai   wa   kirai   **na**   node:
         ah   but   senior   junior   TOP   don't like   COP   because
        'Ah, but I don't like senior-junior thing, so…'
8 **Q:** he   he.
         he   he
        'he he'
9 **R:** ii   keiken   da   to   ***omou.*** (laugh)
         good   experience   COP   QT   think
        'I think it's a good experience.'

However, her speech style changes almost completely when the researcher joins the conversation. See below. In line 10, the researcher interrupts and asks a question using the plain form. R responds to the question in the polite form in line 15 (*shiteimasu* 'I am doing.') and again in line 19 (*hairimashita* 'entered'). It is notable that both cases are marked with a false start: R first replies in the plain form and self-repairs it with the polite form. In line 13, when telling a story about serving tables in a restaurant, R first uses the plain form of the past tense of the verb 'do' (*shiteita*). She immediately repairs it with the polite form (*shiteiamsu*) in her next turn. The instance of self-repair happens again in line 18. When R tells the researcher about a senior person working in the restaurant, she first uses the plain form *haitta* (entered), and then changes the verb to the polite equivalent (*hairimashita*).

R's self-repair to the polite form here is a reflection of her conscious decision. Note that the use of the plain form verb (instead of the polite form) causes no communication breakdown, because the difference between these two forms is localized in the area of verb conjugation and does not affect semantic meaning at all. In either form it is perfectly understood that the person in the topic was acting as a senior because she started working in the restaurant before R did. Still, R repaired the form by replacing it with the polite ending. This self-repair is an indication of her attentiveness to the indexical meaning of the polite and plain forms. Generally, the polite form indexes distance, power difference, and formality, while the plain form indexes solidarity, familiarity, and closeness. These conventional rules of the speech styles are not fixed. Speech styles are dynamic and change according to the shifting interpersonal relationship, flow of conversation, and the image of the 'self' that one wants to project. R consciously shifted from the plain to polite form across different participant structures (i.e. from a dyad with a peer to a triad with a peer and the researcher). This style-shift seems to reflect her understanding of speech boundaries and specifics of different discourse contexts – whom she is talking to and in what situation. In other words, she employed different speech styles skillfully as her interactional resources in order to project a different 'self' to her peer and to the researcher. After these two cases of a false start and self-repair, R's use of the polite forms to the researcher becomes stabilized. In lines 27 and 31, she produces the polite form in the first instance.

Excerpt 6.2 (*continued*)

```
10  T:  senpai    koohai?      do,    donna           keiken       shi-ta?
        senior    junior       what   what kind of    experience   do-PST
        'senpai-kohai? What kind of experience did you have?'
11  R:  hh.    ano,     a::,    senpai          wa:
        hh     well     ah      senior          TOP
        'haha, well, ah... senior is...'
12  T:  un.
        uh-huh
        'uh-huh'
13  R:  watashi         wa       ho:ru    [no      shi-tei-ta
        I               TOP      hall     LK       do-PROG-PST
        'I was doing hall-related work'
14  T:                                    [un.
                                          uh-huh
                                          'uh-huh'
15  R:  shit-imasu,     ano      soshite          isshoni        ho:ru      o      suru
        do-PROG         well     then             together       hall       O      do
16      hito    wa      watashi
        person  TOP     me
        'I am doing hall-related work. Well, then, there is another person
        who is doing hall-related work together.'
17  T:  un      un.
        yes     yes
        'yes,   yes'
18  R:  no:     sakini       kono     resutoran       ni        hait-ta
        LK      before       this     restaurant      LOC       enter-PST
19      [hairi, mashi-ta.
        enter-PST
        'She entered this restaurant before me.'
20  T:  [aa     aa.
        ah      ah
        'I see.'
        (1.0)
21  R:  kono    hito      wa
        this    person    TOP
        'This person'
22  T:  un.
        yes
        'Yes.'
```

23	R:	*nanimo:*	***shi-nai***	*ano*	*hashi*	*dake*	*ano:*	
		nothing	do-NEG	DM	chopsticks	only	well	
		'does nothing. Well, just chopsticks, well...'						
24	T:	*a!*						
		ah						
		'Ah!'						
25	R:	*u:n,*	*fui-*	*fuite:*				
		yes	wi-	wipe				
		'yes, wipe (chopsticks) and...'						
26	T:	*un*	*un.*					
		yes	yes					
		'yes, yes'						
27	R:	*i-masu.*						
		wipe-PROG						
		'wiping.'						
28	T:	*un*	*un.*					
		yes	yes					
		'yes, yes'						
29	R:	*ho:ru*	*no*	*koto*	*wa*	*zenbu*	*watashi*	*hitoride:*
		hall	LK	thing	TOP	all	I	by myself
		'All hall-related work, I (did) by myself'						
30	T:	*un.*						
		yes						
		'yes'						
31	R:	*ano,*	*shi-mashi-ta.*					
		DM	do-COP-PST					
		'well, I did (by myself.)'						

While the excerpt above illustrates R's linguistic adaptability to changing participant structure, the next excerpt displays her adaptability to the sequential organization of talk. Here again, she exploits the two speech styles strategically in order to demonstrate her adaptability. Although R consistently uses the polite form when speaking to the researcher (line 7 and 13), there is one instance in which she opts for the plain form – line 20. Here, R's plain form is embedded in the foregoing turn by the researcher and co-constructs the researcher's utterance.

In the earlier part of the conversation, she tells the researcher about her experience of not using the polite speech style to her senior when working in a restaurant. Because the polite form is the norm when speaking to someone superior in a work place, R thinks that she probably annoyed the senior, which was hinted by the change of the senior's facial expression. In line 17–18 the researcher shows alignment and supports R's interpretation by saying that the senior was probably annoyed because R did not use the polite language (*teineina kotoba*). Notice that the clause of reason (because

R didn't use the polite language) is jointly produced with R. In line 18, the researcher produces the object (polite language) and stops with the object marker particle *o*, signaling that the verb predicate (transitive verb following the object maker *o*) is to follow. Succeeding this, R provides the predicate in the plain form *tsukawamanakatta kara* 'because I didn't use (the polite language).' When the researcher comes to the transition relevance point, R anticipates the researcher's conclusion and says it in the plain form. The use of the plain form here (instead of the polite form) is appropriate because R's voice emerges from that of the researcher, and in this unfolding the plain form grammatically fits the co-construction of the joint voice. Because R's utterance becomes part of the researcher's utterance, R's plain form does not index closeness or equal status with the researcher; it is a resource for the co-construction of the voice with the researcher.

Observe that R produces another clause of reason in line 7. Here R is presenting her own reason as to why she might have annoyed the senior in the restaurant. She says that it was because she did not use the 'politeness thing' (*teinei no koto*). The subordinate clause of reason in line 7 involves the polite form, *tsukawanai desu kara* (because I don't use.). In sharp contrast with the case of turn co-construction described above, R's use of the polite form here is appropriate because the speech is directed to the researcher, not co-constructing the researcher's voice. The choice of the polite form here signals R's perceptions of the situational subtleties and understanding of the speech style that best represents the situation. She uses the polite form to index social meaning of formality and distance with the researcher.

Excerpt 6.3 (post-test): R is talking about her work experience in a Japanese restaurant.

```
1    R:  ano     aruhi:,
         DM      one day
         'well, one day...'
2    T:  un.
         yes
         'yes'
3    R:  senpai  to      hanasu          toki:
         senior  with    talk            when
         'when I talk with the senior'
4    T:  un.
         yes
         'yes'
5    R:  ano::   ano::   u::n,   teinei          no      koto    o:
         DM      DM      uhmm    politeness      LK      thing   O
         'well, well, uhn, politeness thing'
```

6	**T:**	*un.*					
		yes					
		'yes'					
7 →	**R:**	*ano,*	<u>*tsukawa-nai*</u>	<u>*desu*</u>	*kara:*		
		DM	use-NEG	COP	because		
		'well, because I don't use'					
8	**T:**	*un.*					
		yes					
		'yes'					
9	**R:**	*ano*	*senpai*	*no*	*kao*	*ga*	*nanka*
		DM	senior	LK	face	SUB	DM
		'well, senior's face, well'					
10	**T:**	*un.*					
		yes					
		'yes'					
11	**R:**	*kawaru::*		*to*			
		change		QT			
		'change'					
12	**T:**	((laugh))					
13	**R:**	<u>*omotte-imashi-ta*</u> ((laugh))					
		think-PROG-PST					
		'I thought'					
14	**T:**	*sokka:.*					
		I see					
		'I see.'					
15	**R:**	*un.*					
		yes					
		'yes'					
16	**T:**	*sore*	*wa*	*chotto*	**kawaru**	**kamo**	**ne:.**
		that	TOP	a little	change	might	FP
		'That (the senior's face) might change a little.'					
17		*senpai*	*chotto*	*iyana*	*omoi*	**shi-ta**	**kamoshirenai.**
		Senior	a little	annoying	feeing	do-PST	might
		'The senior might have had annoying feeling'					
18 →		*ano, kotoba¿*		*teineina*		*kotoba*	*o*
		DM, language		polite		language	O
		'Well, language¿ Polite language'					
19	**Q:**	*uh huh.*					
		uh-huh					
		'uh-huh.'					
20 →	**R:**	**tsukawa-nakat-ta**		*kara.*			
		use-NEG-PST		because			
		'because I didn't use.'					

Summary

This chapter has presented an analysis of interactional competence as indexed in learners' ability to use appropriate speech styles that correspond to changing situations in talk-in-progress. Specifically, this study examined learners' style-shifts from the plain to the polite form in three-way conversations when they talked with their peers and the researcher at the same time. During the 20 minutes of recording, I (the researcher) joined the conversation occasionally by asking questions or commenting on the ongoing topic. My intention was to see whether this change in the participant structure would affect the students' choice of speech style, because I was clearly in a different position than their conversation partner: an older, Japanese speaking instructor.

Contrary to my expectations, at group-level, the proportion of the plain and polite forms was the same regardless of my participation in the conversation, and the proportion remained unchanged over a semester of study abroad. However, at the individual level, several learners showed signs of sensitivity to the changing participant structure and demonstrated the ability to differentiate speech style according to the addressee. These learners took into account both static and dynamic features of the interaction (e.g. status, interpersonal distance) and strategically manipulated their use of speech style moment-by-moment in order to index different social meanings across contexts. Moreover, as illustrated in Excerpt 6.3, one learner became able to shift between speech styles in order to adapt to the sequential organization of talk. She used the polite form when she was directing her speech to the researcher, but shifted to the plain form when she was co-constructing the researcher's utterance. The plain form as co-construction of an utterance fit the grammatical form and completed the researcher's turn in a sequentially appropriate manner. These instances revealed the learners' incipient ability to use speech styles to index social meaning across discourse boundaries. For a small number of learners, both polite and plain forms – together with the sequential organization of talk – served as resources for the creation of different social meanings and social acts across discourse boundaries.

These learners' abilities to adapt their speech styles to the changing course of interaction can be identified as their development of interactional competence (e.g. Hall, 1995; Young & He, 1998; Young, 2002, 2011). Interactional competence views language knowledge as locally situated. Learners' resources are not determined in advance but are dependent on the specifics of the dynamic context. In the cases described here, the contextual 'specifics' involved participants' status, roles, and relations. When the third person of a different background joins in the middle of the conversation, it changes the flow of interaction, which requires participants to respond to this change competently. Their response has to be prompt and spontaneous so that the ongoing conversation continues seamlessly, because even when the participants' dynamics change, the task of conversation – collaborative construction of meaning – remains, to which all participants must continuously orient their attention. In the case of these few students, they reacted to the change with their 'resources' – their speech styles. The students switched between the polite and plain forms within a single discourse, turn-by-turn, responding to the contextual specifics. Hence, speech styles play a two-part function in interaction. First, learners respond to contextual requirements by drawing on interactional resources (speech styles) that can be used to coordinate their actions. Second, using speech styles, learners signal boundaries between practices and transitions. Style-shifting reveals L2 learners' ability to move between multiple boundaries and discourse practices, and to adapt and align their communicative behaviors to a dynamic, changing context.

Building on the discussion of interactional competence, the next chapter (Chapter 7) presents analyses of another utterance-ending structure examined in this study – incomplete sentences, which revealed the most notable change in participants over the semester. My analysis will show how the increased use of this utterance pattern serves as an indicator of interactional development.

7 Incomplete Sentences in Joint Turn Construction[1]

The last two chapters documented L2 Japanese learners' changing usage of the two primary speech styles at utterance-ending (the polite and plain form) during a semester abroad. The learners' use of the plain forms increased by 22%, while that of the polite forms decreased by 33%. However, the most notable change found in the learners' utterance-ending forms was their increased use of incomplete sentences, which is the focus of this chapter.[2] Incomplete sentences occupied only about 5.7% of the learners' utterances at pre-test, but the percentage tripled at post-test, comprising almost 17% of their utterance-ending forms, thus demonstrating a greater degree of change than that of the polite or plain form.

In Japanese conversation, speakers typically choose between the polite and plain form at the utterance-ending position, or opt for an incomplete ending. The ubiquity of incomplete endings is a well-known characteristic of Japanese conversation (see Chapter 2). By leaving a sentence unfinished, the speaker can avoid explicitly marking interpersonal relationships coming from the choice of a particular speech style (e.g. Chen, 2000; Cook, 2006). The speaker can also appeal to the listener to complete the sentence initiated by the speaker (e.g. Hashimoto, 2007; Hayashi, 2003; Lerner, 2004) or to take over the turn and branch off to a new topic.

Incomplete sentences, particularly those occurring at turn transition points, serve as important linguistic and interactional resources that L2 learners draw in conversation. The very function of incomplete sentence endings at turn-taking position – transition of the speakership, co-construction of a turn, or take-off to a new topic, is an indicator of interactional competence because the ability to integrate incomplete sentences in discourse signals learners' ability to monitor the direction of talk and make sequentially-appropriate contributions to the ongoing conversation. Being able to recognize incomplete endings and respond to them properly show learners' ability to align their speech action to the unfolding discourse and design their contribution in a way that appropriately responds to co-participants' actions. This ability finds synergy with interactional competence because they both capitalize on the ability to accomplish meaningful social actions in cooperation with co-participants. Knowledge of incomplete sentences and the ability to use them to co-construct a turn is a critical component of the linguistic and interactional resources that learners bring to the process of joint meaning making, and thereby contributes to learners' interactional competence.

This chapter describes learners' use of incomplete sentences for the purpose of joint turn construction. I will illustrate how learners interactively achieved shared perspective in the talk-in-progress through collaborative turn construction. Although the majority of the incomplete sentences by the speaker at turn transition points was followed by the listener's simple acknowledgement, I found a small but growing number of incomplete endings followed by the listener's joint turn construction at the end of the semester. At pre-test, there were only two instances of a collaborative turn construction in which the listener completed the sentence left unfinished by the speaker, but at post-test, frequency of such joint turn completion increased to 20. This change indicates the learners' development in their ability to handle sequential exchanges surrounding incomplete sentences. Over a period of one semester, the learners became able to monitor ongoing turns, coordinate their actions with one another, and collaboratively achieve talk-in-progress.

Functions of Incomplete Sentence Endings in Joint Turn Construction

An incomplete utterance was defined as a sentence with an omission of a predicate or, in the case of a compound sentence, an omission of a clause (Usami, 1995). Incomplete sentences serve an important interactional function in that they present an opportunity for joint construction of talk (see Chapter 2). Hayashi (2014) presents a variety of social actions performed by collaborative turn constructions in Japanese. One such action is perspective sharing. When completing the turn initiated by the first speaker, the second speaker imitates the voice of the first speaker by projecting a shared stance. Another common social function behind collaborative turn constructions is the display of sympathy. The second speaker can display empathetic understanding of the first speaker's experience by completing his/her turn. Finally, joint turn construction often occurs for the function of assisted explanation: the second speaker assists with the first speaker's explanation by completing his or her turn. Below I will illustrate these functions in the participants' data.

Joint turn construction around a communication problem

The data in this study revealed many instances of joint turn construction occurring around a linguistic problem. When the first speaker stumbled over a word, the second speaker provided the missing word. This is a case of repair (Schegloff et al., 1977). A repair sequence starts with a repairable, an utterance that is spotted as a source of trouble. When facing the trouble source, the speaker of the repairable initiates a self-repair, or others provide an other-initiated repair. The following excerpt illustrates a repair occurring around an incomplete ending. This is a conversation between E, an American male, and F, a Chinese male, talking about their housemates. Incomplete endings are indicated by a wavy line.

Excerpt 7.1 (post-test): F is talking about his housemates.

```
1:   F:   demo   cho:         <chokusetsu   no:>    (1.4)   tto:
          but    di           direct        LK              QT
2:        komyunikeeshon                    wa:    ii    to    omoimasu
          communication                     TOP    good  QT    think
          'But direct communication is good, I think.'
          (1.1)
3    E:   u:n.=
          yes
          'yes'
4 →  F:   =chokusetsu         no    s- s- ts-
          direct              LK    HES
          'Direct (hesitation)'
5 →  E:   kaiwa               no
          conversation        LK
          'conversation'
6    F:   [hai.   kaiwa              no
          yes     conversation       LK
          'Yes, conversation'
7    E:   [(aa)  >soo    soo   soo   soo<
          Ah     so      so    so    so
          'Ah, so, so, so, so'
8    F:   hai.
          yes
          'Yes.'
```

Prior to this segment, F had explained his living situation to E. There are five residents in F's house: a Singaporean male, a Japanese male, an older couple who owns the house, and F. F complains about the Japanese person in the house because he is unfriendly and rarely communicates with other residents. After a brief complaint, in line 1–2, F reiterates that direct communication is important. E agrees with this statement in the following turn (u:n or 'yes'). Latching on to E's response token, in line 4, F tries to restate the idea with a paraphrase, but cannot produce the complete phrase. He produces the adjective *chokusetsu* (direct) followed by the possessive particle *no*, but cannot produce the noun that comes after the particle. E acknowledges F's linguistic problem and completes the turn by providing the noun that F cannot produce (*kaiwa*, 'conversation') in line 5. Here, E co-constructs F's turn by providing the other-initiated repair to the trouble source.

A collaborative turn completion usually involves a brief post-sequence – acceptance or rejection of the proffered completion (Lerner, 1996). The first speaker either accepts the completion that the second speaker has offered with a minimal response token or rejects the completion and offers an alternative completion. In the L2 data analyzed here, most instances of joint turn completions were followed by the acceptance by the initial speaker. In the excerpt above, after E's turn proffered in line 5, F accepts the repair with a brief acknowledgement (*hai*, 'yes') and confirms the word that E has supplied by repeating it.

The next two excerpts are from a conversation between the same students at post-test recorded 12 weeks later. One notable change from the pre-test data is that the joint turn construction occurred more frequently at post-test in a longer conversational sequence. In the pre-test excerpt above, the turn completion sequence ends after E supplies the missing word to complete F's utterance. Both participants confirm the meaning and move on to a new topic. In contrast, as shown in the post-test excerpts below, after E supplies the trouble word, F maintains the word in his turn-in-progress: F uses E's word in his syntactic unit and presents a new assessment. In other words, collaborative turn construction extends over a longer sequence of exchange at post-test: the first speaker leaves a sentence unfinished; the second speaker completes the sentence; and the first speaker builds on it by making it part of his/her syntactic unit and thus moves the conversation forward.

See Excerpt 7.2, a case of lexical repair. In line 1, F tells E that he goes to his *aikido* practice many times a week. The word *aikido* becomes a trouble source, as E signals his incomprehension in line 2 with a hesitation marker. F does not immediately pick up on this cue; instead, he continues with this topic and utters the word *aikido* again in line 3. Overlapping with this turn, in line 4, E gives a confirmation check by using a similar sounding word, 'hiking.' In line 6, F once again tries out the word but provides only a portion of it in line 6 (*aiki*) and stops there. Following this, in line 7, E finally understands the word *aikido* and produces a confirmation question (*aikidoo↑*) – checking whether his understanding of the word is correct or not. In the subsequent turn, F integrates E's confirmation check into his syntactic unit, *da to omou* (I think that...). In this utterance, the copula *da* signals that there is a word before the copula. The fact that F produces this copula *da* tells us that he has borrowed E's word (*aikidoo↑*) from the preceding turn and integrated it into his own utterance, demonstrating the act of collaborative sentence completion.

Excerpt 7.2 (post-test): F is talking about his club activity, *aikido* (Japanese martial art).

```
1   F:  tatoeba: (1.0)    mai-      maishuu      nankaimo              aikidoo
        for example       every     every week   time and time again   aikido
        'For example, every week, time and time again, aikido'
2   E:  nn [::::
        HES
        'uhmm...'
3   F:  [aikidoo    it::-te:
        aikido      go-TE
        'I go aikido'
4   E:  [haikingu¿
        Hiking
        'Hiking?'
5   F:  [(tto:)
        Well
        'well'
6 → haiki-      haikidoo¿         [aiki-
        hiki        hikido              aiki
        'Hiki, haikidoo¿ Aiki...'
7 → E:                                [hai-  aa aa aa aa aa aa   ha-   aikidoo¿
                                       Hai   ah ah ah ah ah ah  ha    aikido
                                       'Hi, ah, ah, ah, ah, ah, ah, ha, aikido?'
8 → F:                                [da           to        omou
                                       COP          QT        think
                                       'I think it is (aikido).'
9       hai.
        yes
        'yes.'
10  E:  aa:::::
        DM
        'Oh...'
```

A similar case of joint turn completion happens later in the same conversation (see below). In line 13, F introduces another club activity in which he regularly participates on weekends: the China-Japan relation group. E interprets it as a club activity at Waseda University, but F responds to that assumption in the negative in line 17 by saying that the group is not part of Waseda University. Here the utterance *Waseda ja nakutte* (Not Waseda University) is an incomplete ending with the conjunctive particle *te*, which signals that the explanation is not yet over and another clause is expected to follow. The clause to follow is the explanation about the China-Japan relation group, which F cannot supply immediately. In line 19 he supplies a portion of the explanation (*nihon no*, 'of Japan'). This is an incomplete utterance ending with the possessive particle *no*. The softer speech and the discourse marker *ano* (well) indicate that F is not completely self-assured. Following this, in line 20, E provides assurance that he understands what F is trying to say by giving the acknowledgment *un* (yes) and a paraphrase of F's utterance, *nihonjin ga* (Japanese are). Here, the utterance with the subject marker particle *ga* is an incomplete utterance with a missing predicate. In line 21, F repeats the incomplete utterance (*nihonjin ga*), to which E supplies the missing predicate (*ooi*, 'many') in line 22. Here, E and F again collaboratively construct a syntactic unit. By completing a sentence together, they contribute to the joint meaning making process and establish mutual understanding.

Excerpt 7.2 (*continued*)

```
            (Lines 11 and 12 are omitted)
13          shuumatsu    toki:    ano      nicchuu:        kankee
            weekend      time     well     China-Japan     relationship
            'On weekend, well, China-Japan relationship'
14     E:   [u:n
            yes
            'Yes.'
15     F:   [saakuru     ano      saakuru         mitai    na      guru-
            circle       well     circle          like     COP     grou(p)
            'circle, well, it's a group like circle.'
16     E:   a            waseda           waseda          no
            ah           waseda           waseda          LK
            'Oh, Waseda, Waseda's'
17     F:   waseda       ja::     nakut-te        etto     >tabun<    nihon
            waseda       COP      NEG-TE          DM       maybe      Japan
            'Not Waseda, well, maybe, Japanese'
18     E:   aa    [aa
            DM    DM
            'Oh, oh'
19     F:         [°nihon         no (1.2)        ano°
                  Japan           LK              DM
            'Japanese, well...'
20 →   E:   un.   nihonjin        [ga:
            yes   Japanese        SUB
            'Yes, Japanese'
21 →   F:                         [nihonjin       ga:
                                  Japanese        SUB
                                  'Japanese'
22 →   E:   ooi↿=
            many
            'many↿'
```

23 → **F:** =*ooi.*
　　　　many
　　　　'many'
24　**E:** *a   sokka:=*
　　　　ah   I see
　　　　'I see.'

These excerpts demonstrate how these two learners worked collaboratively to solve a communication problem and co-construct meaning. The turn completed by the second speaker provided the crucial piece of information that was necessary to establish meaning and to move the conversation forward. This is evident in the manner in which the first speaker used the second speaker's turn completion unit as part of his continuation of talk-in-progress. By collaboratively completing turns, the participants constructed meaning together and developed a shared mental context in discourse. Learners' joint turn completion around a language problem also signals their alignment and intersubjectivity. As Lerner (1996) claimed, 'early opportunistic completion of a word search is a device that can be used to initiate or sustain a special alignment with a speaker, one of story cosociateship or association co-membership, rather than recipientship' (pp. 262–263). Development in this alignment resource allows for greater success in the co-construction of communication.

Joint turn construction for the display of empathetic understanding

In addition to resolving communication problems, joint turn construction also served the social function of displaying shared understanding. This activity involves demonstrating empathetic understanding of a co-participant's experience: the first speaker tells his/her personal experience to the second speaker and the second speaker displays a vicarious understanding of the first speaker's experience by completing his or her utterance (Hayashi, 2014).

The following excerpt from a conversation between K and L, female American students, and the researcher (T) illustrates this action of empathetic display. The topic of the conversation is transgenderism in Japan. Transgender personalities have recently become popular in Japan, popping up everywhere in the Japanese media as 'new-half' celebrities. In line 1, the researcher solicits the students' opinions about this trend. It is evident that these two students share a similar view toward this topic by the manner in which they co-construct their assessment turn-by-turn. In line 2–3, L explains that there are transgender people in the US too, but broadcasting them on TV is not socially accepted. K joins this explanation in line 4, as she repeats a portion of L's speech (the particle *de*) from the previous turn. This joint explanation is also seen in line 7–8. Overlapping with L's statement that people would get angry if transgender people appeared on TV, K presents her own prediction of people's reactions (*bikkuri*, 'shocked.') in line 8. By doing so, K not only shows alignment with L's point of view but also adds to it.

Collaborative meaning making continues in line 9 where L integrates K's word *bikkuri* into her own syntactic unit and produces an incomplete sentence with a *te*-form ending (*bikkurishite*). With a stretch added to this *te*-ending word, L's turn signals that the topic is still in progress and a clause is still to come. Immediately following this, K meets this expectation by taking over the turn and supplying the clause *tabun dameto omou* ('Maybe it's not good, I think.') to L's incomplete turn. By completing the turn originally initiated by L, K displays empathetic understanding to L's perspective. At the same time, L signals her stance that she is of the same standpoint as K. Series of collaborative sequences in this excerpt present a compelling example of the joint meaning making process. Cooperative overlap, joint turn completion, and recycled use of the co-participants' speech serve as important linguistic and interactional capitals for the learners to skillfully co-construct meaning turn-by-turn.

Excerpt 7.3 (post-test): K and L are talking about transgenderism in Japan

```
1   T:  do      omou,    aayuu    hitotachi  ga    hayatteru  no=
        how     think    those    people     SUB   popular    NOM
        'What do you think about those people (transgender people)
        being popular?'
2   L:  =omoshiro:i.     ano:     amerika    ni    wa,        mo,
        interesting      DM       America    LOC   TOP        too
        'Interesting. Well, in America too'
3       ooi              kedo:    terebi     de
        many             but      TV         LOC
        'many, but, on TV...'
4   K:  de:
        LOC
        'on (TV)...'
5   L:  hair-eba:
        appear-if
        'if appear...'
6   T:  un.
        yes
        'yes'
7   L:  mina       wa:    >nanka<    [okoru
        everyone   TOP    DM          get angry
        'everybody will, well, get angry.'
8   K:                                [bikkuri=
                                       shocked
                                       'shocked'
```

9 → L: =*bikkuri   shi-te:*
        shocked   do-TE
        'shocked...'
10 → K: *tabun   dame: to   omou.*
        maybe   not good QT   think
        'maybe it's not good, I think.'

This excerpt illustrates that turn constructional units (TCUs) (Schegloff, 1996) are interactive units formatted through a step-by-step incremental organization of interaction. TCUs are locally managed and interactively negotiated by the participants in conversation. The central feature of TCUs is the notion of projectability: the next speaker not only identifies the turn completion point but also predicts it before it occurs, anticipating transition-relevance points and locating the upcoming place where he or she should begin to speak (Sacks, 1995; Sacks *et al.*, 1974). An incomplete sentence contributes to this projectability. It signals transition-relevance points and prompts the second speaker to take over the turn and complete the TCU initiated by the first speaker. By completing the original speaker's turn, the second speaker performs a variety of social actions, such as the display of empathy and perspective sharing, as illustrated in this section.

Joint turn construction for assisted explanation

Another common social activity accomplished through joint turn construction is assisted explanation. Assisted explanation occurs when one participant is explaining something to a co-participant and a third participant enters the explainer's turn in order to team up with him or her as a co-explainer (Hayashi, 2014). This type of joint turn construction was absent at pre-test, but was found three times in post-test conversations.

Excerpt 7.4 from a conversation among C, D, and the researcher (T) illustrates this activity. The researcher asks the students whether their classes are difficult this semester. In line 4, D self-selects and responds to the researcher's question with *sonnani* ('not so'), but leaves the sentence unfinished. The phrase *sonnani* is the degree adverb, typically followed by the negation form of an adjective or verb. Meeting this expectation, C takes over the turn and supplies the missing predicate – negation form of the adjective 'difficult' (*muzukashikunai*, 'not difficult'). By completing the turn-in-progress in this manner, C accomplishes participation in D's act of explaining as a co-explainer. As Hayashi (2014) claims, this type of collaborative talk happens in multi-party conversation: it is often used to form 'a local alignment' of two participants as an 'interactional team' 'vis-a-vis a third party' (p. 245). D's completion of C's response in this excerpt indicates that she shares C's perspective about the difficulty level of the Japanese classes.

Excerpt 7.4 (post-test): C and D are talking about their classes.

```
1   T:   ano    kongakki:       ano    doo    dat-taʔ    jugyoo    waʔ
         DM     this semester   DM     how    COP-PST    classes   TOP
         'Well, this semester, well, how were the classes?'
2   C:   ju:
         cla
         'jyu...'
3   T:   muzukashikat-taʔ
         difficult-PST
         'Were they difficult?'
4 → D:   sonnani=
         not so
         'Not so...'
5 → C:   =muzukashiku-nai:     kedo:    donna    jugyoo     mo
         difficult-NEG         but      any      classes    too
         'difficult... Any classes...'
6   T:   un.
         yes
         'yes'
7   C:   shukudai     o     dasu:    kara
         homework     O     give     because
         'because give homework'
```

Another instance of assisted explanation is seen again in the same conversation. In Excerpt 7.5 below, the researcher (T) asked C and D about negative aspects of the Japanese company system. D does not think that the Japanese company system is disadvantaged and instead claims that experiencing Japanese business practices enriches her knowledge of Japanese culture. In line 7, D's opinion statement is left unfinished; there is no clause following the clause ending with the conjunction *kara* ('because'). Taking over the turn, in line 9, C supplies the missing clause (*sore wa ii keiken da to omoimasu* 'I think it's a good experience.'). By doing so, C assists D's explanation: these two learners form a local alignment as an interactional team against the researcher. C's completion of D's opinion statement also indicates that C shares the same perspective toward Japanese business practice as D.

Excerpt 7.5 (post-test): C and D are talking about Japanese company systems.

```
1   C:   u:n     soo     [nee.
         uhmm    so      FP
         'uhmm, let's see'
```

2 **D:** [*un.*
         yes
         'yes'
3 **T:** *un.*
         yes
         'yes'
4 **D:** *ano,*   *(ki ni naru¿)*   *ka,*   *demo yappari   ii   bunka: o:*
         DM   become mind   FP   but   after all good culture O
5   *so-*   *nanka setsusuru   no   wa: jibun no chishiki   mo:*
         right   DM   contact   NOM   TOP self LK   knowledge   also
6 **T:** *un.*
         yes
         'yes'
7 → **D:** *fueru*   *da-*   *fueru*   *to*   *omoimasu   kara:*
         increase   COP   increase QT   think   because
         'Well I mind? But after all, because I think contacting good culture
         also increases self knowledge'
8 **T:** *un.*
         yes
         'yes'
9 → **C:** *sore*   *wa:*   *ii*   *keiken*   *da*   *to*   *omoimasu.*
         that   TOP   good   experience   COP   QT   think
         'I think it's a good experience.'

Joint turn construction for elaborating on the topic-in-progress

The last case of joint turn construction surrounding incomplete sentence endings involves interactive clause chaining in which participants co-construct discourse by linking multiple clauses turn-by-turn. Hashimoto (2007) calls this phenomenon 'interactive clause chaining.' A good example of a grammatical marker that occurs in the clause chaining is the conjunctive particle *te*. In Japanese, nouns, verbs, and adjectives often take *te*-form ending and combine with other words or clauses. Because the occurrence of the *te*-form ending indicates that the current sentence is not complete and a predicate is to follow, the current speaker can continue speaking after the *te*-form or invite the listener to take over the turn. As Hashimoto (2007) illustrates, in a Japanese conversation, speakers use the *te*-form construction repeatedly and systematically to achieve a co-construction of turns (see Chapter 2). In the present data, the *te*-form did not appear at pre-test for the function of collaborative turn construction, but occurred five times at post-test over four student pairs. This suggests that, similar to the practice of assisted explanation and display of empathy, clause chaining for collaborative turn completion is slow-emerging.

Excerpt 7.6, taken from a conversation between O, P, and the researcher (T), illustrates this interactive clause chaining. The conversation revolves around the characteristics of female speech. In lines 1–4, O shares her observation that female speakers use polite speech more frequently than male speakers. Her sentence in line 4 ends with the *te*-form, signaling that the utterance is not yet complete and another clause is to follow. Meeting this expectation, in the subsequent turn, P repeats O's sentence using another *te*-form sentence. This *te*-form ending, once again, signals the continuation of the topic-in-progress. In line 11, O contributes another observation of female speech with the *te*-form ending, which is acknowledged by both P and the researcher.

This pattern is analogous to that of the native Japanese speakers found in Hashimoto's (2007) data. Just like in a typical Japanese conversation, these learners take turns, co-construct discourse, and establish meaning together by conjoining a series of *te*-form clauses. The *te*-form ending, which signals incompleteness, is a useful resource for this activity because it sets out to invite the second speaker to speak in the first speaker's turn space and continues the turn-in-progress on the condition that the second speaker uses the opportunity to advance the first speaker's turn (Hayashi, 2013; Lerner, 2004). This is seen in this excerpt: both learners succeed the turn initiated by the other speaker and develop it by expanding on the topic of female speech.

Excerpt 7.6 (post-test): O and P are talking about female speech.

```
1    O:  ta-   tashikani    teineina::
         cer   certainly    polite
         'Certainly, polite...'
2    T:  u:n.
         yes
         'yes'
3    P:  teinei
         polite
         'polite'
4 →  O:  na         kotoba      tsukat-te
         (polite)   language    use-TE
         'use (polite) language'
5    T:  u:n.
         yes
         'yes'
6 →  P:  tsukat-te:
         use-TE
         'use'
```

7	T:	un.					
		yes					
		'yes'					
8	O:	demo	'wa'	toka	hhh	amari	kika-nakat-ta.
		But	'wa'	like		much	hear-NEG-PST
		'But like wa (sentence final particle), I didn't hear much.'					
9	T:	'naninani	yo'		toka	ne:	
		'something	FP'		like	FP	
		'like something yo'					
10	O:	minna:	minna	no	hanashikata,	tatoeba	
		everybody	everybody	LK	way of speaking	for example	
11 →		anosa:	naninani	sa:	o	<u>tsukat-te</u>	
		DM	something	DM	O	use-TE	
		'everybody's way of speaking, for example, use ano sa, something sa'					
12	P:	[aa.					
		DM					
		'Oh'					
13	T:	[un.	a::	sokka:.			
		yes	ah	I see			
		'yes, I see.'					

Excerpt 7.7, from a conversation between I and J, two Chinese students, is another illustration of the clause chaining with the *te*-form ending. Although in the previous excerpt the same verb *tsukau* ('use') was recycled with the *te*-form ending, in this excerpt, different verbs occur in *te*-form, contributing new information each time.

In line 1, J initiates the topic of Japanese summer festivals (*natsu matsuri*). We can see that I is unfamiliar with this word because she asks for a confirmation check in line 2 and whispers the word again in line 4. To help with her understanding, in line 5, J translates the word into Chinese (*chūnjié*). This self-initiated repair is successful, as seen in I's acknowledgment in line 6. Following this, J continues with her description of summer festivals. In line 8–9, J asks I if she knows about the goldfish game, a common fishing game in a festival, by demonstrating the movement (line 11). Overlapping this turn, in line 12, I joins in this description of the game. This turn-initial overlap indicates that I self-selects the next turn. Since the fishing game is already in her realm of understanding, in line 12, I incorporates the topic of the goldfish game into a general description of summer festivals (*kingyo atte* 'There are goldfish'). Here her sentence is incomplete due to the *te*-form ending of the verb *aru* ('exist'). By leaving the sentence incomplete, she signals that the description is not yet over. Recognizing this, J adds another description of summer festivals (*minna yukata kite* 'Everyone wears *yukata*.') by using another *te*-form construction.

Excerpt 7.7 (post-test): I and J are talking about Japanese summer festivals.

```
1    J:   natsu      matsuri
          summer     festival
          'summer festival'
2    I:   °natsu     matsuri¿°
          summer     festival
          'summer festival¿'
3    J:   °un.°
          yes
          'yes'
4    I:   °natsu     matsuri.°
          summer     festival
          'summer festival'
5    J:   natsu      matsuri    wa,    nanka  chungoku   chūnjié              no
          summer     festival   TOP    DM     Chinese    spring festival      LK
          'summer festival is Chinese spring festival'
6    I:   aa.=
          uh-huh
          'uh-huh'
7    J:   =nanka     chūnjié          no     toki   minna      atsumat-te:.
          DM         spring festival  LK     time   everyone   gather-TE
8         soreni     tabun    nan°ka: nanka na° (1.6) a kingyo no >nanka<
          moreover   maybe    DM       DM           oh goldfish LK  DM
9         geemu   shitteru¿   (1.2)
          game    know
          'At spring festival people gather. Moreover, well, maybe, well, oh,
          do you know goldfish game¿'
10   I:   ↑aa:
          oh
          'oh'
11   J:   a    [ano kingyo   o    (koorase-)   sooyuu           (chichi)
          ah   DM goldfish   O    (unclear)    that sort of     (unclear)
          'Ah, well, goldfish, that sort of'
12 → I:        [sono kingyo    at-te
               that goldfish   exist-TE
               'there are goldfish'
13 → J:   minna      yukata    [ki-te:.
          everyone   yukata    wear-TE
          'everyone wears yukata'
14   I:                        [aa.
                                uh-huh
                                'uh-huh'
```

Summary

This chapter has described the development of interactional competence among 18 learners of Japanese during their semester study abroad program. The learners in this study revealed a marked increase in their production of incomplete sentence endings over a 12-week period. In the post-test data, this sentence pattern consistently appeared around joint turn completion in which one speaker initiates a turn and another speaker finishes it. This knowledge of the structure and function of incomplete sentences in a sequential organization of talk served as a linguistic and interactional resource that the learners employed mutually and reciprocally in their practice of joint meaning making. The learners developed the interactional ability to make use of joint turn construction in order to effectively participate in the activity-in-progress.

As Sindnell (2010: 171) claims, a turn is a 'product of an interaction between speaker and recipient.' Joint turn construction is a clear illustration of co-participants' interaction within a single turn-at-talk because it presents evidence for the projectability of the turn-in-progress. As mentioned earlier, projectability is a characteristic of the turn-taking mechanism. When the current speaker is holding a turn, the next speaker monitors the turn word-by-word for a possible point of turn completion and transition of speakership. Incomplete sentences serve as a strong cue for the transition of speakership and contribute to this projectability. By leaving a sentence designedly incomplete, the speaker can signal a turn completion point and thus prompt or invite completion of the unfinished turn by another. In Japanese, grammatical structures such as *te*-form endings, particles, and certain adverbs signal that the sentence is unfinished and is still in progress. Specifically, these grammatical forms maximize projectability in the turn-taking system, thereby contributing to interactive turn construction.

Understanding these mechanisms of turn co-construction is a direct indicator of interactional competence in a second language (Young, 2002, 2008a, 2008b, 2011). Collaborative turn building with incomplete endings increased in both quantity and quality over the semester. The learners were able to understand what kind of action their co-participant was performing when he or she produced an incomplete utterance and what responsive action would be appropriate. By collaboratively completing each other's turn, the learners were able to intently align to this projection of the unfolding course of the co-participant's action and shape their contribution to the discussion in order to accomplish pertinent participation. As the speaker, they displayed attention to the speaker transition point by leaving a sentence unfinished and signaling the possibility of the next speaker's self-selection of a turn. As the listener, they oriented the speaker transition point by targeting places in which they could initiate their own turn. Additionally, the learners became able to perform a variety of social actions when completing each other's turns. They learned how to use this sequential practice of joint turn building to recover from communication breakdowns, to assist the speaker's explanation, to demonstrate empathy and shared perspective, and to elaborate on the topic-in-progress. Hence, collaborative turn construction is a visible illustration of how learners cooperated to achieve mutual understanding of the talk-in-progress.

Notes

(1) A portion of the findings in this chapter appeared in the *Modern Language Journal* (Taguchi, 2014). Exerpts 7.5 and 7.6 were reproduced from the article with permission from the publisher.
(2) In the conversation data, all the incomplete sentences were identified first. Then, the rest of the utterances (excluding fragments) were categorized as complete sentences involving two speech forms: the polite and plain.

8 Case Histories of Interactional Development and Study Abroad Experience

The previous three chapters documented 18 Japanese learners' changes in their interactional competence during study abroad by illustrating their register-appropriate use of speech style, style-shifts between the plain and polite form across discourse boundaries, and the use of incomplete sentences as turn-taking resources. Shifting from group- to individual-level analysis, this chapter presents findings from interview data featuring four case histories that revealed individual variation in the extent of social networking and the degree of community involvement during study abroad. The types of social interactions that learners have access to and the personal relationships that they develop through such interactions are part of learners' social affordances, and thus are highly relevant to the concept of interactional competence. If we consider the notion that language use and language development take place in social interactions, it is vital to discern change in linguistic abilities and change in social interactions. The four cases in this chapter illustrate the link between these two.

Interview Participants

In selecting the interview informants, I took the following steps. First, I asked the 18 participants individually about their interest in participating in the interviews. Eleven participants indicated interest. Of the 11, I selected four participants that demonstrated diversity in terms of nationality, gender, length of previous Japanese study, living arrangements, and purpose of study abroad. Table 8.1 summarizes background information of the four informants. The names are pseudonyms. Participant ID corresponds to the code assigned to individual students (see Chapter 5). The informants represented four different nationalities. They varied considerably in the length of their Japanese study, ranging from three months to four years. The students were

Table 8.1 Background of the informants

Name	Participant ID	Gender	Country	Age	Level	Previous Japanese study (years)	Major	Living Arrangement
Dewi	A	Female	Brunei	20	3	3.0	Comparative studies	Dormitory
Lin	J	Female	China	19	3	0.3	Political science	Dormitory
Ann	G	Female	U.S.A.	21	3	4.0	East Asian Studies	Homestay
Adrian	Q	Male	France	26	4	4.0	Environmental science	Dormitory

Note: Participants' names are pseudonymous. Level: Level in the Japanese program (total of eight levels). Previous Japanese study: the number of formal Japanese study before coming to Japan.

living in an international students' dormitory, except for Ann who had a home stay arrangement.

Table 8.2 summarizes participants' reasons for studying Japanese and their expectations in Japan. Lin, a Chinese student from Beijing, had instrumental motivation toward Japanese study. She was admitted to the Department of Political Science and Economics with a recommendation from her high school. The department provided a special program for international students and offered courses in English. Different from other students who came to Japan for one or two semesters, Lin's study abroad was a long-term commitment. She planned to stay in Japan for four years until she completed her degree. Unlike Lin, Dewi's reason to study abroad was integrative. She practiced *kendo* (martial art) for seven years in Brunei, which cultivated her interest in traditional Japanese art such as the tea ceremony and flower arrangement. Similar to Dewi, Ann's motivation for Japanese study was integrative. She expressed interest in learning about Japanese pop culture such as *manga* and *anime*, in addition to traditional cultural practices related to Buddhism. She has a Japanese relative living in the USA. who cultivated her interest in Japanese study. Adrian, on the other hand, had career-oriented motivation. He came to Japan with a hope that his Japanese skills and study abroad experience would help him find employment in Japan. He was interested in expanding Japanese contacts and networks to achieve this goal.

Tables 8.3 and 8.4 present results of the motivation survey (Fantini, 2005) given at the end of the semester (see Appendix C for a copy of the survey). All four participants were similarly high in the level of motivation toward study abroad before arriving in Japan, although Lin's motivation was somewhat weaker than that of other students (see Table 8.3). Her motivation

Table 8.2 Informants' reasons for study abroad and their expectations in Japan

	Why do you study Japanese?	Why did you come to Japan?	What expectations do you have for your stay in Japan?
Dewi	Because of interest in traditional martial art and cultural activities; Interest in Japanese people and culture	To earn credits via student exchange program; To experience Japanese culture; To improve Japanese skills	Developing fluency; Expanding vocabulary; Sharing Brunei culture with Japanese people; Learning about Japanese culture; Practicing Japanese traditional art; Communicating with local Japanese people
Lin	Because she got accepted to the political science and economics department in the university (English-medium curriculum)	To complete degree in the political science	Developing fluency
Ann	Because she developed interest in Japan through her Japanese relative. Because she became interested in *manga*, *anime*, and religions in Japan	To study Japanese religions; To improve Japanese	Improving Japanese; Learning Japanese religions; Deepening understanding of Japanese society; Developing fluency
Adrian	'First by chance, then by passion'	To improve speaking skill in Japanese; To gain experience for future career opportunities in Japan	Developing fluency; Gaining career and business opportunities; Making Japanese friends

Table 8.3 Level of motivation toward study abroad in Japan

	Dewi	Lin	Ann	Adrian
Motivation before arriving in Japan	5	4	5	5
Motivation upon first entering Japan	5	5	5	2
Motivation in mid-way through semester	3	5	4	3
Motivation at the end of semester	4	3	5	5

Note: The numbers indicate the degree of motivation toward study abroad on a five-point Likert scale with 1 indicating 'extremely low' and 5 indicating 'extremely high.' See Appendix C for the survey items.

Table 8.4 Characteristics of motivation toward study abroad in Japan

	Dewi	Lin	Ann	Adrian
I sometime wanted to return home	5	1	4	3
I felt I was not learning very much	4	2	5	4
I tried to survive as much as possible	4	4	5	4
I wanted to get along well with Japanese people	5	5	3	4
I wanted to adjust to Japan as much as possible	5	5	5	5

Note: The numbers indicate the degree of agreement with each statement on a five-point Likert scale with 1 indicating 'completely disagree' and 5 'completely agree.' See Appendix C for the survey items.

at the end of the first semester was also low compared with that of other students. Adrian's motivation was low upon first entering Japan and midway through semester, but it went up toward the end of the semester and achieved the highest score. Ann's motivation was most stable, ranging between 4 and 5 before and throughout study abroad. Dewi showed a similar pattern, although her motivation went down by one point mid-way in the semester.

In terms of the characteristics of motivation, as shown in Table 8.4, Lin was the only student who expressed no desire for returning home, which could be a reflection of her degree-seeking status and commitment for long-term stay in Japan. At the same time, she was the only student who reported satisfaction with the level of learning in study abroad. All four students expressed a strong desire to adjust to Japan.

Table 8.5 displays average weekly hours spent communicating in Japanese based on the Japanese contact survey given at the end of the semester (See Appendix D for the survey questions). Dewi was the only student who reported spending time with instructors, which probably reflected her extraordinary involvement in club activities. Ann's reported time communicating with friends, classmates, and the host family was the highest among

Table 8.5 Amount of reported Japanese language contact hours per week

Average weekly hours spent in Japanese	Dewi	Lin	Ann	Adrian	Group mean (SD) ($n = 18$)
Communicating with teachers	5.0	0	0	0	0.73 (1.26)
Communicating with friends, classmates, or host family members	9.0	7.5	30.0	1.0	6.25 (7.02)
Communicating with service personnel	10.5	3.5	4.5	0	2.85 (2.93)

Note: The numbers show average number of hours that the students reported spending in communicating in Japanese. See Appendix D for a copy of the survey.

the members, reaching 30 hours per week, probably because of her home stay arrangement. Adrian's language contact was notably low, only one hour per week.

Interviews with individual participants took place three times over the semester, 40–60 minutes each time. The interviews were semi-structured: it included certain pre-selected themes but allowed flexibility in incorporating themes nominated by the informants. My questions revolved around three themes: Japanese language abilities, study abroad experience, and communication and social contact (see Chapter 4 for the questions used in the interviews). The following case histories present variations in these four participants' social contact and involvement during their study abroad.

Findings

Dewi[1]

Among the four informants Dewi made the largest progress over the semester. Her speech style in the pre-test conversation was predominantly in the polite form, occupying over 60% of the utterance-ending forms. The plain form, the expected style in a conversation with a same age peer, appeared only about 40% of the time. Incomplete sentence ending, a common feature of Japanese conversation, was completely absent in her speech. In sharp contrast, her use of the plain form at post-test jumped to 82% and that of the polite form dropped to 12%, which indicates her understanding of register-appropriate language use. Most notably, incomplete sentences appeared in 6% of the utterance ending forms, moving toward the prototypical pattern of Japanese conversation.

Interview data revealed evidence supporting this strong development in Dewi's ability to use different utterance-ending forms in spontaneous conversation. Dewi expanded her personal network during her stay in Japan to include different types of contacts and social relations. The number of Japanese friends that she reported was five at the beginning of the semester, but it increased to 20 at the end of the semester. This large growth of her social circle seemed to be the result of her outgoing personality, positive attitude, and firm commitment to exploring culture. These personal characteristics led to a range of strategies that Dewi employed in order to initiate and sustain relationships with local members, which represents the case of personal investment leading to linguistic development.

Dewi was a 20-year-old student from Brunei who came to Japan through the exchange program. She was a student in the Department of International Liberal Arts and was taking courses to fulfill her major in Comparative Studies. She was enrolled in the Intensive Japanese Level 3 (12 hours per week) and an elective course (1 hour per week). She had studied Japanese for five semesters at her home university before coming to Japan. Her primary instructor was Japanese. The medium of instruction was a mix of Japanese and English in the first two years and Japanese-only in the third year. In a class of 15 students, she named *kaiwa* as a primary activity in which students engaged in a free conversation based on the theme that they nominated.

Japanese martial art, *kendo*, originally piqued her interest in Japanese study and culture. She practiced *kendo* for seven years in Brunei under a Japanese instructor. The practice was conducted in the bilingual mode with the instructor using Japanese for basic techniques, rituals, and instructions, followed by an English translation.

During her study abroad, Dewi established a number of social networks and played a legitimate role in each of them. Her primary Japanese network was student clubs. She belonged to four different clubs: cultural exchange club, tea ceremony, *shamisen and koto* (traditional Japanese musical instruments), and *soranbushi and nihonbuyo* (traditional Japanese dance). She devoted more than 15 hours per week to club activities. She said that 70% of her interaction in these clubs took place in Japanese. Her communication with club instructors was mostly in Japanese because many of the instructors did not speak English. As shown in Table 8.5, she reported spending five hours per week communicating with instructors, which was notably high compared with other students.

In addition to language practice, these student clubs served as a platform for cultural learning. Dewi talked about the senior-junior relationship and related language use that she observed during club activities. She told me that freshmen always use the title (*senpai* 'senior') and the polite (*desu/masu*) form when talking to seniors, but in the same age group, they use the casual form. Adopting this practice was not particularly difficult for Dewi because she was accustomed to the age-based hierarchy through *kendo*. She told me that she usually spoke in the polite form with everyone and switched to the plain form only when her same-age peers talked to her in the plain form. She also developed a habit of asking age and year of study when she met someone for the first time so she could confirm her position in the relationship, which guided her choice of speech style.

Dewi mentioned that club activities were the highlight of her stay in Japan. She played *shamisen* and performed *nihonbuyo* in front of people, which she called a 'once-in-a-lifetime-experience.' She came to Japan as part of the 'third-year-discovery-year' – time to broaden world perspectives. She set the goal of absorbing as much cultural content as possible while in Japan. The fact that the majority of her club activities involved traditional Japanese art also confirmed her investment in cultural learning. The word *bunka* (culture) appeared seven times during my interviews with Dewi.

Beside clubs, Dewi talked about three other primary Japanese contacts. One was a group of Japanese friends who she met in Hokkaido when she travelled to practice *kendo* on a tour. She maintained contact with them via

Skype, Facebook, email and phone. Another opportunity to practise Japanese was provided by her international friends in the dormitory. She became friends with a few Koreans and Taiwanese who were fluent in Japanese. Dewi spent two to three hours with them every day speaking Japanese. Dewi also became friends with Japanese returnees from the USA.

Dewi considered all of these social networks as invaluable opportunities for her Japanese practice. I asked her whether speaking Japanese was important for her relationship building. She responded in the affirmative, emphasizing that Japanese is an essential tool in order to communicate with people from different language backgrounds. Japanese was instrumental for Dewi in expanding her zone of social contact and establishing membership in the local community. Referring to study abroad as a 'once-in-life-time experience,' Dewi was clearly committed to speaking Japanese at every single opportunity that she could seize.

The extensive social network and friendship she established over time, however, did not come by without difficulty. Dewi had to consciously seek out the opportunities available around her and make the most of them when they actually arrived. I asked her what she learned most during her stay in Japan. Her response was how to make new friends:

Excerpt 8.1

I also learned how ... ah to make new friends you have to, ah, make an effort. You can't just sit there alone and stay quiet and expect people to talk to you. You have to ... ah, you have to be the one who is friendly and makes an effort and become friends with people even though you don't really know them. (Researcher: How did you learn that?) How did I learn that? Ah, I wondered why I only have international friends, not many Japanese friends, and ... I realized not many Japanese people would ... approach international students randomly unless they are very good in English or fluent in English.

I tried to talk to them in Japanese. Just talk about their activities, how has life been, which teachers they like, what's interesting ... those sorts of things, and you automatically become friends. (Researcher: Was it easy to make friends?) It was a bit difficult because you have to constantly keep talking to them. If you talk only once, they don't really talk to you a lot unless they are very friendly people, yeah. I just kept talking to them once or twice and kept saying hi to them. Most people in this university prefer Facebook, so I just add them to Facebook. If I see them on campus I go up to say hi to them. So constantly saying hi to them, constantly going up to talk to them ... help make them feel comfortable talking to us. If you are friendly and are not hesitant to talk to them, it shows them you see them more as friends rather than as acquaintances. (July, 2012)

Dewi was aware that building personal relationships in a foreign country would not come easily if she did not act on her own initiative. Although she came to Japan with a high expectation of making many Japanese friends, she realized that the majority of her relationships were with international students mainly because she was living in the international students' dorm and studying in the international department. Because opportunities to connect with Japanese students were not abundant, she learned to invest in those connections whenever they arose. One of the strategies she used to transform initial interactions into stable friendships was frequent communication via Facebook. She 'friended' people immediately and reached out to them online. Whenever she saw them on campus, she went up to them to initiate small talk.

This persistence was also evident in her response to my question: What personal qualities and abilities are necessary in order to fit in with Japanese society? She listed perseverance and endurance as important qualities. She said that she had to be *genki* (energetic) and *akarui* (cheerful) so people would approach her. After becoming homesick in the middle of the semester, she stopped being *genki*, and as a result, she lost many friends. After this experience she forced herself to become *genki* and *akarui* again. Once these qualities returned, her friends returned. She was aware what kind of self-image to project to attract people to her friend zone and what strategies to implement in order to sustain new friendships.

Dewi's Japanese ability served both as a strategy and outcome of this process of friendship building. As Dewi mentioned, she had to use Japanese to communicate with Japanese students because they did not speak much English. Her Japanese improved because of these relations and connections she established over time. Her ability to speak informally was one of the byproducts of the network building process. Because her previous education focused on the polite forms, she came to Japan with little experience with informal speech used among close friends. She encountered difficulty with controlling her speech style and often ended up juxtaposing the polite and plain forms in conversation. Although this odd mixing of the two forms still remained after a semester in Japan, her understanding of these two forms, as well the social meanings that they express, was evident in the last interview. She shared her observations of the Japanese speech style as follows:

Excerpt 8.2

If they don't know the person or hierarchy going on, ah … like boss or *kohai*, they use *desu/masu*. When children are speaking to their parents, they speak in the casual form. I always hear them speaking on the train or when I'm walking home. They speak in the casual form. Basically everyone around me speaks casually, so I realized the *desu/masu* is a bit too polite to use in a normal, everyday conversation. (July, 2012)

Dewi was also aware how language functions to structure social relations:

Excerpt 8.3

Yes (studying Japanese) is important because there are some expressions or some sorts of politeness in Japanese language that we can't express in English. (Researcher: What kind of politeness?) Umn ... I'm not sure, ah ... in English we have just 'you' and 'me', but in Japanese, we have *anata, kimi, watashi, atashi, boku,* and *ore*. So I think in Japanese there is a more defined boundary between very polite, polite, informal, and rude, but in English, it sounds almost the same unless you use your own expression. (May, 2012)

These excerpts revealed Dewi's interest in different layers of politeness expressed through Japanese language. During her stay in Japan, she had opportunities to observe and practice this sociocultural aspect of language in a variety of communities and social networking that she established over time. Club activities, classmates, friends in the dormitory, and previously-established connections (her friends in Hokkaido) all provided important language practices that complemented her interest. Diverse social situations, personal relations, hierarchy and power, and formality involved in these interactional circles gave her exposure to different forms and styles of communication. Dewi practiced them in order to fit in and function appropriately in each community. Her strong progress with the use of speech style and incomplete sentences found in the conversation task was likely a byproduct of this socialization process and exposure to sociocultural variation in language use.

While the link between social practice and linguistic gain is plausible in Dewi's case, it is also important to consider the role of intercultural competence mediating the link. Intercultural competence is defined as a 'complex of abilities needed to perform effectively and appropriately when interacting with others who are linguistically and culturally different from oneself' (Fantini, 2006: 12). Common behavioral traits of intercultural competence – flexibility and openness to new ideas and practice, empathy and sympathy, tolerance of ambiguity, ability to interpret cultural cues, psychological strength in coping with new situations, and ability to abandon ethnocentrism – are considered critical for successful cultural integration (e.g. Byram, 1997; Fantini, 2006; 2012; Hammer *et al.*, 2003; Olson & Kroeger, 2001). In the process of cultural integration, people gain opportunities for interaction through social networks involved in the process. Linguistic competence is likely to develop as a byproduct of this cultural adjustment process.

Dewi's case fits in this profile of successful integration into the host community, supported by a high level of intercultural competence, leading to opportunities for communicative practice and linguistic development as a result. Dewi made a seamless adjustment to a new culture as shown in the range of interpersonal relationships and social connections that she was able to establish in the short period of three months. Interview data provided concrete illustrations of her cultural adaptability. Dewi's positive attitudes and perseverance, self-initiated access to the community, commitment to staying in touch with newly acquainted people, and continual reflection of what works and what doesn't work in making friends were all essential elements in the process of cultural integration and optimizing her study abroad experience.

Lin

Similar to Dewi, Lin also demonstrated a dramatic change in her use of the speech style. In the pre-test conversation with a peer, she used the polite form more frequently than the plain form (54% vs. 36%), but the pattern was reversed at post-test, with the plain form occupying 83% of the utterance-ending forms. Her use of incomplete sentences also increased slightly, from 10% to 13% at post-test. Another notable change was found in the range of communicative functions that she became able to express with the plain form. Initially her plain forms mainly appeared when presenting information and expressing her feelings, but she expanded her repertoire at post-test and became able to use the plain form for a variety of functions, including joint meaning making.

Interview data revealed insights for these positive changes in Lin's conversation data. Similar to Dewi, Lin successfully established membership in the local community by actively participating in their social activities, but compared with Dewi who had a broad range of social network, Lin's network was limited to a few intimate groups. Nevertheless in each group she developed a deep relationship with individual members, which led to a consistent and systematic exposure to target language input and practice.

Lin was the youngest in the group, a 19-year-old high school graduate from Beijing. Lin came to Japan because she was admitted to the Department of Political Science and Economics upon a recommendation from her high school. The university is well-known for its Political Economics major, which influenced her decision of taking up this study abroad opportunity with the hope that it would help her employment after graduation. Different from other students who expressed cultural learning as a primary purpose of stay in Japan, Lin's motivation to study abroad was instrumental: she had planned to stay in Japan for four years until she received a diploma. Her department offered separate programs for international and Japanese students. International students were enrolled in the English-only curriculum where all courses were taught in English, while sharing a few core courses with Japanese students. Lin studied Japanese for three months prior to coming to

Japan, the shortest length among the participants in this study. Only after she learned about her acceptance to the university, she enrolled in the Japanese language school and received instruction four hours per week, taught in Chinese using a textbook written in Chinese. The class was grammar-based with little communication practice.

These descriptions present a profile of Lin as a student driven by instrumental motivation with almost no explicitly-stated goal of cultural leaning or integration into the Japanese community at the time of entry. She reported only a medium level of motivation (three on the five-point scale) in the motivation survey given at the end of the semester (see Table 8.3). Minimal background in Japanese language study also indicates that Lin was less prepared for her stay in Japan compared with the rest of the group who had more than two years of Japanese study. Considering her background, it was remarkable that Lin made a swift cultural adjustment and showed strong improvement with Japanese skills. The patterns of social contact and involvement emerged in her interview data help us understand the reason behind her progress.

There were three primary social networks that Lin belonged to and actively participated in during the semester. One was the university-based club called *himawari kodomokai* (sunflower children's association), to which she went by recommendation of someone in her department. She liked it so she started participating regularly once a week. Main activities involved interacting with children. Every Saturday club members got together with first graders and played in the park or went on a picnic. There were about 40 members in the club from freshmen to seniors. All of them were Japanese, except Lin and another Korean student.

In addition to the *himawari kodomokai*, Lin belonged to the self-organized student group called the Language Exchange Group. The group started out with five Japanese students, one Korean student, one Australian student, and Lin, who were all same-age peers in the Political Science and Economics Department. They met during the orientation week and decided to meet regularly to practice their language skills. They gathered in the library once a week for two hours and discussed current topics first in Japanese and then in English. When asked about the highlight of her stay in Japan, Lin responded that it was her involvement in this group. The group developed a strong, cohesive relationship over time. Members occasionally went on a weekend trip, besides socializing over lunch, dinner, and *karaoke* on weekly basis. The group also expanded over time both in number and nationality: by the end of the semester, there were 15 members representing five nationalities.

Lin's third community was her part-time job. She started waitressing in a nearby French restaurant twice a week, three hours each time. The restaurant was new and small with space for seven tables and 20 chairs. There were only Lin and the owner (and the cook) of the restaurant working at the same time. She spoke *keigo* (honorifics) to the customers, which was a new experience for her. Although she studied honorifics in class, she was not used to using the special terms and conjugations in honorifics. The owner gave a list of basic honorifics phrases necessary for interaction with customers, which Lin studied and memorized.

Lin sustained her involvement in these three Japanese-speaking communities that presented diverse purposes and activities, as well as different participant roles and membership structures. By attending their activities regularly, Lin established her space in each community and contributed to their goals. However, her participation was not easy at the beginning because of her limited Japanese abilities. Despite the challenge, she had to commit to using Japanese. Because not all Japanese people speak English, Lin felt compelled to speak their language if she wanted to expand her network. See the excerpt:

Excerpt 8.4

Maybe ah at first, because I couldn't speak Japanese, it was really difficult for me to communicate. I couldn't say a word. Inside I was very like ... upset. I wanted to say something but I didn't know how to say it. So I was like, *gan, ganbatte* ... I know a lot of grammar, but I don't know how to use it. (Researcher: How did you overcome the difficulty?) I was just, like, trying to speak in Japanese as much as possible. I wanted to say things in English but I always tried to say in Japanese. (May, 2012)

Among these three distinct social networks, Lin was most invested in the Language Exchange Group. Mid-way into the semester, a time conflict arose between this group and the *himawari kodomokai* so she decided to quit the *himawari kodomokai*. I asked her why she chose the Language Exchange Group over the *himawari kodomokai* when the latter offered far more opportunities for direct contact with Japanese students. She told me that she preferred the multicultural composition of the Language Exchange Group that allowed an open exchange of ideas and perspectives from different cultural standpoints.

Excerpt 8.5

I think like in *himawari kodomokai* there are so many people, and they are all Japanese. They have their common topics, so it's hard for me to get into, like, to talk to them. They are really like, friendly, but I am closer to, like, to my friends in the group, Language Exchange Group, and I really enjoy talking to them. We have different cultures, and we can exchange the cultures. (July, 2012)

Lin also shared her resistance to the strict hierarchy practiced in the *himawari kodomokai* and different speech forms (the polite and plain) used to implement the hierarchy.

Excerpt 8.6

In the *himawari kodomokai*, we need to pay attention to the *senpai-kohai* (senior–junior relationship). We need to use the *desu/masu*. And for the circle they are really like, ah, strict with the hierarchy ... It's hard to communicate with them because, maybe, grade difference is clear. (Researcher: Do you like using *desu/masu*?) No, just like because ... because I feel distance between us if I use the *desu* and *masu*. I feel like, it's strange. (July, 2012)

As these excerpts show, Lin was more content being in the multicultural group than in the Japanese-only environment. Although native speaker input and contact have been claimed as primary benefits of study abroad which lead to language development, the data here suggest that second language learners sometimes develop psychological conflict with the native speaker norm practiced in the community, and as a result, they may distance themselves from interacting with locals. Lin experienced difficulty in accepting certain aspects of Japanese culture practiced in the *himawari kodomokai*, in particular the senior–junior relationship and different speech styles used to signify the relationship. Distancing from these practices, Lin devoted her time to the multicultural group that composed of same-age members from diverse cultural backgrounds. She invested in the intercultural communication occurring in this tight community of international students and Japanese students. In their communication, Japanese language functioned as a lingua franca, rather than the target language of study.

These findings support potential benefit of multilingual communication as a space for linguistic development. In the multicultural group in which people represent their own cultural background, each member is entitled to present their views and ideas from their cultural standpoints. This 'right-to-speak' gives members legitimate roles and responsibilities as participants in the community. A sense of contribution to the group helps reinforce members' feeling of belonging to the group, which in turn leads to a stable and sustainable relationship. Japanese serves as the common language for communication among group members. Students speak Japanese in order to participate in the shared activity and goal, and linguistic gain is likely a byproduct of this participation. This situation may be different from the community of predominantly Japanese people because they might take ownership of the language spoken and topics to be discussed. This was evident in Lin's comment in Excerpt 8.5 when she said that Japanese students in the *himawari kodomokai* talk around common topics, which might isolate foreigners from participating, albeit unintentionally.

Turning to the analysis of Lin's development of speech styles, her participation in three different networks brought opportunities to observe and practice different speech styles. The *himawari kodomokai* served as a place to practice language used to encode age-related hierarchy. As shown in Lin's comment above, there was an underlying rule of speaking practiced among members: seniors using the plain form to juniors and juniors using the polite form to seniors. Lin was explicitly and implicitly socialized into this norm as she participated in their activities. During the second interview, she shared an instance that happened between her and a senior member of the *himawari kodomokai* over Facebook:

Excerpt 8.7

Once on Facebook, ah, *kanjicho, kanjicho*, ah, the highest ... ah, *kanjicho*, ah, the manager of the club, he asked me something, and I ... like, wrote in informal *kotoba*, without *desu* or *masu*. I used the *futsutai* (plain form) in all of my sentences. After that, he wrote to me and said, 'I am *sannen-sei* (junior) now.' But he didn't say, like, directly, like you should use the *desu/masu*, but after he said that, I changed it to the *desu/masu*. (Researcher: Do you think that's what he meant?) Because he said it twice. I'm not sure but maybe ... (May, 2012)

Lin was aware of the social meanings that the polite and plain forms index (age-rank difference). She resisted the norm, because the use of the polite form creates distance between speakers (Excerpt 8.6). At the same time, she understood that Japanese people conform to the age-related language use even when the age difference is only a few years. As illustrated in the excerpt above, Lin understood the implied meaning behind the senior's assertion ('I am a junior.') and his expectations that she conforms to the norm by adopting appropriate speech style as a freshman. At the end, she elected to meet these expectations despite her gut feelings against them. The *himawari kodomokai* served as a venue for learning the distinction between these two forms and social meanings they express through observation, modeling, and feedback.

Her interaction in the Language Exchange Group, on the other hand, presented a site for practicing the plain form. Like other students in this study, Lin initially expressed difficulty in adopting the plain form because the polite form (*desu/masu*) became her default style after learning it first in class. However, by the second interview, she started using the plain form as her dominant style because her friends used it all the time. In the Language Exchange Group she had daily exposure to the plain form spoken by native speakers and international students, which served as her primary input. At the same time, by participating in discussions around cultural exchange, Lin gained opportunity for output. Through this repeated cycle of input and output practice, the plain form gradually entered Lin's system and established its use as default speech style in casual talk.

In addition to the plain form, Lin picked up slang and youth speech through her participation in this group, another domain of informal, in-group speech:

Excerpt 8.8

When I talk to my Japanese friends, I always learn new words. I write them down, remember them, and ah ... sometimes I have a chance to say them in class. I ask teachers to explain them. For example, like, ah ... *dekiru danshi*, meaning a man who is capable of doing things. And *charao*, a guy who is always talking about girls. I shared these words in my class. (June, 2012)

When the *himawari kodomokai* and the Language Exchange Group served as a venue for learning the plain and polite forms, the third social network, the part-time job at a French restaurant, provided space for Lin to learn honorifics, which was the essential form of communication with her customers. Japanese honorifics, linguistic devices that encode politeness, involve three levels: the respect form (*sonkeigo*), the humble form (*kenjyogo*), and the polite form (*teineigo*). Although students in this study received explicit instruction on honorific forms, they often expressed difficulty with the forms because of their linguistic complexity. Honorifics take complicated morpho-syntax structures and unique lexicons, which learners have to simply memorize by heart. Honorifics are functionally complex as well. Honorific expressions encode relative social status between participants and referents, and depending on the degree of politeness to express for the addressees and referents, people differentiate among the levels of honorific forms to use (i.e. the respect, humble, and polite form). Learners of Japanese often struggle with these social meanings that different honorific forms express, in addition to the complexity of the forms.

This was the case with Lin too. When she first started working at the French restaurant, she could not say certain expressions in the respect or humble form. Instead, she used equivalent expressions in the polite form, which was her familiar speech style. It was her boss and the owner of the restaurant who provided direct instruction on higher-level honorifics.

Excerpt 8.9

(Honorifics is) very difficult. When they (customers) asked me something, I just said *wakarimashita* ('I understood' in the polite form), and after I left, I realized that I should have said like, *kashikomarimashita* ('I understood' in the humble form). I don't use *keigo* outside the part-time job. It's a small restaurant, just *tencho* (owner of the restaurant) and me, so I asked *tencho* what *keigo* I should use, and *tencho* gave me a list of easy words and phrases in *keigo*, like *sugu omochishimasu* ('I will bring it right away.') or *menu de gozaimasu* ('This is menu.'). (June, 2012)

This explicit socialization into honorifics though direct teaching, combined with practice in authentic, high-stake interaction, assisted Lin's development of her knowledge of honorifics and confidence in using them. In the last interview, Lin expressed:

Excerpt 8.10

I think I'm improving, because first, like first, I could only use *shitsureishimasu, shitsureiitashimasu,* and *hai*. Now I learned a lot of, like ... if a guest asks me to bring water, before I could say only *hai* ('yes'), but now I can say like, something like ... *omochishimasu* ('I will bring it' in the humble form). And also when I ask, like, what your after dinner drink, I can say *shokugono onomimonowa ikaganasaimasuka* ('What would you like to drink after dinner?' in the respect form). So I think I'm improving. Actually my *tencho* is really kind. He made a list of for me. With those phrases. So I'm *ganbatteiru* (working hard). (July, 2012)

As described above, by transiting three different social networks composed of distinct social settings, goals, memberships, and participant structures, Lin gained access to different types of context-rich input and opportunities for interaction. Communication with the same-age friends in the Language Exchange Group, the senior-junior relationship in the *himawari kodomokai*, and the formal, role-based interaction at the French restaurant presented different social relationships and settings, which resulted in different range of linguistic practice and input. In the Language Exchange Group, Lin learned how to speak in the plain form, the speech style that she had almost no experience with prior to coming to Japan. The *himawari kodomokai* provided an occasion to evaluate and reflect on the social meaning of hierarchy and power that the polite and plain forms index in the interaction between different age groups. Her part-time job in the restaurant served as a place for socialization into honorifics language use, the language of respect and extreme formality, which students learn in class but have little experience using it outside the classroom. These diverse opportunities for practice available in the local communities are the prime advantages of study abroad contexts for language development pointed out in a number of previous studies (e.g. Cook, 2008; Hernandez, 2010; Isabelli-Garcia, 2006; M. Ishida, 2011; Iwasaki, 2011; Kinginger, 2008, 2013; Knight & Schmidt-Rinehardt, 2002; McMeekin, 2011; Shively, 2011, 2013; Wilkinson, 2002). The present findings add to this literature. Lin's case revealed that the local community is structured according to different sub-communities or domains of practice, each of which presents exposure to and practice of unique patterns of speaking that learners use to their advantage for their linguistic growth.

Lave and Wenger (1991) define communities by their membership and practices, including ways of doing things, beliefs, and values shared among members. Communities are characterized by participants' mutual engagement in a social activity from which a certain repertoire of practice emerges, such as ways of thinking and speaking, discourses, tools, and memories (Wenger, 1998). Communities of practice can be beneficial for L2 development because the practice involves direct interaction and negotiation with community members using the target language as a medium of communication. Likewise, through participation in the communities, learners can build their social capital and establish an identity within local communities. Borrowing Gee's (2004: 77) term, 'people learn best when their learning is part of a highly motivated engagement with social practices which they value'.

Lin's case portrays the example of this L2 development occurring through participation in communities and linguistic socialization. Communities formed effective platforms for learning linguistic variations – the polite form, plain form, and honorifics – because these three communities presented different social configurations and distinct linguistic repertoires reflecting those configurations. Lin had to practice forms of speech unique to individual communities in order to participate in their shared social activities and to establish membership and identities within them. In this process, speech styles were both resources and outcomes of her participation in the communities of practice.

Ann

Dewi and Lin's cases revealed a pivotal role of social networks and communities in assisting linguistic development. Ann, too, had her own social networks that provided access to linguistic practice. Being the only participant with a home stay arrangement, Ann's communities of practice concentrated around her interaction with her host family. In the Japanese contact survey, Ann reported the largest amount of time speaking Japanese with friends and host family, recording 30 weekly hours, whereas the other three students' reported time ranged from one to nine hours (see Table 8.5).

Ann's host family had four members: host father, host mother, a host brother, and a host sister who was a high-school student. Ann told me that she spent three hours every day talking with her host family, particularly at dinner time when they sat together and discussed things around TV. Almost 100% of the conversation there took place in Japanese.

Ann was a junior at a university in Ohio majoring in religions with a concentration on East Asian religions. Like Dewi, she came to Japan through the exchange program at the Department of International Liberal Arts and was enrolled in courses taught in English. She studied Japanese for three years in her home university, taught by a Japanese instructor in Japanese. She was the only student who expressed strong frustrations toward the courses offered in the Department of International Liberal Arts. She was 'bored' because the classes took a lecture format and did not encourage critical thinking. The only class that she felt worth taking was the class on religion, which was offered outside her department. It complemented her senior thesis project on women's roles in the Buddhist communities. At the time of the interviews, she was involved in the fieldwork with the *Sotozen* and *Ishokoseikai*, major Buddhist sects in Tokyo, through interviews and observations.

Although the amount of speaking in class was only moderate, Ann absorbed opportunities to practice Japanese in a variety of venues outside the classroom. In response to my question about the skill areas that she improved most in Japan, she immediately said speaking. When she first came to Japan with a group of international students, she had her peers speak for her because she did not have confidence. But after she started home stay and joined a couple of clubs, she started speaking out of necessity. Once she got separated from the international students group, she realized that she had to speak because she no longer had her friends translating for her. She described her early transition from English- to Japanese-speaking country as a 'severe uphill battle' and 'sink-or-swim-situation': her confidence grew only gradually as she was immersed into Japanese on a day-to-day basis.

In regards to the aspect of speaking that she improved most, Ann was the only one in the group who named speech style as the area. She told me that she became skilled in switching between different forms according to whom she was speaking to. See the excerpt:

Excerpt 8.11

When I talk to friends I speak in the casual form, and when the teacher comes, like, I switch to the polite form and speak more respectfully? Before I couldn't do that. I would screw up with my forms, and you know, I spoke to teachers very disrespectfully. I knew I was doing wrong, but I was like, very, ah ... had hard time switching. But I am getting better ... In the States too, mostly because in class we are used to speaking English a lot, so you don't really use the, ah, casual form? And then in class you mostly use you know, the long form (polite form). (May, 2012)

Although her understanding of speech style was somewhat superficial (associating the form with the addressee type, teachers vs. friends), her incipient ability to maneuver between different forms was noteworthy in her comment. Moving away from the classroom use of the polite style as the only form of communication, Ann developed an understanding that there are variants in speech style and that people shift from one form to another in order to index different social relationships, power, and personal distance. In this excerpt we also recognize that Ann was making a conscious choice of speech style as a means of conveying personal stance. For her, the polite form is an expression of respect: not speaking to teachers in the polite form is considered 'doing wrong.'

I asked her what promoted her understanding of different speech forms. She named her interaction with host family as a primary reason. When she first moved in with her family, she was using the polite form with everyone, even with her host sister, because she was unsure about family dynamics and thought that she should speak in the *desu/masu* form simply to be safe. She felt uncomfortable using the casual form after learning the polite form in all of her Japanese study. She described her first few weeks with her host family as 'awkward' because she felt like she was a stranger in a house and wanted to 'stay out of their way as much as possible.' But one day, a host student from last semester visited them for dinner. After observing how comfortable the student was around the family members, Ann started to feel relaxed, accepting her position in the host family. The host family explicitly asked her to use the plain form, which she started to incorporate in her routine.

Although the host family was certainly her primary Japanese contact which provided sustained communication practice, Ann also had access to two groups of Japanese on a regular basis. One group was her Japanese friends in the *nijinokai*, the university-based club that organized weekend activities for international students. She mostly spoke in the plain form with this group. The other group was the informants for her senior thesis project. She got to know three Buddhist scholars through her advisor's connections and interviewed them about their roles in the organization. Ann attended their meetings and contacted them individually to solicit their participation in her project. All the arrangements involved in this process – sending an initial email, introducing herself, and scheduling the interviews – were conducted in Japanese, although actual interviews were about 80% in English. She made bilingual business cards and wrote a consent form in Japanese. Ann was extremely excited about her research, but at the same time she felt nervous about her interaction with professionals. Although she was not very concerned about 'getting things right' with her friends, she was keen on correctness and precision of her language use with the religious groups. At the same time, she tried to be much more polite with the religious members and used honorifics in her speech.

Similar to Dewi and Lin's cases, participation in different social groups assisted Ann's transition from the default polite form to incorporating the plain form and honorifics into her linguistic repertoire. However, in sharp contrast with Dewi and Lin, Ann's change in speech style was observed in the opposite direction. Her use of the plain form decreased slightly, from 57% at pre- to 43% at post-test. The proportion of the polite form remained the same, about 40% each time. Yet, positive change was found in her production of the incomplete sentences: they appeared for 14% of the time at post-test, whereas they were completely absent at pre-test.

Reflecting these findings, conversation data revealed a great degree of style-mixing of the polite and plain forms in Ann's speech, and the mixing persisted at the end of her study-abroad period. We can turn to the interview data to gain insights about these patterns unique to Ann. One noticeable trend found in Ann's data was that, compared with other participants, Ann often appeared ambivalent about the relationship between context and speech forms. There were frequent comments about uncertainty, doubt, and ambiguity related to the choice of speech style, as well as expressions of contradictions or inconsistency between her understanding of speech style and observation of actual use.

These moments of ambivalence and uncertainty were largely triggered by the complexity and dynamicity of the association between context and speech forms that Ann experienced in real-life situations. In day-to-day interactions with her host family, Ann realized that there is no fixed, one-to-one mapping between the linguistic form and social setting. Context is not a fixed, static variable. It changes across time as well as within single interaction corresponding to changing interpersonal relationships, participant structure, and the direction of talk, among other factors. Responding to the change in context, speech style also changes. In her interaction with her host family, Ann had to weigh different social factors before making a decision on what forms to use; often the decision was made case-by-case, because configurations of the factors were unique to situation.

Ann shared her observation that the host family members occasionally switched between forms when speaking to her. She realized that they sometimes talked to her in the casual form and then changed to the polite form, but she was not able to discern the reasons behind their style-shifting. Ann was also ambiguous about her own choice of speech style. She routinely spoke in the plain form at home, but when a different contextual element such as 'setting' came into play, she was indefinite about which form to use, plain or polite. See the excerpt for illustration:

Excerpt 8.12

With my host family sometimes it's hard because they talk to me in the casual form sometime and then other times in the *desu/masu*, and also, ah ... there are different relationships, like between my host father and me versus my host mother and me, so ... It's like, you know, who should I use the *desu/masu* in what situation.

Like, when we went to the tea ceremony, I was like, should I use the *desu/masu* or casual here because it was a different situation, around different people. I wonder, ah, when I meet my host mother's friends, should I talk casual with them or should I use the *desu/masu*, because we are with different people, and you know, I want to show some respect around them. When we go out together, I wonder which form I should use. (July, 2012)

When Ann and her host mother entered a new location outside the home, such as a tea ceremony, Ann became suddenly uncertain about her choice of speech style. Although the plain form was the norm of communication between her and her host mother at home, the formality of the tea ceremony occasion brought an entirely new contextual parameter, which consequently complicated her selection of speech style. Combined with Ann's subjectivity of wanting to show respect to her host mother in public, she was no longer sure whether everyday use of the plain form still applied to this situation.

There was another episode of contextual complexity and dynamicity affecting Ann's linguistic choice. Ann shifted between the plain and polite forms when she considered the degree of imposition in her speech act. Although the plain form was the default style in her communication with her host mother, she switched to the polite form when she had to make a request with a high degree of imposition, like asking her host mother for permission to use kitchen. As she expressed in the excerpt below, the style-shifting here was a way of reducing the potential face-threat coming from disrupting her host mother's territory (i.e. kitchen). This style-shift can be considered Ann's politeness strategy. Although Japanese speakers in this situation probably use syntactic mitigations and indirect expressions to do the face-work, Ann used the style-shift as a tactic to express her consideration and respect to her host mother.

Excerpt 8.13

With my host mom, I use the *desu/masu* when I'm asking her something, like...for example, when I asked her if I can make my *obento* (lunch box), I used the *desu/masu* because kitchen is her domain, and I didn't want to impose, so I'd rather be more respectful with my question. (May, 2012)

Ann's subjectivity was also observed in her patterns of interaction in the home stay setting. She consciously elected different speech forms depending on which family member she was speaking to. Although she maintained the plain form in her communication with her host mother and sister, she was less consistent with her host father. Her host father always used the plain form with her, but Ann used a mix of the polite and plain forms because of his position in relation to her in the family. Since he was the head of the household who ultimately made the decision to host Ann, she had a strong desire for expressing respect to him, reserving the polite form in her communication with him. Here Ann used the polite form as a tool for presenting her desired identity – a humble, respectful student. See the excerpts:

Excerpt 8.14

It's sometimes uncomfortable using the casual form with my host father so I switch to the *desu/masu*. (Researcher: Why do you feel uncomfortable?) With *otosan* (host father), he is kind of like, the head of the household, and I feel weird speaking to him in the casual form, so I use the *desu/masu* mostly with him. (May, 2012)

Excerpt 8.15

In Japanese there are different forms. So, like I use casual with my friends. With my family, I switch forms, between the *desu/masu* and casual. I speak in the casual form with my host mother and host sister, but I use the *desu/masu* with my host father. I want to show respect to him. He is the head of the household and he allows me to stay with them. He uses the casual form with me, but I use the *desu/masu*. (June, 2012)

These excerpts further illustrate the complexity of context affecting Ann's linguistic choice. Ann's perception and understanding of the status and role of family members essentially guided her choice of speech style. Ann was not forced into using the polite form with her host father. Rather, her choice came along naturally from her internal self as a way of expressing respect and deference to him. In the same household where the plain form was the normative practice, Ann's perception of her position in the family (an outsider who temporarily entered their living space) and her perception of her host father (the head of the family who makes decisions) led to the (perceived) unbalanced power relationship between her and her host father. By using the polite form to her host father, Ann positioned herself as someone with less power. Hence, context was configured beyond the typical sociocultural parameters of social relationships, distance, and power. Learner-internal parameters such as perception, subjectivity, and desired identity equally serve as essential dimensions of context that affect Ann's linguistic choice.

In summary, Ann developed a nuanced understanding of speech style through her daily interaction with her host family. She sometimes expressed ambivalence about the choice of speech style because of the idiosyncratic nature of context where multiple speech forms co-exist and shift according to contextual dynamics. Ann observed that a particular speech style (plain or polite) routinely practiced between the same individuals or within the same household is not fixed or stable across contexts. Because real-world situations do not always present one-to-one mappings between the form and context, Ann was often ambivalent about how to speak when multiple competing elements (e.g. setting, occasion, degree of imposition, and participant role) came into the configuration of context. Over time Ann learned to become sensitive to the changing contextual specifics, and adapted and aligned with different linguistic forms responding to a dynamic, changing context. What is more, her linguistic choice was also guided by her subjectivity – the desired 'self' that she wished to project to the community. This was observed in her use of the polite form when addressing to her host father while reserving the plain form with other family members.

Ann's case underscores the importance of the indexical approach in understanding L2 learners' use of speech style. The traditional structuralist approach associates the polite form with formal speech addressed to out-group members (people who are older, of higher status, and non-intimate), and the plain form with informal speech addressed to in-group members (people of lower status and age, and in intimate relationship) (e.g. Harada, 1976; Ide, 1989; Niyekawa, 1991). Real-life situations are not that simple, however. The recent indexical approach refutes this static view and argues that speech style indexes a variety of social identities and self-presentational stance (Cook, 2006, 2008; Fukushima, 2007; Ikuta, 2008; Nazkian, 2010). Under the indexical approach, the *desu/masu* form is not merely a marker of politeness or formality: it is an index of social meaning that one wishes to express in interaction with others. This indexical approach was in practice in Ann's case. Just like native speakers, she used speech style as a tool to express her personal stance of respect and formality. She considered different contextual factors when making a decision on what forms to use, and often, the decision was made case-by-case, because configurations of the factors were dynamic and unique to the situation.

Adrian

Dewi and Lin's cases revealed social contact and involvement leading to linguistic practice and development. Ann's data illustrated a case of observation, practice, and learner subjectivity leading to a nuanced understanding of speech styles. Adrian, the last case in this chapter, displays a complex interplay among a participant's investment in social networking, social affordances, and opportunity to practice language. Different from other three participants, Adrian experienced a constant struggle integrating into the local community. He developed only a sparse social network, which essentially restricted his linguistic practice, despite his expressed desire for connecting with Japanese people. Conversation data, however, revealed a change in his speech style: shifting from the dominant polite form at pre-test (85%) to dominant plain form at post-test (60%). The use of incomplete sentences also increased to 7.5% from 1.2% at the beginning of the semester. As I will show later in this section, it was his interaction style and orientation to the task that were found underdeveloped.

What was interesting in Adrian's case was that he was by far the most motivated toward his study abroad in Japan. He explicitly said that he came to Japan to gain experience and skills for future internship and career opportunities in Japan. He even founded his own club called Japan Investment Club in which a few international students gathered and studied market financing, while connecting with alumni for job opportunities. Reflecting these goals, Adrian's motivation toward study abroad and desire for expanding Japanese network were high, as shown in his responses to the motivation survey (see Tables 8.3 and 8.4).

Adrian possessed many of the desired qualities of a student who can make the most of his study abroad experience: positive attitudes and interest in Japanese culture; strong integrative motivation and desire in assimilating into the Japanese community; commitment to improving language skills; clear vision about the takeaway from a semester stay in Japan; out-going, assertive personality and risk-taking disposition; and intercultural mindfulness. Despite these qualities, Adrian's social contact and involvement remained only at the superficial level, limited to sporadic participation in student clubs and local events. He made almost no Japanese friends during his study abroad: the number of friends he reported was only one at the end of the semester (zero at the beginning). He reported speaking Japanese only one hour per week, the smallest amount in the entire group of 18 students (see Table 8.5).

Adrian presents a case of a highly-motivated student who came to Japan invested in networking and finding career opportunities, but ended up not finding sustainable social networks to belong to. These findings are somewhat counter-intuitive, considering that motivation, commitment, and positive attitudes are considered to be the prime driving force for successful cultural integration into the community. Interview data suggest that these personal qualities have to be supported by other characteristics such as threshold proficiency, learning style, and communication strategies in order to gain regular access to local communities and establish membership within them.

Adrian was a 26-year-old student from France majoring in Environmental Science. He had abundant intercultural experience prior to coming to Japan. He grew up in the Caribbean and immigrated to France with his parents when he was young. After staying in France until the age of 20, he moved to Moscow and worked in a company for a year and a half. Then, he went to Canada and studied in a university for five months. He spoke four languages fluently: French, English, Russian, and Spanish.

Like Dewi and Ann, Adrian belonged to the Department of International Liberal Arts taking courses taught in English, while enrolled in the intensive Japanese language program. He studied Japanese for four years in France. His encounter with the Japanese language was by chance. He failed classes in economics and ended up repeating a part of the high school program. Because he did not want to retake economics courses, he explored other options and discovered Japanese. One day, he came across an exam written in Japanese; he developed an instant attraction to the Japanese characters, which he found unique and exotic.

Adrian said that he could 'breeze through' in the Japanese class. Compared with other subjects that were work intensive with exams, he found the Japanese class 'pleasant' and 'interesting.' He was enrolled in a class taught by a team of a French instructor and a Japanese teaching assistant. The class size changed over time, with 6–7 students in the first year to over 20 students in the second and third year. The profiles of the students changed too. His first-year class was filled with students who were marginalized in school due to their poor achievement in the mainstream classes. However, in the final year after the instructor changed, the class became intense and attracted more serious students. Adrian expressed difficulty in keeping up with the classes in the Japanese university. Pace was fast, and teachers did not take time to explain things thoroughly. They would often go over general meaning without clarifying details of grammatical rules or exceptions of the rules. Adrian told me that in France both teachers and students have a strong taste for debate and discussing problems, but in Japan teachers do not take students' questions in class.

Adrian was committed to his long-term goal of becoming fluent in Japanese. I found his dedication to language and cultural learning exceptional based on a number of unique, powerful expressions he used to characterize his goals. He said that he wants to 'express everything in Japanese at the same level as English.' He would enjoy 'being in a 100% Japanese environment where he needed to solve problems by himself.' One of his intentions for coming to Japan was 'to get lost' so he can discover his potential.

The excerpt below illustrates Adrian's unique stance toward his study abroad in Japan. He believed that hardship and challenge can cultivate people's growth and independence in a foreign country. For him, culture shock was a highly desired condition in the process of cultural integration. He had an ideal self-image of being in the Japanese-only environment and overcoming cultural gaps despite the language barrier. In a sense, Adrian viewed cultural adaptation as a course for self-actualization or a process in which he could realize his potential. Reaching the point of understanding the culture and language would give Adrian a 'proud feeling' and a sense of 'freedom,' which contributes to his internal growth towards the fulfillment of his life. See the excerpt for illustration:

Excerpt 8.16

I really, really loved it (Ontario, Canada), but Canadian culture is close to French culture. It's Anglo-Saxon. There is no, no cultural gap, no cultural shock. I'm really, I'm really looking forward to being in a place where there is strong, strong culture shock. (Researcher: Why do you enjoy culture shock? Some people take it as a difficulty.) Ah, of course it's difficult but it's interesting to be in a difficult situation. And then, when you finally get to the point where you understand the culture and language, it's a really good feeling, proud feeling. And also, it's ... unusual. I don't know how to explain it, but it's a feeling of freedom. I remember my first few months, my first months in Russia were very difficult, because I had a job which was quite technical, and I was there in 2008, and the crash of economy happened and the company I was going to work for one year went bankruptcy. I happened to be in Moscow, but I had no money, no job ... Plus, I didn't have an apartment for a few, a few weeks, so I had so many problems at the same time, but finally I was able to ... it took me some time, but I was able to, finally ... find a solution. And this is very good for pride. It's a very good feeling. It's a very good story afterwards. (May, 2012)

In this excerpt we recognize that Adrian's positive attitudes toward studying abroad were shaped by his previous experiences in living in foreign countries. He had hard times in Russia in 2008 when the Lehman Shock hit world markets. He lost his job, money, and apartment in a foreign environment. He was alone. Despite the desperation, stress and anxiety, however, he managed to turn his life around. This experience functioned as confidence building and led him to appreciate the challenge that a life in a foreign country presents.

Building on these intercultural experiences, Adrian also expressed a nuanced understanding of culture by acknowledging the complexity involved in it. One of the questions I asked the participants in the second and third interview was about their views of ideal personal qualities in the Japanese society. I asked them what abilities and qualities they think are important in order to function effectively and appropriately when interacting with Japanese people. Adrian was the only student who refused to answer this question. Although other students came up with a list of general ideas such as patience, perseverance, ability to follow rules, indirect way of speaking, knowledge of hierarchy, and basic Japanese skills, Adrian's answer was 'I don't know.' He said that he did not want to respond because it is the kind of question that people can answer only when they speak the language well and after spending much time with Japanese people.

Similarly, in response to my question about his cultural expectations prior to coming to Japan, he was the only student who overtly reported having no expectations. He said that he did not like making a general comment about culture and people because it leads to stereotyping, which means little in reality. Before coming to Japan, he even quit reading the Japanese magazine that he had subscribed to for seven years because he did not want to develop any expectations or generalizations about Japanese culture. Here again, we can observe his self-discovery mindset. For him, culture is something to discover on his own through exposure and experience, not something to be taught by others. See the excerpts:

Excerpt 8.17

There are so many, ah, there are so many interesting things about Japan (in the magazine), but there is a moment when you feel you are reading generalizations. And there is moment when you can't think too much about the country in terms of culture...When you talk to someone, you can't assume that everything he says or does leads to the culture. So I, I, I stopped reading things about society and culture for many months before I came here, because there is no culture shock if you try to explain everything by what, what you read or by what some other people said. So I decided to come to Japan with no expectation, no . . . no . . . pre, pre-made ideas¿ (May, 2012)

Excerpt 8.18

Many foreigners (in Japan) have a plenty of stories about what they like and what they don't like about being here, ah . . . but I try not to listen to these because you have to make your own judgment. If you just come to Japan, to the country, and if you adapt opinions from other people, I guess you are missing something. (July, 2012)

These descriptions portray Adrian as someone who is open to new ideas and practices and has psychological strength in coping with difficulties. However, despite his strong interest in exploring culture, Adrian's actual cultural contact remained low throughout his time in Japan. Adrian told me that his greatest difficulty in Japan was making friends and communicating with people. Early in the semester, Adrian joined the magic club where majority of the students were Japanese. While participating in their weekly practice, he developed impression that 'they did not want him in the group' and 'there was no welcoming atmosphere.' As shown in the excerpt below, Adrian felt that the small talk he had with Japanese members never developed into a real conversation: it did not have much substance and did not flow naturally from one topic to another. Japanese students showed almost no reaction to Adrian's questions. He attributed their lack of interest to his limited knowledge of cultural practice. He shared an episode in which he violated the norm of interaction and deviated from the expected behavior as a junior member:

Excerpt 8.19

I am trying not to make any generalizations, but so far people whom I've been speaking, so far, haven't, ah, said much about themselves. Even if we talk for a long time there is no natural flow of conversation going on, ah, so I try to make a conversation. I ask questions about people, but I have an impression that it's not the communication they are expecting. I am feeling that it's not a good way because maybe you are not supposed to provoke, to create discussion ... or maybe, maybe, maybe they are not talking to you because ... you, you haven't proved you are worth talking, I don't know.

Or maybe I made a little mistake when we were doing some magic session. Some guy showed magic trick, and I said wow, that's very interesting, and I showed him the same trick done in another way. I said, I gave him some advice (in Japanese). I think I shouldn't have given him advice or taken the deck from his hands to show him, because I had this feeling something went wrong because I didn't see anyone else showing the tricks. So I said, wait, how come people are not showing secret to each other. I mean, they said, they said actually *senpai* can show how it's done, but you are not supposed to show to someone else if you are not *senpai* or without the approval of *senpai*. (Researcher: Why did you think so?) I asked a girl, girl that I've been talking much. I said, hey, is it OK to show something to someone or should I, should I wait for *senpai* to do it? It's not what I'm used to do – everyone shows everything. So I had, I had a feeling that there is hierarchy. And she confirmed that indeed my feeling was true. It had to come from *senpai*.

Something I'd like it here is ... someone gives me good tools, good cards. Once I know what is happening, what are the good things to pay attention to, little details that foreigners would not notice but actually Japanese people would notice, ah, well, once I know which exact things I should direct attention to understand underlying, underlying, ah, process, I'd be much more confident in such social gathering. (May, 2012)

In the midpoint of the semester, Adrian still had no Japanese friends and expressed his strong desire for connecting with Japanese people. His situation remained the same in the third interview at the end of the semester. He was still seeking opportunities to speak Japanese.

Parallel to his limited opportunities to speak Japanese, Adrian's participation in social networks was slim and short-term throughout the semester. He moved from one group to another without participating in their activities regularly. As a result, he was not able to establish a long-lasting relationship with any of the groups. He was proactive and had no fear of starting new things, but his initiative was short-lived each time. Adrian quit the magic club after attending three meetings, mainly because he did not understand what was going on around him and people were too busy to explain things to him. Mid-way in the semester he launched the Japan Investment Club with a few international students, but the club became inactive after a few periodic activities. At the same time, he joined the salsa club and *karate* club. Members in the salsa club were mostly international students. He quit the club after attending a few times. The *karate* club was a local group of Japanese, including both students and working adults. Although he joined the group late, he continued attending their weekly practices until the end of the semester, six times total.

As illustrated above, Adrian's motivation to make the best of study abroad experience, his desire for assimilating to the Japanese community, his commitment in improving Japanese skills, and other personal qualities that are likely to contribute to successful cultural adjustment did not align perfectly with the outcome of his study abroad. In the last interview Adrian said that, although he had no regrets, next time he comes to Japan he wants to be in a 'real Japanese environment' and be 'active in socializing with Japanese people.'

Three interviews were probably not enough to discern the complexity involved in Adrian's case, but a tendency emerged in the data as an area that might have led to his imperfect experience. This tendency was related to his inadequate Japanese ability, pooled with his demand and expectation for a complete control of the language. Compared with other students, I found Adrian to be exceptionally meticulous and thorough with language. His stance for precision was seen in his comment related to his learning style, particularly in his approach to improving fluency. When asked about an effective way to develop fluency, he responded that the best way is listening to a Japanese conversation and going over the exact transcript, word-by-word. He said that he wanted a complete transcript for everything including hesitations and discourse markers as they appear in a naturalistic conversation.

As another approach to fluency development, he shared his vocabulary learning method that involved intensive repetition and memorization. Whenever he saw a new word, he entered the word and example sentences into a free app called *anki* (memorization). The app asked for translation of the words and checked answers so people learn vocabulary. The program automatically recycled vocabulary every 5 to 10 minutes for a repetition program. He accumulated about 1200 words during the semester. He told me that most of his learning took place alone using this app. He spent 'every day, hours and hours with the phone' to learn words one by one so he would become fluent in Japanese.

Adrian's habit of checking vocabulary in a dictionary was noticeable during the interviews. He often asked for a translation of the words that came up in my questions. Most surprisingly, he was using a dictionary while conversing with his peer during the conversation test. In a face-to-face, spontaneous conversation people would typically try to guess meaning or let go unknown vocabulary, and instead focus on continuing conversation, but this was not the case for Adrian. He did not care about stopping the flow in the middle of the conversation. He had his partner wait until he recorded the new word into his app and resumed conversation.

Adrian's low tolerance toward ambiguity, attention to details, and precision for meaning were also evident in his day-to-day interactional style. As shown in the excerpts below, Adrian explained his tendency to make 'everything clear' about a situation – 'what it is about, how many people are there, and how they know each other.' He believed that vocabulary is necessary for accurate understanding of situations and emphasized that he would need 'precise and specific situational words' to understand everything. However, he also acknowledged that complete understanding of situations is impossible to achieve. According to Adrian, the most challenging part of being in Japan was accepting that he would not understand everything. There are 'mysterious parts', but people still have to know how to react accordingly.

Excerpt 8.20

> I need to learn better Japanese to really understand what's going on, because in order to understand this kind of thing, you need to, you need to have enough vocabulary to have more, more, accurate, accurate, ah, impression of, I need to have enough vocabulary to have more accurate understanding of what's going on. You don't need general idea. In order to understand what's happening, you need to have very precise and specific situational words, and even after this … ah, I guess, you need to, you need to accept the idea that you are not going to understand everything. That's the difficult thing here.
>
> I believe … ah … I could be wrong, but I have the impression that you have to accept a situation where you don't understand everything. Ah … usually, wherever I go, usually, I try to make it clear beforehand, like where we are, in which context, who is the organizer of the party, what it is about, how many people, how they know each other. If I don't know all of these, I will ask people … I try to make everything clear. I have the impression here, ah, sometimes, ah, people accept not knowing exactly what's going on, and you have to, ah, accept that there are mysterious parts. It's very difficult to say but sometime, ah … I don't know even … Even after a lesson or even after *nomikai*, sometimes you ask questions, and you understand that some people don't know more than you do. I don't know … It's very difficult, very difficult to say. (July, 2012)

As revealed in the data, Adrian was oriented toward details and precision with a high expectation of understanding everything happening around him. But his intermediate-level language ability did not allow complete understanding in communication. Instead, his tendency might have worked against improving on his interactional competence. Authentic interaction is filled with ambiguity and unknowns that L2 learners have to cope with using communication strategies to their advantage. Given the on-line demand of communication that involves turn-taking and negotiation, one often has to sacrifice attention to detail for fluency. In reality, adhering to correctness and precision might be ineffective at the task of achieving a successful interaction. It is possible that Adrian's meticulous personality and style interfered with developing abilities to navigate through authentic situations which one has to adapt to and respond to promptly. With an inadequate ability to sustain and develop conversations, he was not able to cultivate relationships with local communities on a level that he could establish stable membership and identity within them.

Interactional competence requires participants to make a skillful use of a variety of linguistic and interactional resources for the task of joint meaning making (Young, 2008a, 2008b, 2011). Successful interaction is a matter of collaborative effort of participants working toward shared understanding. Prerequisite to this process is participants orienting themselves to ongoing talk, and constantly monitoring and regulating their contributions to the talk. Adrian's priority of understanding every single word did not fit well in this scope of interactional competence, because his orientation toward his own goal, not a joint goal of his and his interlocutor, was likely to block a smooth, flowing conversation. The occasional 'timeout' that Adrian took to record vocabulary in his cell phone app created an awkward moment of silence during the conversation task. As a result, the conversation became his self-seeking learning material, rather than the place for collaborative meaning making.

Note

(1) Portion of Dewi's data appeared in Taguchi (in press).

9 Conclusion

In the process of second language learning and acquisition, the ability to interact effectively is critical. But what does it mean to say that one is interactionally competent? This study directly addressed this question in the area of Japanese as a second language. The study investigated the development of interactional competence among 18 learners of Japanese in a study abroad program. Adapting the theoretical framework of interactional competence (Hall, 1995; Young & He, 1998; Young, 2008a, 2008b, 2011), the study documented learners' skillful use of linguistic and interactional resources for joint meaning making. Through a comparative analysis of peer-to-peer conversation data collected over one semester, the study traced changes in learners' interactional competence as observed in their use of two features of spoken interaction in Japanese: speech styles (the polite and plain form) and incomplete sentence endings. A conversation analytic perspective provided an illustration of learners' development of interactional competence, as they gradually expanded their repertoire of interactional resources for the joint creating of meaning in talk-in-interaction. The present findings generate implications in two areas: (1) the theoretical construct of interactional competence and (2) second language development in a study abroad context.

Implications for the Construct of Interactional Competence and Development

This study adopted the theoretical framework of interactional competence, which originated in Hymes' (1970) notion of language as a means of performing social interaction. Incorporating Hymes' insight, Hall (1993, 1995) and Young (2002, 2008a, 2011) proposed a framework for the study of interactional practices. Different from the traditional models that view linguistic competence as psycholinguistic ability residing within individuals' traits (Bachman & Palmer, 1996, 2010; Canale & Swain, 1980), interactional competence views language knowledge and ability as locally situated and jointly constructed by participants in discourse. Interactional competence involves a variety of linguistic and semiotic resources that learners bring into the co-construction of talk and joint creation of meaning. These resources include knowledge of rhetorical scripts; register-appropriate use of lexis and syntax; the turn-taking system; topic management; repair; and recognition and production of boundaries between speech activities (Young, 2002, 2011; see Chapter 1). Most importantly, interactional competence is not the ability of an individual to use those linguistic and interactional resources; rather, 'it is about how those resources are employed mutually and reciprocally by all participants in a particular discursive practice' (Young, 2011: 428). Following this theoretical framework, my study documented the development of interactional competence as it manifested in peer-to-peer conversation among learners of Japanese in a study abroad context.

Individual languages have different linguistic and interactional resources that are important for the structure of discourse and contribute to interaction. This study examined two linguistic structures unique to Japanese: speech styles and incomplete sentences. The polite and plain forms signal register-appropriate language use, which help speakers construct interpersonal, ideational, and textual meaning across different contexts. Learners of Japanese need to know which form to use (polite or plain) to index power, formality, distance, or affect, and their choice is guided by their understanding of the specifics of context. In addition, speech styles mark the transition between discourse boundaries. The polite form is typically reserved for formal situations and the plain form is associated with informal situations. Learners' choices between the two forms can signal their understanding of the interactional situation in which they participate. For example, an informal conversation with a same-age peer might entail the use of the plain form, whereas a formal talk with someone with different status and background might provoke the use of the polite form. Style shifts between the plain and polite forms, on the other hand, serve as learners' resources to transition from one discursive practice to another. These shifts also reflect learners' sensitivity and reciprocity toward the changing state of discourse, as well as their ability to mark discourse boundaries.

Participants in this study demonstrated a marked improvement in their use of speech styles, as shown by the sharp increase in their use of the plain form in a conversation with a same-age peer (see Chapter 5, Table 5.1). In the pre-test peer-to-peer conversation, the polite and plain forms appeared at similar rates (about 47%). However, at post-test, the polite form dropped to 14%, while the plain form increased to 70%, indicating the learners' development in register-appropriate language use. Adapting to the situational specifics, they became able to use the plain form when speaking with their peers about mundane topics.

Learners' underuse of the plain form was expected at the beginning of their study abroad. Because classroom teaching and textbooks emphasize the *desu/masu* form, learners are often unfamiliar with when and how to use the plain form (Cook, 2008). They tend to stick to the polite form as their default style and do not attempt to use the plain form. Previous studies showed that exposure to and participation in interactions in the local community facilitated learners' socialization into the use of the plain form, leading to the dramatic increase of plain forms toward the end of their stay in Japan (Cook, 2008; Iwasaki, 2010; Masuda, 2011; McMeeken, 2011). This study adds to the previous findings.

Learners in this study also demonstrated style-shifts between the polite and plain forms across different participant structures to signal transitions between discourse boundaries. Although the conversation task was arranged as a peer-to-peer interaction, the researcher participated in the conversation sporadically and introduced variation as the conversation was progressing. In the peer-to-peer conversation, shared background and status between learners can lead to informality, but this atmosphere might change when the third person with a different background (the researcher as an older Japanese professor) joins the conversation and creates a multi-party dialogue. Contrary to this expectation, however, group-level findings did not reveal any difference in the proportion of the plain and polite forms between these two participant structures (see Chapter 5, Table 5.1).

However, it was at the individual-level where incipient change was observed. Three learners demonstrated marked style-shifting from the dyad to triad (see Chapter 6, Table 6.1). Shifts from the plain to polite form occurred when the researcher joined the conversation, reflecting learners' understanding of contextual specifics – whom they are talking to and for what purposes. Notably, one learner switched from the polite to plain form when co-constructing the researcher's foregoing turn and producing joint voice with the researcher. Style-shifting symbolized learners' adaptability: adaptability to changing participant structure and adaptability to the sequential organization of talk. Learners used style shifts as their interactional resources to project a different 'self' to their peers and to the researcher, as well as to co-construct turn-in-progress.

In addition to the change in speech styles and style-shifting, learners also increased their functional abilities with the use of the plain form. Although the majority of the plain forms occurred when presenting information and expressing inner self, frequency of other functions – request for information, joint meaning making, and response to questions – increased over time (see Chapter 5, Table 5.2). Particularly notable was learners' gain in the function of joint meaning making (e.g. completing the interlocutor's turn-in-progress, expanding on the interlocutor's speech). Although the degree of change from pre to post was small (3% increase), this change suggests the learners' emergent interactional competence – ability to construct meaning collaboratively. A trend of interactional development was also found in the appearance of new functions with the plain form (e.g. making a request, giving a suggestion) at post-test.

The learners also demonstrated development in their use of the plain form with affect keys, i.e. linguistic resources that signal the speaker's feelings and moods (Cook, 2002). The proportion of the four affective keys coded in the data (i.e. sentence final particles, rising intonation, postposing, and coalescence) was small at pre-test, occupying 19%. This percentage increased to 23% at post-test (see Chapter 5, Table 5.3). Although the increase was small, a qualitative change was notable in the area of postposing. Postposing was almost absent in the pre-test data but emerged at over 2% of the time at post-test (see Chapter 5, Table 5.4). Postposing is a phenomenon of casual, spoken Japanese. Because written Japanese rarely exhibits this feature, Japanese textbooks, particularly at intermediate-level, do not typically provide explanations on postposing. This is supported by the near-absence of this form at pre-test when the learners first came to Japan. After being immersed into authentic communication and non-prescriptive discourse structures during study abroad, the learners probably incorporated this construction in their linguistic repertoire and started using it in interaction.

Taken together, these findings indicate learners' development in their use of speech styles as linguistic resources for participating in talk-in-progress. Increased use of the plain forms in the peer-to-peer dialogue was an indicator of learners' developing ability to use language appropriately according to the talk type. At the same time, it was a sign of learners' increasing ability to deal with a range of communicative functions spontaneously. Style-shifting during the conversation with the researcher, on the other hand, was an indication of the learners' ability to signal boundaries between discourse segments corresponding to different participant memberships.

In addition to the speech styles, the learners also showed conspicuous progress in their treatment of incomplete sentence endings. In Japanese, a variety of particles and conjunctions signal incomplete sentences (Chen, 2000; see Chapter 2). Learners gained competence in using those particles and conjunctions and leaving their sentences incomplete, as demonstrated in the striking increase of incomplete endings from 5% at pre-test to almost 17% at post-test. This is a strong sign of their interactional development because it means that the learners stopped using complete sentences (polite and plain forms) exclusively and sounding textbook-like. Instead, they adopted a more naturalistic way of speech by using incomplete sentences as interactional resources. The dramatic increase of incomplete sentences over semester seems to be a positive study abroad effect. Because formal instruction and textbooks rarely teach this aspect of spoken grammar, it is likely that the learners picked it up naturally as they participated in naturalistic conversation and observed when incomplete sentences occur and what functions they play.

Treatment of incomplete sentences is a prime example of interactional resources that correspond to Young's (2008a) area of turn-taking and sequential construction of actions (see Chapter 1). By leaving a sentence unfinished, the speaker projects a point of turn completion and transfer of speakership. Responding to this signal, the listener may complete the sentence initiated by the speaker (joint turn construction), or may acknowledge the end of the talk and initiate a new topic. This coordinated use of incomplete sentences between the speaker and listener promotes their cooperation and reciprocity at the task of turn-taking. Close analysis of data revealed learners' increasing ability to use incomplete sentences as resources for joint turn construction (see Chapter 7). As speakers, the learners became able to produce incomplete sentences as turn allocation devices; as listeners, they came to understand their use as signaling a turn transition point, and learned to react to this resource appropriately. Join turn completion is an indication of learners' alignment in talk-in-interaction – ability to demonstrate shared understanding and to adopt the other's point of view (Dings, 2014). By completing the interlocutor's turn, learners performed a range of social functions: perspective sharing; display of empathy understanding, assisted explanation; and elaboration on the topic-in-progress (Hayashi, 2014). Knowledge of sequential organization adjoining incomplete sentences served as a resource that the learners employed mutually and reciprocally in their practice of joint meaning making.

In summary, conversation data revealed what it means to be interactionally competent in Japanese by explicating linguistic and interactional resources that enable Japanese learners to construct and orient to social actions in Japanese. Those resources were identified in four areas:

(1) Register-appropriate language use as identified in the learners' increased ability to use the plain over polite form in a conversation with a peer.
(2) Ability to mark boundaries by shifting between the polite and plain form.
(3) Expansion in the range of interactional functions performed with the plain form.
(4) Ability to use incomplete sentences as turn-taking resources for the co-construction of turn-in-progress and joint meaning making.

Implications of the findings for the construct of interactional competence are two-fold. First, the results inform us about the nature of interactional competence specific to Japanese language. While some aspects of the linguistic and interactional resources are considered universal, others are understood as language-specific products. Individual languages have unique linguistic resources that are important for the structure of discourse and thus contribute to interaction. In Japanese, sentence final particles (M. Ishida, 2009; Masuda, 2010) and alignment expressions (Ohta, 2001) have been examined as important interactional resources. This study contributes to the existing literature by revealing the construct of interactional competence in additional areas – speech styles and incomplete sentence endings. The findings show how these linguistics structures, when embedded in talk-in-interaction, serve as a benchmark of learners' interactional development. This study contributes a piece of empirical evidence supporting that individual languages have unique resources that facilitate learners' participation in interaction, which directly adds to our discussion on 'interactional competence-specific-to-languages.'

The present findings should encourage researchers of Japanese to explore central characteristics of the construct of interactional competence in Japanese, both from language-universal and Japanese-specific standpoints, and to link those characteristics to principled methods through which the nature and development of interactional competence can be examined. At the same time, the findings should encourage researchers in other language groups to imagine the uniqueness and commonalities of linguistic and interactional resources inherent to individual languages. Such an exploration within and across language communities will promote a more comprehensive understanding of interactional competence, and in turn help advance the practice of SLA research and teaching.

Another area of implication relates to the development of interactional competence. The present study employed a longitudinal design by administering comparative tasks cyclically and comparing the data between two time points to search for any indications of change. As a result, four areas emerged as indicators of interactional development (see above). However, we recognize that these four areas exhibited considerable variation in terms of the pace and size of development. Although the increase of the plain form was most dramatic in terms of frequency, the range of functions of the plain form showed much smaller progress over time, suggesting that the gains in frequency may precede those of function. Similarly, style-shifting across discourse boundaries was observed only at individual-level, and there was no discernible change at group-level. Finally, in terms of the interactional functions of incomplete sentences, the functions of assisted explanation, display of empathy, and elaboration on topic-in-progress were late-emerging, compared with L2-specific functions such as joint problem solving and repair.

These findings suggest that the construct of interactional competence is multi-faceted and multi-dimensional. Linguistic and interactional resources are not one uniform construct. Different sub-constructs exhibit different developmental pace and patterns, depending on the nature of the sub-constructs and processing mechanisms involved, as well as the modality and task type used to examine the sub-constructs. For instance, a large increase in the use of the plain form and a small increase in style-shifting suggests that learners can progress with utterance-ending forms (use of the plain form) relatively quickly as long as they understand the associations between context and form. In contrast, their ability to transit across discourse units with different speech forms (style-shifting) could be slow-progressing because learners have to attend to a large range of contextual parameters and discourse units that are shifting on their own. A combined analysis of different linguistic structures in a longitudinal design could help us gain a more complete understanding of learners' interactional competence and development.

Implications for Study Abroad as a Site for L2 Learning

Young (2011) observed that most previous studies gave detailed descriptions of learners' changes in interactional competence, but they have provided little evidence of how the changes happened. To address this concern, this study described changes in learners' interactional competence and, at the same time, sought to understand the meaning of those changes by collecting qualitative data on individual learners' study abroad experiences. Interview data from four learners were cross-examined with conversation data to see whether or not different patterns of development can be explained by different degrees of intensity and types of sociocultural experiences among individuals.

The four case histories exemplified individual learners' variation in their investment and linguistic outcome of their study abroad experience (see Chapter 8). Learner characteristics such as motivation, personality, subjectivity and desired identity, learning styles and learning strategies were found to interact with each other and with the context of study abroad, and jointly accounted for the unique trajectories of interactional development. For example, Dewi, a student from Brunei, and Lin, a student from China, were exceedingly successful in their cultural adjustment and integration into the Japanese community. During the short period of three months, they both established roots in local communities by regularly participating in their routine activities. Positive changes with speech styles and incomplete sentences found in their conversation data seem to be the results of this cultural assimilation.

Dewi's social networks were primarily in the area of students clubs. She joined four different clubs at the beginning of the semester, most of which involved traditional cultural practices (e.g. tea ceremony), and spent more than 15 hours a week on these club activities. Her club participation was motivated by her strong commitment to making the best of her study abroad experience. Coming to Japan through the 'third-year-discovery-year' – a time to broaden intercultural perspectives – Dewi was invested in her study abroad as a 'once-in-a-life-time-experience.' Club activities served to maximize her cultural learning in Japan.

Through her participation in these clubs, Dewi became acquainted with Japanese students. But getting to know people did not necessarily lead to establishing long-term friendships with them. After realizing this, Dewi became more proactive with opportunities to connect with Japanese people by using a variety of self-initiated strategies. She 'friended' people she just met and followed them on Facebook. She also developed a habit of running up to Japanese friends for small talk whenever she saw them on campus. Persistence and perseverance in this process seemed to have led to the depth and breadth of the social networks that she established in Japan.

Although Dewi's social networks were the product of her conscious effort and investment, Lin's involvement in communities of practice was rather circumstantial. She joined the student club called *himawari kodomokai*. Her friend was a member and started participating in the activities that involved interacting with elementary-school children. Another community was the informal gathering of Japanese and international students from her department, Political Science and Economics. The group self-formed as a language exchange group where discussion on contemporary issues took place in a bilingual mode. The third community was the French restaurant where she worked part-time as a waitress through her instructor's connection. Although these social networks occurred incidentally in Lin's case, similar to Dewi, Lin was committed to speaking Japanese and participating in her activities consistently, because members might 'forget about her if she doesn't show up every time.'

Each of these communities provided exposure to and practice with different ways of speaking that reflected diverse activities, memberships, and participant roles. The *himawari kodomokai* served as a place for practicing the polite and plain forms and senior-junior relationship indexed by the forms. Lin eventually developed resistance toward this local norm, but this is considered as a reflection of her subjectivity and refined understanding of the normative association between the form and social meaning. On the other hand, in the language exchange group, Lin received intensive practice with the plain form. In the group of same-age peers with common professional goals and multicultural backgrounds, Lin gained a space to exercise her identity as a student from China and to represent a voice from Chinese culture. Her role in the French restaurant provided opportunities to practice honorifics with customers, which were not available in other places. Like Dewi, she took these opportunities seriously because of their high-stake nature involving real-life consequences.

The commonality between Lin and Dewi's cases is that they were exposed to different registers, communicative practices, and linguistic experiences through different domains of social interaction available in the local community. Opportunities to observe and practice speech styles in diverse social settings seemed to have facilitated their development with using and understanding different speech styles. What is more, consistent and sustained participation in these social networks helped them cultivate long-term personal relationships.

While Lin and Dewi's cases demonstrated the quality and quantity of social contacts leading to linguistic development, Ann's case was an example of observation of authentic interaction leading to ambivalence and uncertainty with her choice of speech style. Through her daily interaction with her host family, Ann observed style-shifting happening quite casually among family members. She noticed that her host family sometimes switched between the plan and polite form when addressing her, without any obvious reason she could find. She also shifted style herself in her interaction with her host family without knowing any of the rules. Although the plain form was the primary style she used at home when speaking to her host mother, she switched to the polite form when they were placed outside of the home and interacted in the public eye. At home too Ann occasionally shifted between forms. When asking a favor of her host mother, she elected to use the polite form to reduce potential face threat. Ann's style-shifting with her host father, on the other hand, stemmed from her subjectivity and desired identity. Perceived status difference between her and her host father made her feel uneasy with using the plain form. Style-shifting was the result of her internal conflict between her desire to express respect to the head of the household and her appeal to solidarity and reciprocity in response to her father's use of the plain form.

A substantial amount of style mixing remained in Ann's speech in the peer-to-peer conversation at the end of the semester, demonstrating a contrasting pattern from Dewi and Lin's data. Ann's persistent style mixing could be attributed to her real-life experience with the complex and dynamic relationship between speech styles and context of use. Routine style-shifting in her day-to-day interactions made her realize that there is no static, one-to-one mapping between speech style and context. Context is complex; it involves a number of parameters, not limited to setting or relationship, but extending to occasion, role, and degree of imposition. Responding to the change in context, speech style also changes. Different from Dewi and Lin, Ann's development was most evidently found in her nuanced understanding of this complexity among context, forms, and social meaning that they index. She was living in the midst of style mixing occurring in the same physical environment (i.e. home), among the same participants (i.e. host family and her). Through exposure to style-shifting in day-to-day interactions, she observed that different speech forms co-exist and shift according to contextual dynamics. For Ann, working out the choice of speech style in the real world was much more complicated than rules she learned in the textbook (i.e. the plain form used for informal talk and polite form for formal talk). In authentic interactions, she had to configure a number of contextual parameters, along with her subjectivity and desired identity, before making a decision on what forms to use. Results of this process were her incipient but still ambivalent understanding of the associations between speech style and context of use.

While these three learners' cases suggested that the role of social contact and participation in the community assisted their linguistic development and understanding, Adrian, a student from France, was not quite successful in cultivating sustainable social relationships during his stay in Japan. He came to Japan highly motivated and invested, driven by instrumental motivation of finding internship and career opportunities. Oriented toward this goal, Adrian had a strong desire to improve his language skills and connect with locals. Adrian's abundant intercultural experiences, motivation and interest, desire for cultural assimilation, and outgoing personality, however, did not line up with the outcome of his study abroad. Adrian's social contact and involvement remained sporadic, inconsistent, and short-term. He made only one Japanese friend during his study abroad. His reported time speaking Japanese was the smallest in the participant group: one hour per week.

From interview data, a tendency emerged in Adrian's personality and learning style as a potential reason for his rather unproductive integration into the community. Adrian was meticulous and detail-oriented with a high expectation of understanding everything happening around him. This tendency might have restricted his participation in real-world interactions where he had to navigate through a great deal of ambiguity, unknowns, and guesswork. With an inadequate ability to sustain communication without understanding details, it is possible that Adrian could not cultivate relationship with local communities or establish long-term membership within them.

The central question addressed in previous literature in the area of study abroad and SLA is what makes the study abroad context unique for second language learning and development (see Chapter 3; for a review, see Collentine & Freed, 2004; DuFon & Churchill, 2006; Kinginger, 2009, 2011, 2013; Llanes, 2011). The study abroad program, defined as a pre-scheduled, temporary stay in a foreign country for educational purposes, is considered to provide a unique context of learning where learners have access to both formal instruction in class and authentic interaction outside of the classroom. Researchers have revealed the specifics of the study abroad context that actually drive language development. Japanese has been one of the target languages in such research (e.g. Cook, 2008; M. Ishida, 2009, 2011; Iwasaki, 2011).

Based on the four case histories, this study offers implications about the types of opportunities, learning resources, and experiences available in Japanese study abroad programs that are likely to assist learners' progress toward becoming a competent speaker of Japanese in the target community. Cultural adaptation and assimilation promoted through extensive social contact and networking were found to be the basis for language development. However, Dewi and Lin's cases and the contrasting case of Adrian suggest that social contact has to be systematic, sustainable, and enduring for learners to establish and maintain membership in the community. Because sporadic, intermittent participation does not seem to provide sufficient time and practice to grow linguistically and culturally, learners need to be committed to long-term involvement and pledge to practice on a regular basis.

From the interview data, learner-specific and contextual-related reasons emerged as primary factors that make longstanding, sustainable social involvement possible. Learners' motivation and commitment, interest in culture, openness, and positive attitudes are important characteristics because they provide initial access to the local communities; however, in order to transform initial interactions to longstanding relationships, learners have to use other resources skillfully. Communication strategies and personal qualities such as patience, perseverance, flexibility, and ambiguity tolerance are some of the factors that contribute to the stability of learners' community membership. Other factors such as the amount of intercultural experience were found to be no guarantee for a successful transition to a new culture, at least in the context of this study. This is because Adrian experienced a struggle integrating into the Japanese community, whereas Lin and Ann, both first-time long-term visitors in a foreign country, made a seamless adjustment. Although there might be universal, culture-generic attributes that are useful in any cultural context or encounter, a new culture presents new demands and challenges that learners have to cope with on a case-by-case basis.

In terms of the context-learning connection, the present findings support the claim that opportunities to observe and practice language in diverse social settings contribute to the acquisition of speech styles. The community consists of a number of different domains of practice, each of which is characterized by different membership, goals, conventions, and norms of interaction. Each domain presents unique patterns of speech (e.g. the polite and plain form, honorifics) that learners have to practice in order to participate in shared activities and to cultivate membership. During this process, explicit and implicit socialization into different speech forms takes place through feedback and modeling by community members, and learning of speech styles is a byproduct of this process.

An implication from this observation is that the concept of *domains of practice* can be used as a frame of reference to examine study abroad experience. By typifying membership, activity, and patterns of interaction within and across domains, linguistic features and ways of speaking specific to individual domains emerge. Those linguistic features can be used as a yardstick to analyze learners' linguistic abilities, which, in turn, reveal meaningful interpretations about the connection between a study abroad experience and language development.

Future Directions

This study involved participants with diverse first languages, educational backgrounds, and living arrangements, which contribute to the generalizability of the findings. However, because the participants were limited to adult learners of Japanese in a study abroad context, findings cannot be generalized to other age groups, language groups, or learners in an at-home instructional context. Because interactional competence is concerned with language use in social contexts, interactional performance is sensitive to the sociocultural backgrounds and experiences of those who interact. Language-specific means of organizing interactions might generate distinct patterns of interactional development across language groups. Likewise, differing patterns may arise from differing learning environments. This study was conducted in a second language context where learners had frequent exposure to a community-wide practice of speech styles and incomplete sentences, but such practice may not be available in a foreign language context where linguistic input and practice tend to be restricted to the classroom. Hence, future studies involving different participant characteristics and contexts of learning are necessary in order to build on the validity of the present findings.

This study conceptualized indications of interactional competence rather narrowly, limiting the analysis to two linguistic structures in Japanese (speech styles and incomplete sentences). There are many other features of interactional competence that could be productively examined, for instance backchannels and response forms (*aizuchi*), interactional particles, and expressions of alignment, which were examined in the previous studies (M. Ishida, 2009; Masuda, 2010; Miyazaki, 2007; Ohta, 2001; Yoshimi, 1998). Future research could approach interactional competence more broadly by incorporating the analysis of other characteristic features of Japanese discourse.

Related to this, future effort should be directed to continuing an exploration of the configuration of interactional resources, with the aim of revealing what types of knowledge and ability could promote successful participation in interaction. Japanese-specific resources such as those found in this study help us understand what linguistic and interactional resources enable participants to construct and orient to social actions in a specific language. Once identified, those resources could be used as a basis on which interactional competence is assessed and examined.

Similarly, more research is needed to examine the concept of boundaries in interactional practice. As Young (2008a, 2011) attests, in authentic communication, different assortments of resources are called for, depending on contextual specifics of a particular discourse practice. For example, the ways in which question-answer sequences occur in a classroom setting are different from the ways in which they appear in an academic advising session, even though participants' relationships and roles are the same (i.e. teacher and student). The task for L2 learners involves developing linguistic and interactional abilities to signal boundaries between different discourse practices and to shift between different situations by using linguistic and interactional resources to their advantage. This study examined learners' style-shifting between segments of conversation involving different participant configuration (i.e. one-to-one conversation between peers versus multi-party interaction involving the researcher), but given that the group-level change in style-shifting over these conversational segments was rather negligible, it is possible that the task used in this study was not able to make boundaries explicit across segments. Future research can be more creative in designing a task that reveals L2 learners' ability to move between multiple boundaries and discourse practices. Such a study will also help to discover what interactional resources are specific to practice, and to what extent those resources are shared with other practices.

Finally, interpretations of the participants' interactional development in relation to their sociocultural experiences in the local community were somewhat limited because of the narrow range of the qualitative data collected in this study. Although the study was designed to seek explanations for the individual variations found in the conversation data, three interviews were probably not sufficient to reveal the quality of social contact and involvement among individual learners. In addition, this study relied solely on self-reported data (i.e. interviews); this data should be complemented with observation and field notes to increase the validity of the conclusions drawn from the data. Future research should commit to data triangulation by using a variety of methods such as journals, questionnaires, and interviews to document learners' participation in context and their interactional development. Based on the notion that language use and language development take place as learners participate in social interactions, it is important to discern both – change in linguistic ability and change in social interactions. Future research should focus on this link by attending to how linguistic changes occur through changing social relationships, contact, and participation. Through the process of synthesizing a body of triangulated data, an interesting portrayal will emerge regarding the opportunities for interactional practice, learners' stances in accessing and making use of these opportunities, and context- and learner-specific factors that facilitate or constrain such access.

Appendix A

Transcription Conventions

(3.2)	timed pause longer than 1.0 second
hh	out-breath
.hh	in-breath
hehh, hahh	laughter syllables
wo(h)rd	(h) laughter within words
((sniff))	non-speech sound, non-verbal action, description
cu-	cut-off
lo:ng	stretch
(word)	unclear word
( )	unclear speech with no approximation
run=	run on/latch
=on	
¿	rising intonation
.	falling intonation
,	slightly rising intonation
:	stretch
under	emphasis (dotted underline)
°soft°	softer speech
>fast<	faster speech
<slow>	slower speech
over[lap [overlap	overlap
…	omission
kimasu	polite (*desu/masu*) form
kuru	plain form
hanashite	incomplete sentence ending
COP	various forms of copula verb *be*
LK	linking nominal
NEG	negative morpheme
PST	past tense

PROG	progressive aspect
NOM	nominalizer
O	object marker
SUB	subject marker
Q	question marker
QT	quotative marker
FP	sentence final particle
CP	conjunctive particle
TOP	topic marker
DM	discourse marker, fillers
TE	te-form (conjunctive particle *te*
AUX	auxiliary verb
LOC	locative
HES	hesitation
RES	resultive aspect

Appendix B

Conversation Task

Directions: You will have an informal, casual conversation with a same-age, close friend peer for about 20 minutes.

Talk about your life and experience in Japan, for example:

- Your classes, routine, hobbies, weekend activities, travels, etc.
- Things you like and don't like about Japan.
- Similarities and differences between Japan and your country.

Notes

- Your conversation should be all in Japanese.
- Even if you experience difficulty with speaking, try to continue conversation as much as possible until you are told to stop.
- You and your partner should have equal contribution to conversation. You should not dominate the conversation or be dominated in the conversation. Participate actively and collaboratively.
- The conversation will be between you and your partner, but the researcher will join the conversation occasionally.
- Use a variety of conversation strategies, for example: stating opinions, soliciting opinions, asking and responding to questions, commenting on your partner's responses, asking for clarification, and changing topics.

Appendix C

Motivation Survey
(adapted from Fantini, 2005)

1. What was your level of interest and motivation toward Japan during this semester?

		extremely low	extremely high
a.	Before arriving in Japan	1 ------ 2 ------ 3 ------ 4 ------ 5
b.	Upon first entering Japan	1 ------ 2 ------ 3 ------ 4 ------ 5
c.	Mid-way through this semester	1 ------ 2 ------ 3 ------ 4 ------ 5
d.	Now	1 ------ 2 ------ 3 ------ 4 ------ 5

2. How would you characterize your motivation toward the host culture while in Japan? Indicate the level of your agreement/disagreement with each statement below.

		strongly disagree	strongly agree
a.	I sometimes wanted to return home.	1 ---- 2 ---- 3 ---- 4 ---- 5
b.	I felt I was not learning very much.	1 ---- 2 ---- 3 ---- 4 ---- 5
c.	I tried to survive as best I could.	1 ---- 2 ---- 3 ---- 4 ---- 5
d.	I desired to get along well with Japanese people.	1 ---- 2 ---- 3 ---- 4 ---- 5
e.	I desired to adjust to Japan as best I could.	1 ---- 2 ---- 3 ---- 4 ---- 5

Appendix D

Japanese Contact Survey

- The questions below ask about your experience with using Japanese in your daily activities. Please reflect on your activities in the past few weeks, and respond to the questions by circling the numbers.

1. How much time do you spend communicating in Japanese with your teachers outside of class?	Typically, how many days per week? 0 1 2 3 4 5 6 7 On those days, typically how many hours per day? 0 0-1 1-2 2-3 4-5 more than 5
2. How much time do you spend communicating in Japanese with your classmates, friends or host family outside of class?	Typically, how many days per week? 0 1 2 3 4 5 6 7 On those days, typically how many hours per day? 0 0-1 1-2 2-3 4-5 more than 5
3. How much time do you spend in communicating with service personnel in Japanese?	Typically, how many days per week? 0 1 2 3 4 5 6 7 On those days, typically how many hours per day? 0 0-1 1-2 2-3 4-5 more than 5
4. How much time do you use Japanese outside the classroom for class-related things?	Typically, how many days per week? 0 1 2 3 4 5 6 7 On those days, typically how many hours per day? 0 0-1 1-2 2-3 4-5 more than 5
5. How much time do you use Japanese outside the classroom for non-class-related things?	Typically, how many days per week? 0 1 2 3 4 5 6 7 On those days, typically how many hours per day? 0 0-1 1-2 2-3 4-5 more than 5
6. How much time do you spend reading Japanese newspapers, magazines, books or other materials outside of class?	Typically, how many days per week? 0 1 2 3 4 5 6 7 On those days, typically how many hours per day? 0 0-1 1-2 2-3 4-5 more than 5

7. How much time do you spend on emails or internet in Japanese outside of class?	Typically, how many days per week? 0 1 2 3 4 5 6 7 On those days, typically how many hours per day? 0 0–1 1–2 2–3 4–5 more than 5
8. How much time do you spend watching movies, TV, DVD or other audio-visual materials in Japanese outside of class?	Typically, how many days per week? 0 1 2 3 4 5 6 7 On those days, typically how many hours per day? 0 0–1 1–2 2–3 4–5 more than 5
9. How much time do you spend writing essays, homework assignments or other materials outside of class?	Typically, how many days per week? 0 1 2 3 4 5 6 7 On those days, typically how many hours per day? 0 0–1 1–2 2–3 4–5 more than 5
10. Do you use Japanese in the activities other than the ones listed above? If so, which activity and how much time did you spend? Activity	Typically, how many days per week? 0 1 2 3 4 5 6 7 On those days, typically how many hours per day? 0 0–1 1–2 2–3 4–5 more than 5

(1) Do you take classes with Japanese students? If so, how many hours per week? What is the medium of instruction in those classes, Japanese, English, or other language(s)?
(2) How many close friends do you have in Japan? Of which, how many are Japanese people?
(3) With whom in what occasions do you speak Japanese most? List all. Write who and what kind of communication. (e.g. I speak Japanese most with my host brother when helping his math homework.)

Appendix E

Proportion of the Utterance-Ending Forms by Individuals: Polite Forms, Plain Forms and Incomplete Endings

Learner ID	Test	Polite (%)	Plain (%)	Incomplete	Total number of utterances
A	Pre-test	64.0	36.0	0	86
	Post-test	11.1	79.8	9.1	99
B	Pre-test	43.8	56.3	0	48
	Post-test	28.4	49.3	18.8	73
C	Pre-test	44.0	44.0	12.0	84
	Post-test	6.8	68.2	25.0	88
D	Pre-test	69.5	25.2	5.3	131
	Post-test	11.6	70.5	17.9	95
E	Pre-test	23.9	73.1	3.0	67
	Post-test	1.9	77.6	20.6	107
F	Pre-test	60.8	35.3	3.9	51
	Post-test	6.1	68.3	25.6	82
G	Pre-test	43.1	56.9	0	72
	Post-test	43.5	42.4	14.1	92
H	Pre-test	9.7	82.8	7.5	93
	Post-test	10.2	66.9	22.9	157
I	Pre-test	42.6	46.8	10.6	94
	Post-test	5.3	67.4	27.4	95
J	Pre-test	53.7	35.5	10.7	121
	Post-test	5.7	78.7	15.6	122
K	Pre-test	19.1	71.3	9.6	94
	Post-test	1.2	79.8	19.0	163

L	Pre-test	32.0	64.0	4.0	75
	Post-test	8.5	78.3	13.2	129
M	Pre-test	35.5	61.3	3.2	93
	Post-test	26.8	65.0	8.1	123
N	Pre-test	58.1	38.5	3.4	117
	Post-test	20.6	70.6	8.8	136
O	Pre-test	58.0	35.2	6.8	88
	Post-test	20.4	62.1	17.5	103
P	Pre-test	48.9	40.4	10.6	94
	Post-test	23.7	57.0	19.4	93
Q	Pre-test	80.0	18.8	1.2	85
	Post-test	23.1	57.7	19.2	78
R	Pre-test	83.7	16.3	0	43
	Post-test	17.9	69.0	13.1	84

Note. The learners (A-R) formed a pair and had a 20-minute conversation.

References

Atkinson, D., Churchill, E., Nishino, T. and Okada, H. (2007) Alignment and interaction in a socio-cognitive approach to second language acquisition. *Modern Language Journal* 91 (2), 169–188.
Atsuzawa-Windley, S. and Noguchi, S. (1995) Effects of in-country experience on the acquisition of oral communication skills in Japanese. *Australian Review of Applied Linguistics* 12 (1), 83–98.
Bachman, L.F. (1990) *Fundamental Considerations in Language Testing*. New York: Oxford University Press.
Bachman, L.F. and Palmer, A.S. (1996) *Language Testing in Practice: Designing and Developing Useful Language Tests*. Oxford: Oxford University Press.
Bachman, L.F. and Palmer, A.S. (2010) *Language Testing in Practice*. Oxford: Oxford University Press.
Barron, A. (2003) *Acquisition in Interlanguage Pragmatics: Learning How To Do Things with Words in A Study Abroad Context*. Amsterdam/Philadelphia, John Benjamins.
Brown, L. (2013) Identity and honorifics use in Korean study abroad. In C. Kinginger (ed.) *Social and Cultural Dimensions of Language Learning in Study Abroad* (pp. 269–298). Amsterdam: John Benjamins.
Byram, M. (1997) *Teaching and Assessing Intercultural Communicative Competence*. Philadelphia: Multilingual Matters.
Caltabiano, Y.M. (2008) Consequences of shifting styles in Japanese: L2 style-shifting and L1 listeners' attitudes. In M. Bowles, R. Foote, S. Perpinan and R. Bhatt (eds) *Selected Proceedings of the 2007 Second Language Research Forum* (pp. 131–143). Somerville, MA: Cascadilla Proceedings Project. See www.lingref.com, document #1740.
Canale, M. and Swain, M. (1980) Theoretical aspects of communicative approaches to second language teaching and testing. *Applied Linguistics* 1 (1), 1–47.
Chen, W-M. (2000) Incomplete speech in Japanese native speakers' conversations]. *Kotobato Bunka* [language and culture], 125–141.
Chen, W-M. (2004) The speech style shift in the initial encounter between advanced Taiwanese learners of Japanese and native Japanese speakers: A comparison with conversations by native Japanese speakers. *Nihongo kyoikuronsyuu* [Journal of Japanese Language Education] 20, 18–33.
Churchill, E. (2003) Competing for the floor in the American home: Japanese students sharing host families. *Kanagawa University Studies in Language* 25, 185–202.
Clancy, P. (1985) The acquisition of Japanese. In D.I. Slobin (ed.) *The Crosslinguistic Study of Language Acquisition* (vol. 1, pp. 373–524). Hillsdale, NJ: Lawrence Erlbaum.
Collentine, J. (2004) The effects of learning contexts on morphosyntactic and lexical development. *Studies in Second Language Acquisition* 26 (2), 227–248.
Collentine, J. and Freed, B. (2004) Learning contexts and its effects on second language acquisition. Special issue. *Studies in Second Language Acquisition Special issue* 26 (2).

Cook, H.M. (1996) The use of addressee honorifics in Japanese elementary school classrooms. In N. Akatsuka, S. Iwasaki and S. Strauss (eds) *Japanese/Korean Linguistics 5* (pp. 67–81). CSLI Publication: Stanford.

Cook, H. (1999) Situational meanings of Japanese social deixis: The mixed use of the *masu* and plain forms. *Journal of Linguistic Anthropology* 8 (1-2), 87–110.

Cook, H. (2001) Why can't learners of JFL distinguish polite form from impolite speech styles? In K. Rose and G. Kasper (eds) *Pragmatics in Language Teaching* (pp. 80–102). Cambridge: Cambridge University Press.

Cook, H.M. (2002) The social meanings of the Japanese plain form. In N. Akatsuka and S. Strauss (eds) *Japanese/Korean Linguistics* 10 (pp. 150–163). Stanford: CSLI Publications.

Cook, H. (2006) Japanese politeness as an interactional achievement: Academic consultation sessions in Japanese universities. *Multilingua* 25 (3), 269–292.

Cook, H. (2008) *Socializing Identities Through Speech Style*. Bristol: Multilingual Matters.

Dewey, D. (2004) A comparison of reading development by learners of Japanese in intensive domestic immersion and study abroad contexts. *Studies in Second Language Acquisition* 26 (2), 303–327.

Dewey, D. (2008) Japanese vocabulary acquisition by learners in three contexts. *Frontiers, 15* (Fall/Winter), 127–148.

Diao, W. (in press) Peer socialization into gendered Mandarin practices in a study abroad context: Talk in the dorm. *Applied Linguistics*.

Diao, W. and Freed, B. (2012) Confirmed beliefs of false assumptions: A study of home stay experiences in the French study abroad context. *Frontiers: The Interdisciplinary Journal of Study Abroad* 21 (Fall), 109–142.

Dings, A. (2014) Interactional competence and the development of alignment activity. *Modern Language Journal* 98 (3), 742–756.

Duff, P. (2007) Second language socialization as sociocultural theory: Insights and issues. *Language Teaching* 40 (4), 309–319.

DuFon, M. (2010) The socialization of leave-taking in L2 Indonesian. In G. Kasper, H.T. Nguyen and D.R. Yoshimi (eds) *Pragmatics and Language Learning* (vol. 12, pp. 91–112). Honolulu, HI: University of Hawaii National Language Resource Center.

DuFon, M. and Churchill, E. (2006) *Language Learners in a Study Abroad Context*. Clevedon: Multilingual Matters.

Fantini, A.E. (2005) *Assessing Intercultural Competence: A Research Project of the Federation EIL*. Brattleboro, VT: Federation EIL.

Fantini, A.E. (2006) Exploring and assessing intercultural competence. Retrieved February 15, 2012, from http://www.sit.edu/publications/docs/feil_research_report.pdf

Fantini, A.E. (2012) Multiple strategies for assessing intercultural communicative competence. Language: an essential component of intercultural competence. In J. Jackson (ed.) *The Routledge Handbook of Language and Intercultural Communication* (pp. 390–406). Oxford: Routledge.

Freed, B.F. (1990) Language learning in a study abroad context: The effects of interactive and non-interactive out-of-class contact on grammatical achievement and oral proficiency. In J. Altas (ed.) *Linguistics, Language Teaching and Language Acquisition: The Interdependence of Theory, Practice and Research* (pp. 459–477). Washington, DC: Georgetown University Press.

Freed, B. (1995a) *Second Language Acquisition in a Study Abroad Context*. Amsterdam: John Benjamins.

Freed, B. (1995b) What makes us think that students who study abroad become fluent? In B. Freed (ed.) *Second Language Acquisition in a Study Abroad Context* (pp. 123–148). Amsterdam: John Benjamins.

Freed, B. (1998) Language learning in a study abroad context. Special issue. *Frontiers* 4.

Freed, B., Dewey, D. and Segalowitz, N. (2004) The language contact profile. *Studies in Second Language Acquisition* 26 (2), 349–356.

Fukushima, E. (2007) On the topic of mixed style of *desu/masu* form and non-*desu/masu* form – Taigu communication among Japanese business people. *Waseda daigaku Nihongo kyoikugaku* [*Waseda University Study of Japanese Language Education*] 138, 24–32.

Gee, J.P. (2004) *Situated Language and Learning: A Critique of Traditional Schooling*. New York: Routledge.

Geyer, N. (2013) Discernment and variation: The action-oriented use of Japanese addressee honorifics. *Multilingua* 32, 155–176.

Goffman, E. (1979) Footing. *Semiotica* 25 (1), 1–29.

Hall, J.K. (1993) The role of oral practices in the accomplishment of our everyday lives: The sociocultural dimension of interaction with implications for the learning of another language. *Applied Linguistics* 14 (2), 145–167.

Hall, J.K. (1995) Aw, man, where you goin? Classroom interaction and the development of L2 interactional competence. *Issues in Applied Linguistics* 6 (2), 37–62.

Hall, J.K. and Doehler, P.S. (2011) L2 interactional competence and development. In J.K. Hall, J. Hellermann and P.S. Doehler (eds) *L2 Interactional Competence and Development* (pp. 1–18). Bristol: Multilingual Matters.

Hall, J.K., Hellermann, J. and Doehler, S.P. (2011) *L2 Interactional Competence and Development*. Bristol: Multilingual Matters.

Hammer, M.R., Bennett, M.J. and Wiseman, R. (2003) Measuring intercultural sensitivity: The intercultural development inventory. *International Journal of Intercultural Relations* 27 (4), 421–443.

Harada, S-I. (1976) Honorifics. In M. Shibatani (ed.) *Syntax and Semantics 5: Japanese Generative Grammar* (pp. 499–561). New York: Academic Press.

Hashimoto, H. (1993) Language acquisition of an exchange student within the homestay environment. *Journal of Asian Pacific Communication* 4 (2), 209–224.

Hashimoto, Y. (2007) Clause chaining, turn projection and marking of participation: Functions of TE in turn co-construction in Japanese conversation. In Y. Takubo, T. Kinuhara, S. Grzelak and K. Nagai (eds) *Japanese/Korean Linguistics* (vol. 16, pp. 250–265). Stanford, CA: CSLI Publications.

Hassall, T. (2013) Pragmatic development during short-term study abroad: The case of address terms in Indonesian. *Journal of Pragmatics* 55 (1), 1–17.

Hayashi, M. (2003) *Joint Utterance Construction in Japanese Conversation*. Amsterdam/Philadelphia: John Benjamins.

Hayashi, M. (2013) Turn allocation and turn sharing. In J. Sindnell and T. Stivers (eds) *The Handbook of Conversation Analysis* (pp. 167–190). Malden, MA: Blackwell.

Hayashi, M. (2014) Activity, participation, and joint turn construction: A conversation analytic exploration of 'grammar-in-action.' In K. Kabata and T. Ono (eds) *Usage-based Approaches to Japanese Grammar: Toward the Understanding of Human Language* (pp. 223–258). Amsterdam: John Benjamins.

Hayashi, M. and Mori, J. (1998) Co-construction in Japanese revisited: We DO 'finish each other's sentences.' In N. Akatsuka, H. Hoji, S. Iwasaki and S. Strauss (eds) *Japanese/Korean Linguistics* (vol. 7, pp. 77–93). Stanford: CSLI Publications.

Hellermann, J. (2008) *Social Actions for Classroom Language Learning*. Clevedon: Multilingual Matters.

Hellermann, J. (2009) Practices for dispreferred responses using *no* by a learner of English. *International Review of Applied Linguistics* 47 (2), 95–126.

Hellermann, J. (2011) Members' methods, members' competencies: Looking for evidence of language learning in longitudinal investigations. In J.K. Hall, J. Hellermann and P.S. Doehler (eds) *L2 Interactional Competence and Development* (pp. 147–172). Bristol: Multilingual Matters.

Hernandez, T.A. (2010) The relationship among motivation, interaction, and the development of second language oral proficiency in a study-abroad context. *The Modern Language Journal* 94 (4), 600–617.

Huebner, T. (1995) The effects of overseas language programs: Report on a case study of an intensive Japanese course. In B. Freed (ed.) *Second Language Acquisition in a Study Abroad Context* (pp. 171–194). Amsterdam: John Benjamins.

Hymes, H.D. (1972) On communicative competence. In J.B. Pride and J. Holmes (eds) *Sociolinguisitics: Selected Readings* (pp. 269–293). Middlesex, Harmondsworh: Penguin.

Iino, M. (1996) 'Excellent foreigner!': Gaijinization of Japanese language and culture in contact situations: An ethnographic study of dinner table conversations between Japanese host families and American students. Unpublished doctoral dissertation, University of Pennsylvania, Philadelphia.

Ikuta, S. (1983) Speech level shift and conversational strategy in Japanese discourses. *Language Science* 5 (1), 37–53.

Ikuta, S. (2008) Speech style shift as an interactional discourse strategy: The use and non-use of *desu/masu* in Japanese conversational interviews. In K. Jones and T. Ono (eds) *Style Shifting in Japanese* (pp. 71–89). Amsterdam: John Benjamins.

Isabelli-Garcia, C. (2006) Study abroad social networks, motivation and attitudes: Implications for second language acquisition. In M.A. DuFon and E. Churchill (eds) *Language Learners in Study Abroad Contexts* (pp. 231–258). Clevedon: Multilingual Matters.

Ishida, K. (2009) Indexing stance in interaction with Japanese *desu/masu* and plain forms. In N. Taguchi (ed.) *Pragmatic Competence* (pp. 41–68). Berlin/New York: Mouton de Gruyter.

Ishida, M. (2009) Development of interactional competence: Changes in the use of *ne* in L2 Japanese during study abroad. In H.T. Nguyen and G. Kasper (eds) *Talk-in-Interaction: Multilingual Perspectives* (pp. 41–68). Honolulu: University of Hawai'i, National Foreign Language Resource Center.

Ishida, M. (2011) Engaging in another person's telling as a recipient in L2 Japanese: Development of interactional competence during one-year study-abroad. In G. Pallotti and J. Wagner (eds) *L2 Learning as Social Practice: Conversation-Analytic Perspectives* (pp. 45–85). Honolulu: University of Hawai'i, National Foreign Language Resource Center.

Iwasaki, S. (1993) *Subjectivity in Grammar and Discourse: Theoretical Considerations and a Case Study of Japanese Spoken Discourse*. Amsterdam: John Benjamins.

Iwasaki, N. (2010) Style shifts among Japanese learners before and after study abroad in Japan: Becoming active social agents in Japanese. *Applied Linguistics* 31 (1), 45–71.

Iwasaki, N. (2011) Learning L2 Japanese "politeness" and "impoliteness": Young American mean's dilemmas during study abroad. *Japanese Language and Literature* 45 (1), 67–106.

Iwasaki, S. and Ono, T. (2007) Kaiwakenkyuuu kara kizukareru bunpoo no sekai [The World of Grammar based on Study of Conversation]. *Gengo* [*Language*], 36, 24–29.

Jones, K. and Ono, T. (eds) (2008) *Style Shifting in Japanese*. Amsterdam: John Benjamins.

Kinginger, C. (2008) Language learning in study abroad: Case studies of Americans in France. *Modern Language Journal, Special issue*, 92.

Kinginger, C. (2009) *Language Learning and Study Abroad: A Critical Reading of Research*. Basingstoke: Palgrave Macmillan.

Kinginger, C. (2011) Enhancing language learning in study abroad. *Annual Review of Applied Linguistics* 31, 58–73.

Kinginger, C. (2013) *Social and Cultural Aspects of Language Learning in Study Abroad*. Amsterdam/New York: John Benjamins.

Kinginger, C. and Farrell, K. (2004) Assessing development of meta-pragmatic awareness in study abroad. *Frontiers: The Interdisciplinary Journal of Study Abroad* 10 (Fall), 19–42.

Knight, S.M. and Schmidt-Rinehart, B.C. (2002) Enhancing the homestay: Study abroad from the host family's perspective. *Foreign Language Annals* 35 (2), 190–201.

Kuno, S. (1973) *The Structure of The Japanese Language*. Cambridge, MA: MIT Press.

Larsen-Freeman, D. and Cameron, L. (2009) *Complex Systems and Applied Linguistics*. Oxford: Oxford University Press.

Lave, J. and Wenger, E. (1991) *Situated Learning: Legitimate Peripheral Participation*. Cambridge: Cambridge University Press.

Lerner, G. (1996) On the 'semi-permeable' character of grammatical units in conversation: Condition entry into the turn-space of another speaker. In E. Ochs, E.A. Schegloff and S. Thompson (eds) *Interaction and Grammar* (pp. 238–276). Carmbridge: Cambridge University Press.

Lerner, G. (2004) Collaborative turn sequences. In G. Lerner (ed.) *Conversation Analysis: Studies From the First Generation* (pp. 225–256). Amsterdam/Philadelphia: John Benjamins.

Llanes, A. (2010) Children and adults learning English in a study abroad context. Unpublished doctoral dissertation. Universitat de Bercelona.

Llanes, A. (2011) The many faces of study abroad: An update on the research on L2 gains emerged during a study abroad experience. *International Journal of Multilingualism* 8 (3), 189–215.

Llanes, A. and Munoz, C. (2009) A short stay abroad: Does it make a difference? *System* 37 (3), 353–365.

Makino, S. (2002) When does communication turn mentally inward: A case study of Japanese formal-to-informal switching. In N. Akatsuka and S. Strauss (eds) *Japanese/Korean Linguistics* (vol. 10, pp. 121–135). Stanford, CA: CSLI Publications.

Makino, S. and Tsutsui, M. (1986) *A Dictionary of Basic Japanese Grammar*. Tokyo: The Japan Times.

Markee, N. (2008) Toward a learning behavior tracking methodology for CA-for-SLA. *Applied Linguistics* 29 (3), 404–427.

Marriott, H. (1993) Acquiring sociolinguistic competence: Australian secondary students in Japan. *Journal of Asian Pacific Communication* 4 (2), 167–192.

Marriot, H. (1995) The acquisition of politeness patterns by exchange students in Japan. In B. Freed (ed.) *Second Language Acquisition in a Study Abroad Context* (pp. 197–224). Amsterdam: Benjamins.

Marriott, H. and Enomoto, S. (1995) Secondary exchanges with Japan: Exploring students' exchanges and gains. *Australian Review of Applied Linguistics* 12 (1), 64–82.

Masuda, K. (2010) Acquiring interactional competence in a study abroad context: Japanese language learners' use of the interactional particle *ne*. *Modern Language Journal* 95 (4), 519–540.

Masuda, K. (2011) *Nihongo gakusshuusha no buntai shifuto nitsuite* [Japanese learners' style-shifting]. In M. Minami (ed.) *Gengogakuto nihongokyoiku* [Linguistics and Japanese Education] (vol. 6, pp. 191–212). Tokyo: Kuroshio.

Matsumoto, K. (1995) Fragmentation in conversational Japanese: A case study. *JALT Journal* 17 (2), 238–253.

Matsumura, S. (2001) Learning the rules for offering advice: A quantitative approach to second language socialization. *Language Learning* 51 (4), 635–679.

Maynard, S.K. (1989) *Japanese Conversation*. Norwood: Ablex Publishing Corporation.

Maynard, S.K. (1991) Pragmatics of discourse modality: A case of da and *desu/masu* form in Japanese. *Journal of Pragmatics* 15 (6), 551–582.

Maynard S.K. (1993) *Discourse Modality: Subjectivity, Emotion, and Voice in The Japanese Language*. Amsterdam: John Benjamins.

McMeekin, A.L. (2007) Learners of Japanese and socialization through expert-novice negotiation in a study abroad setting. Paper presented at the 17th Conference on Pragmatics and Language Learning. Honolulu, Hawaii.
McMeekin, A.L. (2011) Japanese L2 learners' use and acquisition of the plain form during study abroad. A paper presented at the meeting of the American Association for Applied Linguistics. Chicago: IL.
Mendelson, V.G. (2004) Spain or bust? Assessment and student perceptions of out-of-class contact and oral proficiency in a study abroad context. Unpublished doctoral dissertation. University of Massachusetts, Amherst.
Miyazaki, S. (2007) *Japanese women's listening behavior in face-to-face conversation.* Tokyo: Hitsuji Shobo.
Nazkian, F. (2010) *Interviewdanwaniokeru jyotaino kino* [Functions of plain form in interview]. In M. Minami (ed.) *Gengogakuto Nihongokyoiku* [*Linguistics and Japanese Education*] (vol. V, pp. 141–173). Tokyo: Kuroshio.
Nguyen, H.T. (2011a) A longitudinal microanalysis of a second language learner's participation. In G. Pallotti and J. Wagner (eds) *L2 Learning as Social Practice: Conversation-Analytic Perspectives* (pp. 17–44). Honolulu: University of Hawai'i, National Foreign Language Resource Center.
Nguyen, H.T. (2011b) Achieving recipient design longitudinally: Evidence from a pharmacy intern in patient consultations. In In J.K. Hall, J. Hellermann and P.S. Doehler (eds) *L2 Interactional Competence and Development* (pp. 173–205). Bristol: Multilingual Matters.
Niyekawa, A. (1991) *Minimum Essential Politeness: A Guide to the Japanese Honorific Language.* Tokyo: Kodansha International.
Nofsinger, R.E. (1991) *Everyday Conversation.* Thousand Oaks, CA: SAGE.
Nomura, J. (2007) Japanese postposing as an indicator of emerging discourse pragmatics. *BUCLD (Boston University Conference on Language Development) Proceeding* 31, 1–9.
Ochs, E. (1996) Linguistic resources for socializing humanity. In J. Gumperz and S. Levinson (eds) *Rethinking Linguistic Relativity* (pp. 407–437). Cambridge: Cambridge University Press.
Ohta, A. (2001) *Second Language Acquisition Processes in the Classroom: Learning Japanese.* Mahwah, NJ: Lawrence Erlbaum.
Okamoto, S. (1999) Situated politeness: Manipulating honorific and non-honorific expressions in Japanese conversation. *Pragmatics* 9 (1), 51–74.
Okamoto, S. (2011) The use and interpretations of addressee honorifics and plain forms in Japanese: Diversity, multiplicity, and ambiguity. *Journal of Pragmatics* 43, 3673–3688.
Olson, C.L. and Kroeger, K.R. (2001) Global competency and intercultural sensitivity. *Journal of Studies in International Education* 5 (2), 116–137.
Ono, T. and Suzuki, R. (1992) Word order variability in Japanese conversation: Motivations and grammaticization. *Text* 12 (3), 429–445.
Polanyi, L. (1995) Language learning and living abroad: Stories from the field. In B. Freed (ed.) *Second Language Acquisition in a Study Abroad Context* (pp. 271–291). Amsterdam/Philadelphia: John Benjamins.
Regan, V., Howard, M. and Lemée, I. (2009) *The Acquisition of Sociolinguistic Competence in a Study Abroad Context.* Bristol: Multilingual Matters.
Rine, E.F. and Hall, J.K. (2011) Becoming the teacher: Changing participant frameworks in international teaching assistant discourse. In J.K. Hall, J. Hellermann and P.S. Doehler (eds) *L2 Interactional Competence and Development* (pp. 244–274). Bristol: Multilingual Matters.
Sacks, H. (1995) *Lectures on Conversation.* Oxford: Blackwell Publishing.
Sacks, H., Schegloff, E. and Jefferson, G. (1974) A simplest systematics for the organization of turn-taking for conversation. *Language* 50 (4), 696–735.

Saito, J. (2010) Subordinates' use of Japanese plain forms: An examination of superior–subordinate interactions in the workplace. *Journal of Pragmatics* 42 (12), 3271–3282.

Schauer, G. (2006) Pragmatic awareness in ESL and EFL contexts: Contrast and development. *Language Learning* 56 (2), 269–318.

Schegloff, E.A. (1996) Turn organization: One intersection of grammar and interaction. In E. Ochs, E.A. Schegloff and S.A. Thompson (eds) *Interaction and Grammar* (pp. 52–133). Cambridge: Cambridge University Press.

Schegloff, E.A. (2007) *Sequence Organization in Interaction*. Cambridge: Cambridge University.

Schegloff, E.l A., Jefferson, G. and Sacks, H. (1977) The preference for self-correction in the organization of repair in conversation. *Language* 53, 361–382.

Schieffelin, B.B. and Ochs, E. (1986) *Language Socialization Across Cultures*. Cambridge, Cambridge University Press.

Schmidt-Rinehart, B.C. and Knight, S.M. (2004) The homestay component of study abroad: Three perspectives. *Foreign Language Annals* 37, 254–262.

Segalowitz, N. and Freed, B. (2004) Context, contact, and cognition in oral fluency acquisition: Learning Spanish in at home and study abroad contexts. *Studies in Second Language Acquisition* 26 (2), 173–199.

Shibatani, M. (1990) *The Languages of Japan*. Cambridge: Cambridge University Press.

Shimojo, M. (1995) Focus structure and morphosyntax in Japanese: Wa and ga, and word order flexibility. Unpublished doctoral dissertation, State University of New York at Buffalo.

Shively, R. (2011) L2 pragmatic development in study abroad: A longitudinal study of Spanish service encounters. *Journal of Pragmatics* 43, 1818–1835.

Shively, R. (2013) Learning to be funny in Spanish study abroad: L2 humor development. *Modern Language Journal* 97 (7), 939–946.

Siegal, M. (1994) Learning Japanese as a second language in Japan and the interaction of race, gender, and social context. Unpublished doctoral dissertation, University of California-Berkeley.

Simon, M.E. (1989) An analysis of the postposing construction in Japanese. Unpublished doctoral dissertation, University of Michigan.

Sindnell, J. (2010) *Conversation Analysis: An Introduction*. Malden, MA: Blackwell.

Tadokoro, K. (2012) Speech level education in first time conversations – focus on language and consciousness]. *Taigu komyunikeshon kenkyuu* [*Taigu Communication Research*] 9, 81–96.

Taguchi, N. (in press) Cross-cultural adaptability and development of speech act production in study abroad. *International Journal of Applied Linguistics*.

Taguchi, N. (2011) The effect of L2 proficiency and study-abroad experience in pragmatic comprehension. *Language Learning* 61 (3), 904–939.

Taguchi, N. (2014) Development of interactional competence in Japanese as a second language: Use of incomplete sentences as interactional resources. *Modern Language Journal* 98 (2), 518–535.

Taguchi, N., Li, S. and Xiao, F. (2013) Production of formulaic expressions in L2 Chinese: A developmental investigation in a study abroad context. *Chinese as a Second Language Research Journal* 2 (1), 23–58.

Takahara, P. and Peng, F.C. (1981) Gojun toochi. In F.C. Peng (ed.) *Nihongo no Danjosa: Male-female Difference in Japanese* (pp. 97–115). Tokyo: The East-West Sign Language Association.

Talburt, S. and Stewart, M.A. (1999) What's the subject of study abroad? Race, gender, and 'living culture.' *Modern Language Journal* 83 (2), 163–175.

Tanaka, H. (1999) *Turn-Taking in Japanese Conversation: A Study in Grammar and Interaction*. Amsterdam: Benjamins.

Tanaka, K. (2004) Changes in Japanese students' beliefs about language Learning and English language proficiency in a study-abroad context. Unpublished doctoral dissertation, New Zealand: University of Auckland.

Tracy, K. (2002) *Everyday Talk: Building and Reflecting Identities*. New York: The Guilford Press.

Tomiyama, Y. (2009) Progress in acquisition of Japanese discourse structures from intermediate to advanced level learners. Unpublished doctoral dissertation, University of California at Los Angeles.

Uenaka, A. (1997) Intermediate/advanced learners' speech level and speech level shift – comparison with native Japanese speakers. *Nihongo kyoiku ronbnsyuu [Journal of Japanese Language Education]*, 149–165.

Usami, M. (1995) Honorifics from the point of discourse level – conditions and functions of speech level shifting. *Gakuon* 662, 27–42.

Wenger, E. (1998) *Communities of Practice: Learning, Meaning and Identity*. Cambridge: Cambridge University Press.

Wilkinson, S. (1998) On the nature of immersion during study abroad: Some participant perspectives. *Frontiers: The Interdisciplinary Journal of Study Abroad* 4, 121–138.

Wilkinson, S. (2002) The amnipresent classroom during study abroad: American students in conversation with their French hosts. *Modern Language Journal* 86 (1), 157–173.

Yagi, K. (2007) The development of interactional competence in a situated practice by Japanese learners of English as a second language. *Hawaii Pacific University TESL Working Paper Series*, 5.

Yoshimi, D.R. (1999) L1 language socialization as a variable in the use of *ne* by L2 learners of Japanese. *Journal of Pragmatics* 31 (11), 1513–1525.

Young, R. (2002) Discourse approaches to oral language assessment. *Annual Review of Applied Linguistics* 19, 105–132.

Young, R.F. (2007) Language learning and teaching as discursive practice. In Z. Hua, P. Seedhouse, W. Li and V. Cook (eds) *Language Learning and Teaching as Social Interaction* (pp. 251–271). Basingstoke & New York: Palgrave Macmillan.

Young, R. (2008a) *Language and Interaction: Advanced Resource Book*. Oxford: Routledge

Young, R. (2008b) *Discursive Practices in Language Learning and Teaching*. Malden, MA and Oxford: Wiley-Blackwell.

Young, R. (2011) Interactional competence in language learning, teaching, and testing. In H. Hinkel (ed.) *Handbook of Research in Language Learning and Teaching* (pp. 426–443). New York: Routledge.

Young, R. and He, A.W. (1998) *Talking and Testing: Discourse Approaches to the Assessment of Oral Proficiency*. Amsterdam: John Benjamins.

Young, R. and Miller, E.R. (2004) Learning as changing participation: Negotiating discourse roles in the ESL writing conference. *Modern Language Journal* 88 (4), 519–535.

Index

activity types, 5, 37
addressee honorifics, 10
affect keys, 13–14, 41–42, 65–68, 71, 82, 147
affective stance, 14, 19, 41
agency, 18, 35
alignment, 2, 14, 28–29, 80, 88, 93, 104–107, 149, 156
assisted explanation, 99, 106–108, 149–150

Bachman & Palmer, 1, 3–4, 145
boundaries, 2, 4, 8–9, 12, 13, 24, 39, 84, 85, 91, 96–97, 114, 146–150, 156, 157

Canale & Swain, 3, 4
coalescence, 13–14, 43, 66–67, 82, 148
co-construction of turn, 25, 28, 108, 149
collaborative turn construction, 99, 101, 108, 113
communication strategies, 22, 69, 137, 144, 155
communicative competence, 1–10, 12, 20, 24, 27
communicative events, 5, 37
community of practice, 33
context-learning connection, 32, 155
contextual affordances, 36
contextual dynamics, 14, 135, 153
contextual parameters, 18–19, 150, 153
contextual specifics, 12, 19–20, 84, 97, 136, 147, 156
Cook, 10, 12–20, 23, 33, 40–43, 65–66, 85, 98, 124, 129, 136, 146–148, 154
cultural adaptability, 123

deliberate defocusing, 72–74
desu/masu form, 10, 14, 21, 23–24, 132, 136, 146

detached speech style, 13
dialogical construct, 2
dictionary form, 10, 14, 40
discourse boundaries, 4, 12, 24, 39, 84–85, 96, 114, 146–147, 150
discursive practices, 6–7, 12, 37
display of sympathy, 99
[+distance], 17
[–distance], 17
domains of practice, 129, 155

ellipsis, 25
ethnography of speaking, 4
expression of inner self, 42, 57–58, 60, 82

footing, 8
formal register, 11, 81
functional knowledge, 4
functions of the plain form, 59

grammatical knowledge, 3
grammatical repair, 72–74

Hall, 1, 3–8, 96, 145
Hellermann, 1, 3, 6
honorifics, 10, 15–16, 19, 36, 124–125, 128–130, 132, 152, 155
Hymes, 3–4, 145

identity, 5, 8, 12, 15–17, 19, 23–24, 36, 130, 134–135, 144, 151–153
identity resources, 8
impersonal speech style, 13
incomplete sentences, 25–26, 29–30, 40, 43, 50–51, 53, 56–57, 86, 97–99, 101, 103, 105, 107, 109, 111–114, 118, 122–123, 133, 136, 146, 148–151, 156

incomplete utterance ending, 24, 102
indexical approach, 12, 14, 19, 81, 136
individual variation, 3, 32, 35, 37, 56–57, 67, 81, 114, 157
informal register, 11, 50, 81
informal speech style, 13–14, 66–67
in-group members, 11, 14, 35, 136
interactional competence, 1–10, 12, 20, 24, 27, 30, 37, 39, 42, 43, 47, 61, 71, 81–85, 96–11, 112, 114, 143–151, 156
interactional resources, 1–3, 5–10, 12, 26, 28, 30, 37, 39, 40, 42, 47, 84, 91, 97–99, 144–150, 156–157
interactive chain, 28
intercultural competence, 44, 46–47, 122
intersubjectivity, 28, 104

Japanese contact survey, 47–48, 117, 130, 162
joint meaning making, 12, 30, 40, 42, 57–58, 61–62, 82, 84, 99, 103, 105, 112, 123, 144–145, 147, 149

kohai, 92, 121, 126

language socialization, 24, 33
linguistic resources, 2–3, 8–9, 11–12, 24, 41, 49, 65, 81–82, 85, 147–149

motivation survey, 47–48, 115, 124, 137, 161

naked form, 13
negotiation sequence, 21, 78

Ochs, 13, 33
on-stage identity, 17
one-to-one correspondence, 18
organizational knowledge, 4
out-group members, 11, 14, 23

participant framework, 8
perspective sharing, 99, 106, 149
plain form, 10–16, 17–25, 40–42, 50, 51, 53, 56–63, 65–68, 70, 71, 74, 81–82, 85, 88, 90–91, 93–94, 96, 98, 118–119, 123, 127–129, 132–136, 146–150, 152–153
polite form, 10–12, 15–23, 40, 50, 51, 53–54, 56, 68, 81, 85–86, 88, 90–94, 96, 98, 118–119, 121, 123, 127–128, 130–136, 146, 153

postposing, 13, 42, 66–68, 71–78, 80–82, 148
pragmatic knowledge, 4
pragmatic repair, 72–74
projectability, 106, 112

register, 4, 8, 11–13, 24, 49–50, 81, 152
register-appropriate language use, 12–13, 65, 81, 84, 118, 146
repair, 5–9, 70, 73–75, 82, 84, 91, 100–101, 110, 146, 150
repairable, 7, 100
rhetorical scripts, 7, 146
rising intonation, 13–14, 42, 66–71, 82, 148, 158

senpai, 91–92, 94–95, 119, 126, 141
sentence final particles, 13, 34, 40, 49, 67, 82, 148–149
sequential organization, 5, 8–9, 12, 76, 81–82, 93, 96, 112, 147, 149
shared perspective, 99, 113
social actions, 2, 3, 7, 61, 99, 106, 112, 149, 156
social affordances, 37, 114, 136
social contact, 23, 34, 152
social networks, 33, 119–120, 122, 124–125, 129–130, 137, 141, 151–152
social participation, 31
socio-cognitive approach, 1
sociocultural knowledge, 3, 33
sociolinguistic, 3–4, 12, 31, 35
sociolinguistic knowledge, 4
sophisticated pragmatics, 72–75
speech acts, 4, 8–9, 32, 65, 82, 84
speech styles, 2, 3, 9–16, 18–19, 20, 22, 23–24, 39, 40, 43–44, 46, 50–51, 53, 55, 57, 59, 61, 63, 65, 67, 69, 71, 73–75, 77, 79, 81, 83, 85–86, 90–91, 93, 96–98, 126–127, 130, 136, 145–149, 151–153, 155–156
strategy of economy, 26
study abroad, 1–9, 12, 14, 16, 18, 20, 22–24, 26, 28, 30–37, 39–40, 42, 44–48, 52, 54, 56–58, 60, 62, 64, 66, 68, 70–72, 74, 76, 78, 80–82, 86, 88, 90, 92, 94, 96, 100, 102, 104, 106, 108, 110, 112, 114–146, 148, 150–152, 154–156
style mixing, 15–18, 23, 53, 90, 133, 153

style-shifting, 14–18, 24, 49, 83–85, 88, 90, 97, 133, 136, 147–148, 150, 153, 156–157
subjectivity, 12, 23, 28, 81, 104, 134–136, 151–153
sustainable relationship, 126

te-ending, 28–29, 105
three-way conversation, 50, 88, 96
transfer of speakership, 8, 148
transition relevance place, 18, 26

turn allocation, 26, 40, 149
turn construction units, 6
turn-in-progress, 20, 30, 42, 61, 106, 109, 112, 147, 149
turn projection, 26, 28, 40
turn-taking, 4, 8–9, 26, 84, 98, 112, 114, 144, 146, 148–149
two-way conversation, 50, 86, 88, 90

Young, 1–9, 12, 37, 39, 84, 96, 112, 144–146, 148, 151, 156

For Product Safety Concerns and Information please contact our EU Authorised Representative:

Easy Access System Europe

Mustamäe tee 50

10621 Tallinn

Estonia

gpsr.requests@easproject.com

www.ingramcontent.com/pod-product-compliance
Ingram Content Group UK Ltd.
Pitfield, Milton Keynes, MK11 3LW, UK
UKHW021943200326
4879IPUK00004B/66